OCCIDENTALISM

"Death is but one and comes but once,"
Emily wrote, but my brother's visits
over and over the week we had taken to tour
Kent before I attended a conference, and there was
"grief of want" but there was also a want of grief,
an "imitation of a light that has so little oil"

in the vastness of the vow he had taken two years before
to no longer speak to me. I looked away from this
bitter harvest that I was tithed and thought about
the gooseberries and donut-shaped peaches, a more
succulent bounty consumed from Canterbury's
market stalls as we trekked over uneven cobblestones

to the Cathedral and the Tomb of the Black Prince,
where candles burned for those cherished and lost,
and for those who have failed to appear. My brother
had married a Catholic woman and baptized his children
but in a moment of premonition requested a Jewish
funeral. In two months from then, it would be Yom Kippur,

the day we repent our sins and mourn our dead, whether recent
or long past, and we would spark the *yahrzeit* candle for him
to melt into its glass all night and day. I have many deceits
from which I cannot look away but not this: When my father
lifted his head from his empty plate and said, "What's done
is done," I assured him that I had already chosen to forgive.

OCCIDENTALISM

Images of the West

EDITED BY
James G. Carrier

CLARENDON PRESS · OXFORD

Oxford University Press, Walton Street, Oxford OX2 6DP
Oxford New York
Athens Auckland Bangkok Bombay
Calcutta Cape Town Dar es Salaam Delhi
Florence Hong Kong Istanbul Karachi
Kuala Lumpur Madras Madrid Melbourne
Mexico City Nairobi Paris Singapore
Taipei Tokyo Toronto
and associated companies in
Berlin Ibadan

Oxford is a trade mark of Oxford University Press

Published in the United States by
Oxford University Press Inc., New York

© the several contributors and in this volume James G. Carrier 1995

First published in hardback and paperback 1995
Reprinted in paperback 1996

British Library Cataloguing in Publication Data
Data available

Library of Congress Cataloging in Publication Data
Occidentalism : images of the West / edited by James G. Carrier.
Includes bibliographical references and index.
1. Ethnology—United States.   2. Civilization, Western-
-Philosophy.   3. Americans—Public opinion.   4. Public opinion-
-United States.   5. United States—Social life and customs.
I. Carrier, James G.
E184.A1023   1995   909'.09821'0072—dc20   94-49555
ISBN 0-19-827978-7
ISBN 0-19-827979-5 (Pbk.)

Printed in Great Britain
on acid-free paper by
Bookcraft (Bath) Ltd,
Midsomer Norton, Avon

For Roger Keesing
Fondly and respectfully remembered

PREFACE

I TRAINED in sociology, a discipline which encourages attention to industrial capitalist societies—the West. While social diversity was never an explicit topic in the courses I took or in my doctoral research, I was aware of at least part of the complexity that made up what my teachers so casually called 'American society'. That society seemingly dissolved as I listened to my teachers, read my books, and carried out my research. This was because, though I may have perceived American society as an interrelated whole, that whole itself was made up of parts that varied widely, just as the people in that society differed in important ways in their social locations. Class, race, gender, region, educational level, religion, and a host of other variables were the dimensions that my teachers, and ultimately I, took for granted as identifying possible lines of cleavage and conflict within the larger whole.

Entirely fortuitously I drifted out of sociology and into anthropology, helped along by an extended period of fieldwork while I accompanied my wife as she did her doctoral research in Melanesia, and by an extended period of teaching at the University of Papua New Guinea in a combined department where all the interesting questions seemed more anthropological than sociological.

While we were in the field, conversations with villagers occasionally turned to discussions of the United States. Often I was surprised and flattered by the interest people took in different aspects of American life. However, I was just as often dismayed by the rigid, simplistic, and often simply wrong way that they typified the United States, especially when they were contrasting their own society to mine. Of course, there was no reason why they should have been insightful or subtle in their analyses. America was a long way away, they had many other and more important things to do with their time than find out about it, and they made no claims to be skilled social analysts.

I was somewhat more unsettled by the ways that some anthropologists typified the United States in particular and Western society in general. To be fair, the majority of these typifications emerged in casual conversations, though by no means is this true of all of them. It struck me at the time as a professional double standard, and it repelled me. These were conscientious scholars who devoted great effort to uncovering the nuances, complexities, and inter-connections of the societies that they studied. Yet they would casually and superficially characterize Western society in terms so simplistic that they would not be tolerated of an anthropologist speaking about a village society. Like the villagers whose simplifications of the West disturbed me, their simplistic characterizations usually occurred when they were contrasting the West with the society they had studied, but unlike those villagers, these anthropologists should have been insightful and subtle in their analyses. The West was their home and they were skilled social analysts by training and profession.

My dismay at the characterizations made by those whom I have come to think of as my colleagues, as well as my dismay at the vehemence of my own reaction, are what started me along the way that has resulted in this collection.

And along that way my initial dismay and vehemence have lost their rough edge. Instead, they have transmuted into an intellectual puzzle: to what degree do anthropologists characterize the West in essentialistic and simplistic ways? What difference does it make? The pursuit of the solution to this puzzle led in turn to a larger issue, the ways that people identify themselves, others, and the relationship between the two. The anthropologists and the villagers lodged in my memory became two aspects of this single issue, for all were identifying the West, the village, and the relationship between them.

The aspect of this issue the present collection addresses is what I call occidentalism, though I am hardly the first to use the term. The range of analysis presented here reveals, I think, that occidentalism is a protean concept, and one that fits especially well with some recent trends within anthropology itself. Although it anticipates some of what I say in the Introduction, I want to mention those trends here.

One of these trends is the growing self-reflection among anthropologists, especially the growing concern with the assumptions built into the discipline, their own anthropological work, and the products that result. While many works have goaded this self-reflection, an important one is Edward Said's *Orientalism*, which both caught anthropological attention and had a title that encouraged an easy inversion, to occidentalism. Occidentalism is timely here, because it can be a useful concept for prying open the assumptions, often unspoken, that anthropologists have about Western societies. Understanding these assumptions is important because anthropologists often appear to interpret the non-Western societies they study in terms of an opposition to their understandings of the West.

Occidentalism goes with another anthropological trend, the growing concern with *kastom* (in Melanesia), the 'invention of tradition', the creation of distinctive identities by people outside the West. The notion of occidentalism is pertinent for this concern because, frequently, those distinctive identities emerge when, as in Melanesia, people confront an encroaching West. But even though these identities emerge in something like opposition to the West, it is important to remember that 'the West' in this case is a partial construct. It is those bits of Western society and culture that get shipped out to the colonies, so to speak. Further, 'the West' is people's interpretation of those bits, rather than an objective reflection of them. Thus, a concern with the occidentalism of Melanesian villagers, to continue the example, can help explain their emergent self-conceptions, their *kastom*, their regeneration and creation of distinctive practices and identities.

There is a third anthropological trend I want to mention in connection with occidentalism. That is the growing anthropological concern with the West itself. Whether out of intellectual preference, financial necessity, or a growing concern with comfort as middle age encroaches, more and more anthropologists are turning their attention to Western societies, rather than the discipline's more conventional village societies. Occidentalism bears on this trend because, or so I hope, that anthropological attention begins to call into question some of the ways that Westerners represent the West to themselves.

Perhaps because the West is home to most anthropologists, the illumination of the partiality of Western occidentalism can reveal issues that are more difficult to discern in the study of alien places. These issues revolve around the question of *whose* experiences and perceptions of Western society are elevated to the level of public acceptance, and whose are denied—why and how. And this in turn raises a further complication. In defining the quintessential West, Western occidentalism creates an alien within the gates. Put differently, it defines certain sorts of people in Western society as not being valid Westerners—as being backward, and hence subordinate and even dangerous. This has an important practical consequence. It generates and justifies programmes intended to bring those domestic others into line. It can become a fairly straightforward mechanism of social control.

The authors in this collection deal with all of these issues, and help to show why occidentalism is an important and timely concept. Sadly, however, I must point to an important gap in the collection. That gap is the way that scholars in non-Western societies, less likely to share common Western academic occidentalisms, can reveal the ways that those

occidentalisms have shaped Western interpretations of non-Western societies. The importance of the work of non-Western scholars in this regard
is apparent in, for example, Arjun Appadurai's discussion in 'Is Homo
Hierarchicus?' (*American Ethnologist*, 13 (1986): 745–50) of the recon-
ceptualization of India, the West, and their colonial encounter by some
South Asian intellectuals. And, of course, those non-Western scholars
themselves are likely to have their own occidentalisms that would be
interesting to analyse.

Although I began working on this collection in 1990, it was little more
than a promise until the 1992 meeting of the American Anthropological
Association, in San Francisco. Contributors agreed to my suggestion that
I organize a session on occidentalism, and as meeting-day approached,
chapter drafts began to appear. All of the chapters in this collection were
the basis of talks in that session, except my own, Millie Creighton's,
Deborah Reed-Danahay's, and Jonathan Spencer's. I used my allotted
session time to introduce the concept and the papers; Creighton, Reed-
Danahay, and Spencer joined the project too late to be included in the
session.

J. G. C.

ACKNOWLEDGEMENTS

IN developing and thinking through the notion of occidentalism I have been influenced by the work of many people, whom I mention in the Introduction and my own chapter. Clearly foremost among them, though he may not recognize his influence, is Nicholas Thomas.

I owe a debt of a different sort to my wife, Achsah Carrier. Not only did she introduce me to anthropology in the first place, she has constantly goaded me to be a better anthropologist. Especially, she has been an empirical counterweight to my more theoretical flights of fancy, reminding me that the elegant mental edifices I like to construct need to take cognizance of the not-so-elegant reality around me. The result is work that is less spare and tidy, but more subtle and satisfactory.

I owe a debt of yet another sort to Michael Herzfeld. He has been more generous of his time and attention than I had any reason to expect. His suggestions led me to recruit some of the contributors to this collection and were important in securing the interest of the people who agreed to be commentators at the occidentalism session at the 1992 meeting of the American Anthropological Association. Without him, this collection would have taken a very different and less interesting form.

Although I owe special thanks to Herzfeld, and although I take responsibility for what you see, this collection has a distinct air of collaboration about it. I owe more than pro forma thanks to all the contributors for their suggestions about how to proceed at various stages. Their collective wisdom routinely was greater and more sensible than my own.

Finally, I owe thanks to those who agreed to be commentators at the American Anthropological Association meeting where we presented these papers. Jean Comaroff, Jean Jackson, George Marcus, and James Fernandez all made incisive comments about the thrust of the project as a whole and about individual papers. We have ruthlessly taken advantage of what they had to say, and the collection is far better as a result.

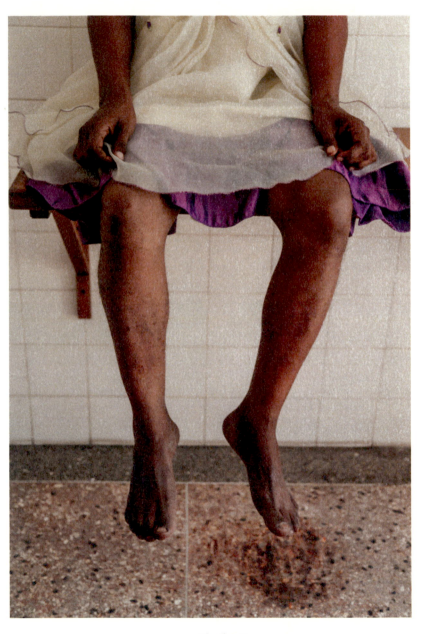

Shaibu 2
Photograph by Aneeta Mitha

CONTENTS

Introduction

This collection is about occidentalism, stylized images of the West. While anthropologists conventionally see themselves as producing, and recently have debated their ability to produce, knowledge of societies and cultures outside the core of the West, occidentalism is the silent partner of their work and debates. The contributors to this collection illustrate the importance of this occidentalism in various ways. My purpose in the first part of this Introduction is to describe occidentalism and locate it within the discipline. To do so I start by looking at one of the ways in which anthropologists have criticized their own discipline, criticism that draws on Edward Said's *Orientalism*. Indeed, Said's work is so influential that 'orientalism' has become a generic term for a particular, suspect type of anthropological thought. (In this collection, 'orientalism' marks the generic use of the term, 'Orientalism' being reserved for the specific manifestation Said describes.)

The critics who invoke Said are part of a growing number of those who reject much that anthropology has been, or at least what anthropologists tell each other it used to be. The evolving collective, informed method and judgement of the body of specialists who existed in the hundred years before the last quarter of the twentieth century seems increasingly suspect. The critics, apparently no longer comfortable as the successors to that body of specialists, have called into question what they see as old-style anthropology. That is the study of simple and stable societies that are radically distinct from the complex and changing West, and the rendering of those societies in terms of the concepts and issues of conventional anthropology. Their criticism is a curious mixture of decreasing and increasing self-confidence. Decreasing, because critics seem less willing to rely on academic anthropology itself as the foundation and justification for the ways that they approach and render the societies they study. There is growing support for the idea that the discipline should be guided, or at least influenced, by outsiders, particularly those whom anthropologists study. But equally, there are signs of an increasing self-confidence, because many anthropologists tell themselves that their task is not the scholarly pursuit of anthropological questions through fieldwork, but instead is the more portentous one of representing and interpreting alien societies to the West (Spencer 1990 describes some of the pitfalls of this assumption).

Said's appeal for these critics is understandable, because of his general concern with the way that the academic discipline of Oriental Studies has represented and interpreted the Middle East to Western society, and because of his particular concern with the inadequacies and undesirable consequences of that representation. Two points that are central to Said's criticism of Oriental Studies resonate with the points made by the critics of modern anthropology. Those are that Oriental Studies constructs an image of the Orient that is 'absolutely different . . . from the West' (Said 1978: 96) and that what is imagined and represented is a 'closed system in which objects are what they are *because* they are what they are, for once, for all time, for ontological reasons that no empirical matter can either dislodge or alter' (1978: 70). The alien Orient, thus, is essentialized, is reduced to a timeless essence that pervades, shapes, and defines the significance of the people and events that constitute it.[1]

Echoing Said, many of the critics argue that conventional anthropology presupposes and presents its own orientalisms, societies rendered in terms of essences that are timeless and radically alien (e.g. Clifford 1988; Fabian 1983). Much of their criticism centres on identifying orientalist elements and assumptions in the descriptions that anthropologists produce, and may go little further than textual analysis itself. In other words, it centres on the product of orientalism in anthropological representation rather than the process of orientalization, by which I mean the activities and factors that Said describes that lead to orientalist constructions of alien societies. (For criticisms of such work, see Errington and Gewertz 1987; Fardon 1990; Keesing and Jolly 1992; Polier and Roseberry 1989; Spencer 1989.)

Orient vs. occident: dialectical definition

Said says that Orientalists 'promoted the difference between the familiar (Europe, the West, "us") and the strange (the Orient, the East, "them")' (1978: 43). Here Said introduces the complements of the Orient and Orientalism, the Occident and Occidentalism. He does so when he says that the Orientalists compared, even if only implicitly, themselves and the strangers they studied in a way that would allow them to identify and heighten distinguishing characteristics. 'The Orient', then, is an example of what Kenneth Burke calls contextual or dialectical definition: 'To tell what a thing is, you place it in terms of something else. This idea of locating, or placing, is implicit in our very word for definition itself' (1969: 24). We may think that we are simply describing something that exists out there in the real world. However, because such definitions are contextual, the thing described is, in fact, unstable. It varies with its context, and so loses its substance or facticity and becomes fluid.

Thus, although 'the Orient' may have appeared in Oriental Studies to be a term with a concrete referent, a real region of the world with real attributes, in practice it took on meaning only in the context of another term, 'the West'. And in this process is the tendency to essentialize, to reduce the complex entities that are being compared to a set of core features that express the essence of each entity, but only as it stands in contrast to the other. In conventional anthropology, the orientalisms that have attracted critical attention, thus, do not exist on their own. They are matched by anthropologists' occidentalisms, essentializing simplifications of the West. Adam Kuper (1988: 5) points to this when he says that anthropologists in the end of the nineteenth and the beginning of the twentieth centuries 'took . . . primitive society as their special object, but in practice primitive society proved to be their own society (as they understood it) seen in a distorting mirror'.

Essentialist, dialectical definition of the sort that concerns the critics of anthropology is not a unique event. Rather, as Said recognizes, it is a manifestation of a more general process, one by which a set of people seeks 'to intensify its own sense of itself by dramatizing the distance and difference between what is closer to it and what is far away' (1978: 55). It is an instance of a larger process of self-definition through opposition with the alien, of the sort that Peter Mason (1990) describes in his history of European understandings of America. In literary terms, Burke (1969: 33–4) says that in this circumstance 'the protagonist is motivated [i.e. identified] by the nature of the antagonist . . . There is a grim little pleasantry that runs, "Of course we're Christians—but what are we being Christians *against?*"' Nicholas Thomas (1992a: 216) makes this same point when he says 'the question . . . is not, How are traditions invented? but instead, *Against what* are traditions invented?'

Thus, it should come as no surprise that twin and opposing characterizations of the modern West and societies in other times and places are a notable feature of the history of sociology and anthropology. They are particularly apparent in formative theoretical works, for often these were intended to describe what their authors saw as the key distinguishing features of the modern West. Marx's pre-capitalist and capitalist societies, Durkheim's mechanical and organic societies, and Lévi-Strauss's hot and cold societies all illustrate the process that concerns me. At a more mundane level, occidentalism is apparent in the way that some anthropologists object to Western intrusions in village life. Wage labour, missions, plantation, or mining projects are seen as tokens of a relatively undifferentiated and essentialized Western social life that will, if un-checked, displace a village life that is itself often seen as coherent and uniform.

Usually, however, the Western half of this dialectic is hidden in mod-ern anthropology, for researchers want to write about the people they have been studying. Some scholars, though, do address both sides of the opposition explicitly. An example is Louis Dumont, whose *From Mandeville to Marx* (1977) lays out his vision of the core of the West, while his *Homo Hierarchicus* (1970) lays out his vision of the core of India. The first book traces the development of the egalitarian individualism and the concern with relationships between individuals and things that Dumont sees as central to the modern West. Such a view does reflect elements of Western thought. However, the arguments presented in parts of this collection, as well as elsewhere (e.g. Abercrombie, Hill, and Turner 1986), show that these elements are partial at best, for important areas of many people's lives, and presumably also their thoughts, appear to operate in terms of rather different principles.

From Mandeville to Marx is not simply a partial rendering of the West, for the ideas expressed in it stand in a distinct relationship to Dumont's view of India. Dumont signals that relationship in *Homo Hierarchicus* when he devotes extended attention in his introductory material to West-ern egalitarian individualism, drawing especially on de Tocqueville. He does so in order to show what Western society and self-understanding lack, the sense of hierarchy that, he says, India embodies and from which we may learn. In one sense, this occidentalist rendering of Western thought appears to be little more than a way of encouraging readers to appreciate the distinctive genius of India. But there is more here than a device to catch readers' attention and make them receptive to the tale that Dumont wants to tell.

At the simplest level, this occidentalist West generates a tone of abso-lutism and essentialism that helps make Dumont's orientalist rendering of India seem unexceptionable, even expected. At a more profound level, however, the occidental and the oriental define and justify each other in Dumont's work. Each defines what is notable about the other, for the image of an individualist West makes non-individualistic elements in India noteworthy, just as the image of a hierarchical India makes indi-vidualistic elements in the West noteworthy. Indeed, this process seems central to Dumont's (1970: 2) vision of the nature of comparative social anthropology. Chris Fuller (1989: 56) describes the dialectical spirit of Dumont's essentialist enterprise, as well as its tenuous links to everyday social life. Fuller says that it

needs to be recognised that the dichotomy [between India and the West] is asymmetrical; it has a thesis: 'modern'—and an antithesis: 'traditional'. The concept of the traditional economy has been generated as the negative of the modern by isolating and defining the traits which are *not* characteristic of modern economies, or rather those which are *not* susceptible to interpretation by Western economic theory.

Dumont's opposition of Oriental hierarchy and Western individuality differs from Durkheim's opposition of mechanical and organic societies, Weber's traditional and rational societies, and a host of others that exist in scholarly and popular thought. Lumping together under 'occidentalism' individuality, organic solidarity, rationality, and the like entails losing some precision. However, there is a gain. The various oppositions that are, in this collection, subsumed under the opposition between orient and occident spring from an implicit opposition between the West and non-Western societies. This implicit opposition does not only underlie more specific oppositions, it also gives them much of their rhetorical force and intellectual appeal. If these various oppositions were not about the distinctiveness of the West, people would pay much less attention to them.

The notion of an opposition between occident and orient allows more than an insight into the nature of Western academic models and understandings. It also makes it easier to recognize similar forms of thinking in other places and times. For example, in his *European Vision and the South Pacific*, Bernard Smith describes European artistic representations of the South Pacific made on early voyages of discovery. Smith points out that, by the time initial sketches were reworked into finished paintings or woodcuts for books, they were distorted in systematic ways that brought them into line with European cultural stereotypes of the Dark Savage, the Noble Savage, the World Turned Upside Down. Roy Harvey Pearce identifies a similar process in early American writings on North American Indians. Whether they described those Indians as noble or savage, as worthy of emulation, civilization, or, ultimately, extermination, the fact was that 'what Indians signified was not what they were'. Instead, 'Americans were only talking to themselves about themselves' (Pearce 1965: 232). And this process continues, as is evident in the recent debate surrounding 'The West as America', at the National Museum of American Art (see Foner and Weiner 1991).

The alien entity that is the antagonist of Oriental Studies and conventional anthropology is far away from those Westerners who do the studying. Baghdad and Nuerland are a long way from Paris and London. However, ultimately 'far away' turns out to be not about absolute distance, but about the relative difference of segmentary opposition, which Michael Herzfeld (1987: chap. 7) says has been recurrent in European thought and which appears clearly in changing conceptions of Europe and the countries within it over the past few decades. Thus, when anthropologists consider the differences between humans and other animals, as when, in *Capital*, Marx contrasts the worst of architects with the best of bees (in Tucker 1978: 344), the alien is restricted to the non-human and the familiar embraces the whole of humanity. However, the familiar can be defined narrowly, in which case the alien can be as close as poor people in Liverpool or religious fundamentalists in Virginia. Because anthropologists are largely white, middle-class, well-educated people, they are able to define much as alien. This fluidity is manifest in the fact that many anthropologists who have turned their attention to the West have analysed yet another set of aliens, closer to home than the Bororo, but still different. They can be different because they are isolated socially, as are Mediterranean peasant villagers or mountain-dwellers of Appalachia. Equally, they can be different because they lack important social or cultural attributes, such as working-class people in Philadelphia who are ignorant of modern medical facts (Balshem 1991) or Montana townspeople who are ignorant of their own history (Errington 1987).

Occidentalism beyond the West

A different sort of occidentalism appears, and is of growing importance in anthropology, in studies of the ways that people outside the West imagine themselves, for their self-image often develops in contrast to their stylized image of the West. The self-imagining that is known most widely in anthropology probably is the concept of *kastom*, the concern to preserve and perhaps recreate what people see as their traditional ways, reported originally in Melanesian ethnography (e.g. Keesing and Tonkinson 1982). Roger Keesing (1982: 298) says *kastom* is 'an idealized reformulation' of indigenous social life by village people. While it need be neither fanciful nor unperceptive, *kastom* is relatively essentialist and static, a result of a sequence of events that led many Melanesians to take a 'sufficent external view of themselves and their way of life to see their culture as a "thing"'

(1982: 300; see also Handler 1988: ch. 3). The sequence of events, says Keesing (1982: 300), that led to this reification in Melanesia was colonization, the relatively rapid and, for Melanesians, unavoidable juxtaposition of Western and Melanesian social forms.

Nicholas Thomas has pursued the link between colonization and *kastom* in his consideration of the emergence in Fiji of *kerekere*, the practice of sharing and lending, as an identified and reified marker of customary indigenous life. He presents this emergence as an instance of 'the process of naming and reifying customs and beliefs [that] takes place in a particularly marked and conspicuous fashion in the course of colonial history' (Thomas 1992*b*: 65). He says that prior to the 1860s, which is prior to intensive colonial intrusion, there is no evidence that *kerekere* was a recognized custom that was taken to be a distinctive marker of Fijian society. Rather, it became such over the course of the next few decades.[2] While the actual social processes that led to the reification of *kerekere* are complex and reflect the contingencies of Fijian colonial history, Thomas's general argument is fairly straightforward.

His point is that the conceptions that indigenous Pacific people have of themselves, conceptions that include notions like *kastom* and the centrality of *kerekere*, are not simple reifications of aspects of social life. Rather, they are reifications in context, and the context is the encounter of the village and intruding colonial Western social forms. But of course Pacific islanders no more perceive the intruding West in neutral, objective terms than intruding Westerners perceive those islanders in neutral, objective terms. Instead, these orientalist imaginings of islanders emerge as part of a dialectic that also produces occidentalisms, which Thomas describes in detail. The result is 'essentialized constructs of selves and others within which particular customs and practices are emblematic' (Thomas 1992*b*: 82).

To complicate matters, what began as image can be self-fulfilling and so become reality. This is illustrated by Eric Hirsch's (1990) analysis of the use of betel nut among the Fuyuge, an inland society in Papua New Guinea. Hirsch says that in Papua New Guinea the chewing of betel nut was confined largely to coastal areas during the early colonial period. However, in the past few decades it has become more widespread. Part of the reason for this, he argues, is that it has become identified as distinctively Melanesian in contrast to European, for Europeans drink beer and disapprove of betel nut. Once this identification emerges, peripheral societies in the country, such as the Fuyuge, are likely to adopt betel nut in order to claim membership in Papua New Guinea centres of power. In

THE WOUNDS WE WEAR

Joy Kennedy-O'Neill

T HE NEW INTERN SMILES AT ME, AND WAVES. HER WRIST HAS a black hole, a gash so deep there's nothing else to see. No bone. No flesh. It's like her hand is floating above her arm. I know the hole is just a projection from her temple's implant, but god, it seems so real. Past suicide attempt? Or maybe she's a cutter?

My boss wears a hole from his heart down to his gut. Daughter died. Messy divorce. The guy pushing the coffee cart has a black gash at his throat. Maybe he said something he regrets. He doesn't talk much.

The new intern takes a coffee from the cart and looks at me again. She motions to a second cup, smiling. An invitation. All I can do is stare at the hole in her wrist—blacker than the dark roast java.

Everywhere I look, I see people's pain. Their neural implants throw it, like magic lantern patterns, all over their bodies. Does it make them proud?

the process, the image of Melanesia as betel territory is reinforced and made more real.

The politics of definition

As the examples of *kerekere* and the use of betel nut point out, there is more to occidentalism and orientalism than the general desire to distinguish the familiar and the alien and to heighten the difference between them. People can distinguish between the familiar and the alien in many ways. Political contingencies, of the sort I have described in the preceding paragraphs and to which I return repeatedly, influence which of the many possible distinctions become important, become taken-for-granted ways of identifying the essence of us and them. The essentialisms of occidentalism and orientalism, then, do not spring unbidden from the differences between groups, but are created in a process of essentialization. In this process political relations within and between societies shape the construction and interpretation of the essential attributes of those societies. Said describes a range of political and economic contingencies that shaped the relationship of Europe and the Middle East. These factors help explain why and how scholars converted into a timeless and alien essence, the 'Orient', what was in fact sets of people existing in history and in relationships among themselves and with others outside the region.

These factors are also important if we are to understand the inadequacies and pitfalls of particular essentializations. After all, it seems unlikely that we can see and make sense of things without using essential notions: the simple act of calling what I am sitting on 'a chair' invokes such a notion to a degree. Thus, the issue is not (or should not be) whether people reduce things to essences, whether an essence of being ('chair') or an essence of relationship ('gift of my wife's mother'). Instead, it is whether those reductions become so entrenched that it becomes difficult to stand back from them and consider whether they help or hinder scholars in the pursuit of the questions that confront them. For Said and the critics, the essentialisms of Oriental Studies and conventional anthropology had become entrenched, and were hindering rather than helping.

Political contingencies shape the orientalisms and occidentalisms of villagers as well as those of academics. When the advocates of the orientalisms of *kastom* distinguish themselves from a West that they construe as essentially materialist and disorderly, they implicitly or explicitly claim power in their own society. Equally, however, reifications of tradition in non-Western societies can be negative. Advocates of *kastom* may well find themselves challenged by those who construct the village and Western life in very different, but still dialectical and essentialist, terms, and who advocate a rejection of *kastom* and an increased involvement with the encroaching Western socio-economic sphere. And, of course, attendant upon their advocacy is a claim to power and influence in the village society for themselves. Recently this political dimension has appeared especially clearly in Fiji, where coup and government reorganization have been justified in terms of a return to traditional Fijian ways in a process that has denied power and legitimacy to those who offer competing conceptions of Fijian tradition and its applicability to modern Fiji (Lawson 1993).

The social and political complexities of conflicting occidentalisms and orientalisms appear particularly clearly in many of the Melanesian millenarian and reformist movements commonly called 'cargo cults' (e.g. Lawrence 1964; Schwartz 1962). However, the processes that are so striking in these movements have been more general, frequently played out in terms of conflicts between younger men, often returning to a village with experience as migrant workers, and their elders, without that experience but attached to the existing village social order and often occupying positions of power in it. The ways that other people's occidentalisms can serve to support or to criticize their own existing social and political practices appear as well in Xiaomei Chen's (1992) study of some modern Chinese renderings of the West and in Eleanor Smollett's (1993) study of some modern Bulgarian renderings of the West.

Laura Nader illustrates this political use of representation in both Western and non-Western societies in terms of gender politics. She says that various commentators in the Middle East construct and present images of the West that portray women there as devalued sex objects, exploited by a flourishing pornography, and constantly threatened by molesting, rape, incest, and family violence. These are paired with orientalisms of Islamic society as one that values women and in which they can be secure. Nader (1989: 333) says that one function of these opposed essentializations is to solidify and legitimize patriarchal gender relations in the Middle East. Equally, she observes an inverse process in the West. There, various commentators construct and present images of the Middle East that portray women as veiled and forced into submission through a double sexual standard, and as victims of everything from arranged marriage and polygyny to clitoridectomy (Nader 1989: 333). And again, one function of these orientalisms, together with the attendant occidentalism of the West as the land of independent and advanced women, is to solidify and legitimize patriarchal gender relations in the West.

Nader's paper presents a neat juxtaposition of two sets of essentialized renderings of West and Middle East that shows how these renderings do not simply generate and define the difference between societies. In addition, they often serve to buttress a particular distribution of power and privilege within a society by showing how awful things are elsewhere. However, it is important to remember the point that twin essentializations can be part of a political criticism. Thus, Smith (e.g. 1985: 80–5) showed that different early renderings of the people of the Pacific were shaped by the way that the representer understood European society and wished to comment upon it, whether to praise or to denounce. Likewise, Orientalisms of the Noble Savage, whether as a person of generosity, peace, and dignity, or more recently as a wise ecologist attuned to a fragile nature, can be paired with occidentalisms of a violent, rapacious, and heedless West in an effort to challenge existing Western practices and structures and advance new ones.

I have described how social strategies and inequalities within a society can shape the essentializations that people put forward. However, inequalities between societies can be important as well. Although dialectical and essentialist definitions of the familiar and the alien can occur whenever two sets of people come into contact, Thomas (1991a: 7) is correct when he points out that 'the capacities of populations to impose and act upon their constructions of others has been highly variable throughout history'. In this larger, inter-social arena, Westerners have been more powerful and hence better able than people elsewhere to construct and impose images of alien societies as they see fit.

At the simplest level, encroaching Westerners can and do employ villagers as performing exotica to enact 'traditional' dances and ceremonies in the tourist business, just as Western merchants can and do ensure that non-Westerners manufacture the sorts of objects that Westerners identify as authentically indigenous (Gewertz and Errington 1991: chs. 1–2; Miller 1987: 123). For example, in 1980 Bloomingdale's, a department store in New York, launched its China sale. The items being touted were identified as authentically Chinese, the result of company buyers' relentless pursuit of examples of ancient Chinese craft and art through Chinese 'warehouses, back alleys, and small markets' (Bloomingdale's literature quoted in Silverman 1986: 22). While the items for sale were produced in China, most 'were designed by Bloomingdale's artists in New York, who projected their fantasies of the opulent, mysterious empire and ordered accordingly' (1986: 24–5). In the more complex patterns of colonization, the British system of indirect rule involved a sort of orientalism made flesh, for the colonizers imposed on the colonized a form of social and political organization that the British saw as traditional and indigenous (for Fiji, see Thomas 1991*b*: 167–75).

A final example will illustrate some of the complexities of the process by which the self-conception of those outside the West can be shaped by Western power. Important in the semi-official self-image of Papua New Guinea by Papua New Guineans are the notions of ethnic diversity and the strength of village ties, which many people see as distinguishing them from a Western world that they characterize as relatively uniform, mobile, and oriented toward urban life. Equally, however, this self-conception reflects and was buttressed by a set of colonial and national government policies that, Peter Fitzpatrick (1980) argues, have served the interests of capital by decreasing the pressure on employers for a living wage, decreasing the pressure on the state for adequate welfare services, and reducing the likelihood that workers would see themselves as sharing a common class situation and so form effective unions. In other words, the process began as something analogous to the logic of indirect rule, in that the colonizers used policies intended, among other things, to preserve what they saw as indigenous social forms. However, as Western encroachment increased, this state of affairs took on a class-based momentum of its own by benefiting capitalists in the country. And, as I described with betel nut, here too the essentialism can become self-fulfilling, for in the economic circumstances I have described it is unlikely that many Papua New Guineans would be able to ignore their village ties and ethnic identities. In the absence of adequate wages and social welfare policies these ties and identities are often necessary for survival, especially in old age.

Thus it is that academic anthropologists and the people they study construct stylized images of the occident and orient in the context of complex social, political, and economic conflicts and relationships. As I have shown, moreover, these stylized images are not inert products. Rather, they have social, political, and economic uses of their own, for they shape people's perceptions, justify policies, and so influence people's actions.

About the collection

The chapters in this collection seek to lay out the existence and nature of occidentalisms among anthropologists and among ordinary people in societies in the West and elsewhere. These two different sorts of essentialist rendering of the West address concerns that, on their face, appear to be of very different salience for the anthropologists who are likely to be reading these words.

Occidentalism within anthropology touches directly on what has been the discipline's primary task since its inception, studying sets of people outside of the core of the West. As I have made clear in this Introduction, this sort of occidentalism is significant because it points out that this task is more difficult than we may think. Increasing the modesty with which anthropologists approach their work is a worthwhile goal. Occidentalism outside anthropology touches the discipline less directly, for it is an object of anthropological study rather than a warning about the difficulties of anthropology itself. As an object of study it relates most directly to the topic of cultural identity and similar phenomena. National, ethnic, and racial identities revolve around an opposition between an us and a them, and in many parts of the world those identities reflect in part an assumption or rejection of 'the West' in one or another of its guises.

It would be dangerous, however, to think that these two sorts of occidentalism, one within and one without anthropology, are so distant from each other. More than history and the other social sciences, anthropology has maintained a principled ignorance of the modern West, though this ignorance was never perfect and has decreased in the last few decades. Perhaps because of this ignorance, anthropologists would seem especially likely to absorb, without noticing that they have done so, those influential occidentalisms that have been shaped by Western world dominance.

In one of his more convoluted sentences, Said (1978: 11) observes: 'I doubt that it is controversial . . . to say that an Englishman in India or Egypt in the later nineteenth century took an interest in those countries that was never far from their status in his mind as British colonies.' In short, what the English thought of India or Egypt was shaped by the relationship between those countries and Britain, a colonial relationship. The converse is also true: it seems likely that an Englishman in the later nineteenth century took an interest in England in which its colonial mastery, its relationship with other countries, was never far from his mind. To the degree that anthropologists have absorbed important constructions of the West, it is likely that what they have absorbed has also been shaped by the distinction between the West and the rest.

The Western occidentalisms that anthropologists absorb are shaped by another political fact, power relations within the West. Several of the chapters in this collection describe how dominant constructions of the West reflect the interests and experiences of dominant groups in the

West. Thus, the Western occidentalisms that anthropologists are likely to absorb are doubly infused with socio-political relations. In being the bearers and manipulators of these occidentalisms, then, anthropologists meet nationalists, for both are engaged in the politics of identity.

In saying that Western anthropologists absorb these identities I do not mean that they support them. In fact, of course, many anthropologists object to the West as they occidentalize it and do what they can to protect the people they study from its more unsavoury effects. When I say that anthropologists absorb these identities, I mean a different point: they accept the occidentalism as a valid representation of the core of the modern West, even if they do so unthinkingly. One point of this collection is not to moralize about these occidentalisms, but to challenge them.

The chapters

The chapter that begins this collection is Lamont Lindstrom's 'Cargoism and Occidentalism'. On its face 'cargo cult' refers to an empirical set of activities and social movements. Lindstrom shows, however, that embedded in the phrase and manifest in its use are a set of renderings that generate and maintain a body of essential distinctions between the rational and empirical West and the irrational and ritual alien. However, as the concept has slipped into popular usage it has come to be applied more promiscuously by and to Western and non-Western people alike. But Lindstrom argues that this is not merely a degeneration of a scholarly concept. Rather, the popular usage helps reveal a key tension that the notion expresses, the tension generated by eternal longing. What this chapter suggests, then, is that the notion of cargo cult involves not the generation of an orient that is an inversion of the occident, but the generation of an orient that is a projection of one element of the West, the perpetual, unsatisfied desire that is so pronounced under capitalism.

Lindstrom's chapter is first because, in addressing his topic, he addresses a range of issues that are important for understanding occidentalism. One is the different ways that people identify the relationship between the orient and the occident. There is a tendency, apparent in this Introduction, to assume that there is a radical separation between the two. Thus, for example, Dumont says that the West can learn from India, but he portrays a profound gap between them. However, Lindstrom is correct when he notes that things are not always this simple. It may be, for instance, that orient and occident are linked in a developmental or evolutionary relationship. Such a view links the two entities in real ways, in the manner of younger and older siblings. Such a linkage can serve what many see as a laudable goal, reducing the sense of profound difference that exists in renderings like Dumont's. However, it can serve other purposes as well. For instance, it easily leads to a universalizing of the more advanced party, typically the condescension that the orient will be just like the occident if only it is given a bit of time, if only inhibiting restraints are removed, if only there are a few more structural readjustments to the economy. This rhetoric justifies the occident, while it denies legitimacy to orientals who seek to change in any way other than by becoming more like the West (see Thomas 1992*a*: 225). But just as the Noble Savage that Smith describes could reflect critically on the West, so the younger sibling, possessed of the wisdom induced by innocence or the clarity induced by necessity, can see and speak the truth about the elder (see Carrier 1992*a*: 15–17).

It is not just Westerners who call Melanesian villagers cargoists. Lindstrom shows that other Melanesians do too, in different ways at different times. Moreover, just as Melanesians give voice to Western orientalism, so Westerners can ascribe to them a flattering occidentalism of kindness, wealth, generosity, and efficiency. Western occidentalisms and orientalisms, then, do not stay at home. They are absorbed by or presented in the voices of the orient. Lindstrom thus points out the permeability of the boundary between occident and orient. This appears particularly in his discussion of the political uses of the orientalism of the cargo cult in the West itself. There it asserts the distinctive superiority of an occidentalized West. At the same time, however, it is a label applied to some people who are aliens within the gates, in the West but not Western enough. In showing that people in the West can be criticized in this way, Lindstrom shows that even within the geographical boundaries of the West are people who can be classed as orientals for certain purposes and in certain contexts.

The ultimate in this border crossing is the claim that cargoism is a universal human attitude. This appears to dissolve the boundary, to do away with the invidious distinction between the West and the rest. However, Lindstrom suggests that it does so on Western terms, and so effectively reasserts the perspectives and biases contained so clearly in the early, pejorative descriptions of the Melanesian cults. It does so because it sees in the cargo cult evidence of the universality of the eternal longing that is a core part of Western capitalist culture. The warning in this tale is clear. Talk of transcending boundaries by a universalistic humanism can easily turn into a universal Westernism, so that we are back where we started.

Finally, Lindstrom raises a point that inevitably bedevils any effort to sketch essentialist renderings of the orient and occident. Frequently, perhaps even typically, people talk about only one part of the opposition, just as anthropologists typically describe the orient and remain silent about the occident. Commonly, then, it is necessary to infer the hidden element of the pair. It is necessary to attend to the nudges, winks, and pauses that encourage those for whom such essentialisms are intended, rarely anthropologists, to fill in what is, as Lindstrom says, always already understood.

The following chapters are presented roughly in terms of a single dimension, defined by two poles. One pole is the analysis of occidentalism in the work of a single academic, the topic of the earlier chapters; the other pole is the analysis of occidentalism in large publics, the topic of the later. While this ordering device is arbitrary, it has the advantage that a number of other factors are associated with it, especially the visibility of political forces in the generation and use of these essentializations, and the degree to which essentializations are unambiguous and the boundary between them impermeable.

The first two chapters are concerned with academic essentializations. One of their key purposes is to bring to visibility the anthropological occidentalisms that are the hidden or forgotten complement to the anthropological orientalisms that have received so much critical attention. In doing so, these chapters directly address the question of the dialectical nature of anthropological essentialism.

The first of these is Deborah Reed-Danahay's 'The Kabyle and the French: Occidentalism in Pierre Bourdieu's Theory of Practice', an analysis of the two most influential of Bourdieu's books, *Outline of a Theory of Practice* (Bourdieu 1977) and *Reproduction in Education, Society and Culture* (Bourdieu and Passeron 1990). Bourdieu is both unusual and intriguing because he has written extensively and influentially both as an anthropologist of a non-Western society, the Kabyle, and as a sociologist of his own French society, particularly the French educational system. Bourdieu has tried to avoid the radical conceptual separation of the West and exotic societies. However, as Reed-Danahay notes, in spite of his efforts Bourdieu's work embodies the juxtaposition of twinned and essentialized visions of France and the Kabyle, each defined in opposition to the other.

Bourdieu's juxtaposition of France and the Kabyle takes many forms, as Reed-Danahay shows. However, an important feature of the juxtaposition echoes a Weberian distinction between the rational and institutional on the one hand, and on the other the non-rational and personal, and thus resonates with some of the uses of the notion of cargo cults. The rational, institutional French have their formal institutions and means of social reproduction and their abstract knowledge. The non-rational, personal Kabyle have only informal institutions, the constant task of regenerating themselves and their relationships through personal action, their practical but unarticulated knowledge. However, Reed-Danahay argues that this opposition does not spring from a comparison of France and Kabylia in any straightforward way. Rather, it reflects among other things Bourdieu's desire to criticize elements of French society. Consequently, if the opposition appears to spring from Bourdieu's presentation of these two societies, it does so because it shapes what is presented and what is ignored. Notably, Bourdieu ignores the importance of individual agency in French society and even in French schools. Equally, he ignores the importance of Algerian state institutions, including schools, for the Kabyle, whom he presents as a self-contained and timeless autochthonous social group.

Bourdieu's occidentalism, however, is not total. He also recognizes that there are aliens within the gates—peasants and the working class—who lack the abstraction and commitment to formal institutions that mark the true France, and through it the true West. In pointing to these groups as anomalies, Bourdieu solidifies a particular view of the West, and so illustrates the politics of occidentalism. If his occident is marked by its opposition to the Kabyle and by its possession of rationality and formal institutions, it is also marked by the power of the bourgeoisie, for that occident is their self-conception writ large.

My 'Maussian Occidentalism: Gift and Commodity Systems' investigates not a single writer, but a scholarly model that draws on the work of Marcel Mauss and is found particularly among anthropologists of Melanesia. The model is the distinction between societies of the gift and of the commodity. I focus on an aspect of the model that has received little critical attention, its characterization of the West as a commodity system. 'The West' may call up images of capitalist logic and markets full of autonomous actors. However, the evidence presented in this chapter shows that many Western people transact objects and services with each other in ways that resemble gift transactions. Moreover, they do so in many areas of life, even in the heart of the commercial realm. In ignoring these transactions, the model occidentalizes the West as a commodity system. Certainly the West is the land of the commodity compared to Melanesian villages. However, this common anthropological model takes the relative difference in the importance of gifts and commodities in these two areas of the world and elevates it to an essentialist rendering.

This model leads ethnographers to shape their representations of Melanesian societies by ignoring the more occidental, which they see as inauthentic, while focusing on the more oriental. Thus, in their interpretations and representations of Melanesian societies anthropologists reproduce the essentialist rendering of the society of the gift. The result is that influential summary analyses of Melanesian ethnography can call on a range of published work to promulgate the model's orientalism, just as influential commentators use this orientalist rendering of the region to regenerate the model's occidentalist rendering of the West.

In demonstrating the inadequacy of the commodity model as a description of the modern West, this chapter raises a question: why should such an occidentalism command such unreflective assent in the West? The answer suggested echoes what Reed-Danahay says of Bourdieu's occidentalism. It has to do with the internal politics of the West. The idea of impersonal transactions and autonomous actors reflects at least the self-image, and probably the experience, of influential parts of Western society. Political relations in the West, rather than just political relations between the West and Melanesia, shape these essentialist images.

Jane Nadel-Klein's 'Occidentalism as a Cottage Industry: Representing the Autochthonous "Other" in British and Irish Rural Studies' returns to an issue raised obliquely by Lindstrom, the location of 'the West', and hence ultimately the nature of that concept. Like Lindstrom, Nadel-Klein looks at both popular and scholarly literature, in her case detective stories and community studies, both representing a single place, the British Isles.

The village people portrayed in these two bodies of literature are aliens within the gates, the insufficiently Western people that Lindstrom decribes. In detective stories the villagers who seem bucolic and familiar prior to the discovery of the crime are revealed by the event to be furtive, secretive, bound by loyalties deeper and older than the allegiances to order and justice that motivate the police or private detectives who investigate the death. They are, in fact, modern heirs to a primordial folk. Even though they may live only a few hours by fast car from London, their geographical proximity belies their cultural distance. Less dramatically, but only slightly less thoroughly, community studies portray a similar, autochthonous social order. These are the self-contained communities that exhibit not the differentiations, trajectories, and tensions of the modern West, but a cohesive and pervasive solidarity that, in anthropological writing, characterizes descriptions of isolated villages in particular and the orient more generally.

It's been nearly a year since cancer took my Alice. I still sleep on my side of the bed. The gauzy winter sky looks flat and pulled tight, like a cold sheet.

⸺•◦•⸺

After work, my sister Janice comes over and I tell her that the intern might be hitting on me.

"It's too soon," I say, fiddling with my coffee spoon.

"Well, how would she know? You don't wear an e-Pat," she says, pointing to the empathy pathos dermal on her temple. It's metal. Small as a B-B, glowing soft blue.

"I don't want to wear one."

"You expect everyone to know what you're feeling, yet don't show it. You don't *project* it."

This from a woman who squirreled four diaries under her mattress when we were kids, and threatened to kill me if I ever read them.

I shake my head. "I just don't want one."

"Why not? You have the latest phone. You wear holo-glasses, buy the latest gadgets."

"It's not the tech," I shrug. "It's just..."

"Remember when everyone thought no one understood them? That no one knew what *they* were going through?"

I wonder if she remembers the day when I read her diaries. The day when I realized all her black eye-liner and one-note "fines" and sarcastic eye rolls meant that she was just as unmoored as I was from our parents' divorce. I wonder if she remembers our big fight, when we broke two lamps throwing books at each other. How we sobbed and hugged in the corner afterwards like two boxers worn out in the ring.

She'd said, "I want Mom back."

And I'd sworn that I'd love someone till death did us part.

Janice taps her dermal once again. "This uncovers the *real* you. Shows it to the world."

My sister has a black hole just under her navel, shaped like lost hope. She had a miscarriage two years ago.

⸺•◦•⸺

For the rhetorics that Nadel-Klein, Reed-Danahay, and Lindstrom describe, the West of occidentalism is not simply a geographic space, for non-Westerners, orientals, can live there too and pose a threat to occidental rationality and order. If it is not simply geographic, what is the occidentalist West? To begin to address this question it is necessary to address the context of the 'West', its distinction from the orient. I have already said that the distinction parallels many others common in scholarly and popular thought, but it points directly to what they often coyly obscure, a concern with the distinctive genius of the modern West. The occident, then, is both spatial, for it is Western, and temporal, for it is modern. This point merely echoes Johannes Fabian's (1983) idea that, for Westerners, the long ago and the far away often overlap.

This dual aspect of the occident is expressed in Nadel-Klein's observation that the rural villages of British detective stories and community studies are anachronisms, like French peasants in Bourdieu's view. They are caught out of time; they are survivals from the past that are geographically Western but not modern. But the time they are out of is not the quantitative time of the clock and the calendar. Rather, it resembles a Melanesian construction of qualitative time that Lindstrom mentions, in which periods of stability alternate with periods of reconstitutive change, what can be called a constitutional view of history (Carrier 1987). Thus, British villagers are of the wrong constitutional period (pre-modern) given their geographic place (the West). In their embarrassment they resemble the modern Japanese. Although Japan is outside the geographic West, at least the economic data seem to indicate that it is fully modern, perhaps more than the West itself. It appears likely that this Japanese anachronism, this being in the wrong time given its place, helps make that country such a focus of attention and concern in the modern West.

Japan is the focus of the first of the chapters concerned with how those outside the modern West generate occidentalist images of a West from which they are distinct. In 'Imaging the Other in Japanese Advertising Campaigns', Millie Creighton analyses the ways that advertisements in that remarkably self-contained country invoke foreigners of several sorts, but especially white occidentals. Japanese advertising is a particularly fruitful source of such images, for it is especially concerned with mood and tone, and generally avoids concrete information about the product involved.

What Creighton describes is the use of white occidentals, *gaijin*, to achieve two main purposes, related to each other because both rely on the strangeness of *gaijin* in Japanese culture. The first of these purposes is a re-affirmation of the value and security of Japan. Advertisements do this when they portray the potentially threatening *gaijin* in ways that eliminate that threat. These are foreigners rendered cute and cuddly, and even at times incompetent. But although advertisements tame *gaijin*, they also use their domesticated exoticness to bend the rules, to express values that, like egoism, are suspect and faintly improper if put in the mouths of Japanese themselves. It is through a consideration of these functions of *gaijin* in advertising that this chapter shows their content, and thus the occidentalism that they embody. For a number of good historical reasons, the Japanese see the West as both a threat to their integrity and a source of technical and cultural value and innovation. *Gaijin* represent taste, beauty, and novelty at the same time that they threaten. Frequently these threats take the form of an individualism and sexuality that challenge the stress on decorum and social cohesion that mark Japanese public life.

Creighton provides something of a point of reference for the chapters that follow, because the situation she describes is, in the context of this collection, extreme. Japan is powerful relative to the West that it confronts, with a strong and established sense of national identity. Further, the images that she describes are not forged in a political struggle for emerging self-definition. Instead, they are formed in a setting that resonates with very different concerns, the creative departments of advertising agencies. But even though the setting may be extreme, the processes are not. Political and economic power are important in the creation of essentialist constructions of the West, just as in the cases described by other contributors to this collection.

For instance, even though the concern with things foreign may be recurrent in Japan, its particular manifestations are the result of pragmatic political and economic processes. The Japanese government was under pressure from Western governments to reduce the country's advantageous balance of trade. It saw internationalization and being open to things foreign as at least a way to placate the complainers. Advertising agencies, on the other hand, were in the business of persuading people to buy, and saw that some of what they wanted to say would create resistance if it were put in the mouths of Japanese. Using *gaijin* allowed a way out of their problem.

But the use of *gaijin* shows that the occident and the orient need not be simply antagonistic. The ins and outs of their relationship that Lindstrom describes are extended in Japan, where exposure to the threatening, challenging, and exhilarating occident does not displace Japanese self-orientalism. Instead, the occident is tamed. *Gaijin* are revealed to be impotent, ignorant, and even amusing foreigners after all. The security and value of the orientalism of Japan are reaffirmed.

Another token of the occident is money. As it is in the present, so for a long time the existence of money has been taken as an indicator of Western superiority, marking the rationality and efficiency that are crucial elements of Western economic dominance. In 'Duelling Currencies in East New Britain: The Construction of Shell Money as National Cultural Property', Deborah Gewertz and Frederick Errington show how the contrast between the moneyed West and moneyless others has been manifest in distinctive ways in the area around what is now Rabaul, in East New Britain province in Papua New Guinea. The reason for this distinctiveness is that the Tolai and other people who live in the area have long had a form of money, commonly called *tambu*. Early Western commentators found *tambu* to be very much like 'true' money and they often took it as evidence of the inherent Westernness of the Tolai and their relative superiority to other Melanesian societies. Westerners and Tolai have continually commented on the similarities and differences between *tambu* and Western money, and these comments themselves contain a dialectic of Tolai and Western identity.

The question of the relationship between *tambu* and Western money became insistent when a Western artefact dealer sought to export shell money. In their description of the successful effort to block the export, Gewertz and Errington show that people from the Rabaul area represented Western money as an asocial corrosive, emblematic of an occidentalized West of impersonal calculation, while they said *tambu* operated as a cohesive social medium, linking people together in an orientalized Melanesia of reciprocation and concern. However, this model of an orientalizing *tambu* and an occidentalizing dollar does not just look outward to the difference between Papua New Guinea and the West. In addition, it looks inward, and so resembles some Western uses of cargoism, British detective stories, and community studies. Gewertz and Errington explore this inward orientation when they locate the incident they describe as part of the political debate by which people in Papua New Guinea both highlight and obscure differences among themselves, a debate through which powerful people and groups extend their power and make it legitimate.

The first of these political processes occurs within the societies of the Rabaul area where people use *tambu*. Those who asserted the sociality of *tambu* in contrast to Western currency and who asserted its status as an emblem of a distinct Papua New Guinea identity were, even if only implicitly, making a claim about relations within these societies. By stressing these features of *tambu* they were obscuring the marked and growing inequalities of wealth and power within their own societies, just as they were using the ideology of *tambu* to make those inequalities legitimate, or at least more palatable. Here, *tambu* operates somewhat as the commodity model does at times in the West. It defines a moral structure that encompasses both the powerful and the weak and so encourages the weak to accept their weakness and vicariously participate in the glories of the powerful.

While the debate over shell money served at least partly to obscure differences within the societies in the Rabaul area, it served (again, at least partly) to strengthen differences between them and societies elsewhere in Papua New Guinea. In seeking to block export, the advocates of *tambu* sought to have it elevated to the formal status of national cultural property. Success would make *tambu* an emblem of the country as a whole, and would thereby elevate the status of the societies that used it. But the game was already rigged in favour of *tambu*'s advocates, for their societies, especially the Tolai, were already disproportionately powerful and privileged. Here those advocates resemble the Western commentators Lindstrom describes who see disturbing signs of cargo thinking among the subordinate in the West. Just as these commentators asserted the legitimacy of their own power by painting themselves as the bearers of an exemplary and valued occidentalism, so *tambu* users painted themselves as the bearers of an exemplary and valued orientalism.

Indigenous constructions of the West emerge through complex processes, as Robert Thornton shows in 'The Colonial, the Imperial, and the Creation of the "European" in Southern Africa', a chapter that is distinctive in this collection. While most others trace the elaboration of existing renderings of orient and occident, Thornton describes what seems to be an initial, or at least early, construction of a new occidentalism by a non-Western group, the Zulu. In doing so, he helps reveal the disorder and uncertainty that exist before the simplifying essentialisms can exert their tidying effect. Put simply, there was no 'West' in the Zulu field of vision, but a confusing array of social arrangements and actors of uncertain power and practice, and hence a confusing array of potentialities. Only with hindsight could we comfort ourselves with the idea that it had to turn out as it did. In this, Thornton echoes Lindstrom's point that orient and occident can speak to and of each other in many different ways, so that their respective unities dissolve into ambiguity.

Thornton shows how, for the Zulus, the encroaching West was highly differentiated. It included English, Dutch, Portuguese, and a range of other European nationalities; the sphere of Western settlement included Indians, Zulus who had fled their homelands, and people from elsewhere on the continent; the English, Dutch, and Portuguese settlements were organized in different ways, dealt with the Zulus in different ways, and often were at odds with each other. There was as well another important source of ambiguity. For much of the nineteenth century it was not clear which of three main groups that Thornton describes, the Zulus, the Dutch, and the British, possessed the greater military power. The Zulus, then were not just reacting to and resisting an overwhelming and undifferentiated European presence.

As such a complex situation might suggest, the Zulus fashioned a complex occidentalism, though they did not fashion it on their own. Their construction of the West and Westerners contained two distinct elements, what Thornton calls the 'inside' and the 'outside'. The occidentalism of the outside reified and essentialized the British Empire, embodied in Queen Victoria, as a key source of beneficent moral and political power that Zulu royals sought to appropriate and invoke in their relations with local whites. Opposed to this was a construction of a malignant inside, the racism that was to become calcified in the policy of Apartheid. To compound this complexity, key elements of Zulu occidentalism did not spring from the Zulu themselves. Instead, they came from a British missionary bishop who constructed an essentialist image of Britain as a pedagogic device, in order to facilitate his missionary and educational activities.

Because the Zulus who elaborated and adopted this complex construction of Westerners were themselves royal, they could assert a commonalty with Queen Victoria and the Empire, not only with regard to the local whites of the inside, but also with regard to Zulu commoners. In doing so, Zulu royalty were looking inward as well as outward in their construction of themselves and others. They resembled, then, the advocates of *tambu*, as they did the sentiments of at least some of the Britons who sought to govern the Empire. One such was Lady Gordon, wife of the colonial governor of Fiji in the 1870s, who wrote that the ranking Fijians were 'such an undoubted aristocracy. Their manners are so perfectly easy and well-bred. . . . Nurse can't understand it all, she . . . looks down on them as an inferior race. I don't like to tell her that these ladies are my equals, which she is not!' (quoted in Thomas 1991*b*: 172).

Like others in this collection, Thornton points out that occidentalisms and orientalisms serve not just to draw a line between societies, but also to draw a line within them. This process is likely to be particularly pronounced in societies that self-consciously stand on the border between occident and orient. One such society is Greece, the concern of Michael Herzfeld's 'Hellenism and Occidentalism: The Permutations of Performance in Greek Bourgeois Identity'. In it he investigates occidentalisms and orientalisms as they are opposed within Greek society itself.

As Herzfeld shows, Greece is unusual because mundane elements of life are frequently seen as reflecting Turkish influence, and hence are oriental. At the same time, Greece claims to be the heir to Hellenism, the very source of the occidental. However, a growing number of Greeks are rejecting elements of their Turkish cultural heritage of the past several centuries, and replacing them with elements that mimic the West. The genuinely local and oriental, then, is being replaced by the alien and occidental, which itself is being redefined as traditional because it reflects Hellenism. This is not some spontaneous, pan-Grecian movement, for it is the Greek élite who promulgate a Hellenist and occidentalist construction of the country, and it is they who justify their ascendancy by pointing to their own Hellenized selves. But while the politics of practical occidentalism may be particularly striking in Greece, they are present in the ideas and situations described by many contributors. Zulu royalty, for instance, are prone to see themselves in a particularly flattering and Western light in comparison to Zulu commoners and local Western administrators. As the case of *tambu* shows, of course, practical orientalism shows a similar political aspect.

Herzfeld brings out yet another important point, that 'occidental' and 'oriental' are not stable and exclusive categories. Instead, in Greece as elsewhere, there is a continuum of the more occidental and the more oriental, and it seems likely that many people see themselves as located ambiguously on that continuum. In the United States, certainly, classes and groups of people are defined both as falling short of the Western pole and as exhibiting some traits held over from their earlier, more oriental origins. This is most notable with blacks and the parasitic intellectual industries that have grown up around them. Alex Haley's search for roots is a search for a non-Western oriental core being. Many academics make a good living spotting traces of African elements in the kinship, music, religion, and the rest in American blacks. These may serve to give blacks an identity independent from that of undifferentiated Americans, an identity that can be a source of personal resilience. The novel end-of-year celebration of Kwanza is an example. At the same time, however, these are clearly oriental identities, and the collective shortcomings of blacks in American society can be attributed easily to the lingering orient within them, as illustrated by the accusations of cargo cult thinking made occasionally against ghetto blacks that Lindstrom describes. What is true of blacks can easily be true, as it has been true, of those with familial origins in eastern and southern Europe or points east.

Herzfeld's discussion of practical Greek occidentalism brings us to the other end of the dimension that orders this collection. We are well beyond the focus of Reed-Danahay's and my own early chapters, academic models that portray a world of abstract and unambiguous categories. Instead, Herzfeld describes the messy practicality of drawing boundaries and calling names, the realm of the practical construction of identity, the choices, activities, and strategies through which people define themselves and the things around them as occidental or oriental.

These two poles come together in Jonathan Spencer's 'Occidentalism in the East: The Uses of the West in the Politics and Anthropology of South Asia'. Not a conclusion in the normal sense, this final chapter illustrates and reflects on many of the points raised in this collection by way of the study of South Asia, and particularly Sri Lanka. It does so by describing and contrasting the orientalisms and occidentalisms of important scholars who have written on the region, both Westerners and South Asians themselves. Even though these scholars have all written about South Asia, they have done so for different audiences and different purposes, so that the occidentalisms they express and the relationships between orient and occident that they assume and espouse have different contents and values.

The Western scholars Spencer describes are Louis Dumont and McKim Marriott. Each has invoked what Spencer calls a 'rhetoric of authenticity' to buttress his arguments about the nature of South Asian society. As Dumont and Marriott use this rhetoric, Westerners can understand South Asia only by abandoning their cultural presuppositions and categories so that they can see the region in its own terms. While they disagree about what constitutes the region's 'own terms', Dumont and Marriott both sees the terms that they identify as being authentically South Asian and radically distinct from the modern West, though Dumont does think the two can be subsumed under a common intellectual framework. For the Sri Lankan scholars Spencer describes, however—Ananda Coomaraswamy, Martin Wickremesinghe, and Munidasa Cumaratunga—the case is different. These writers are as much nationalists as scholars, and while all invoked a rhetoric of authenticity, they did not see the distinction between orient and occident in the way that Dumont and Marriott did. Two saw that Sri Lanka had incorporated elements of the West, both good and bad. Consequently, their 'authenticity' does not entail the purity that it does for the Western writers. The third, Cumaratunga, sought purity, but the introductions into Sri Lanka that most concerned him were those from elsewhere in South Asia, rather than from the West. He reminds us that the West, real or imagined, need not be the pole against which those outside the West define themselves.

For Spencer, these Western and South Asian writers differ fundamentally in their attitudes toward history, and especially the history of the relationship between orient and occident. Dumont's and Marriott's orient is, in its purity, one in which colonization and reciprocal influence are expunged. In this, these writers resemble Bourdieu's construction of the Kabyle that ignores French colonial institutions and the Maussians' construction of Melanesia that ignores Western intrusions. This rhetoric of authenticity undergirds the very notion of the orient as mysterious, so mysterious that the knowledge and skills of the anthropologist are crucial if we are to learn of it and its lessons for us. This anthropologist's charter paints a world very different from that of the Sri Lankan writers. At least for two of them, the occidentalized West is not the inhabitant of a different universe, neither touched nor touching. Instead, the image of the occident includes the history of colonial rule and, more broadly, the vast imbalance of power between nations. Such a West impinges upon the orient in various ways and so helps define it.

Spencer's concluding chapter returns this collection to Lindstrom's opening one. Each describes the relationship between orient and occident in more scholarly and in more popular presentation; Lindstrom through writings on cargo, Spencer through writings on South Asia. Each provides a beneficial warning, but one that poses a problem. The warning is that scholarly renderings of orient and occident, with their neat categories and clear divisions, are likely to be unfaithful to the ways that people actually think and act. The clear distinction between cargo thinking and Western thought, like the clear distinction between South Asia and the West, gives way to much more complex popular images. If we are all ultimately cargoists, if South Asia is shaped by the West, then our neat, essential academic categories cannot be sustained. Here, however, the problem lurking in the warning appears. We cannot do other than simplify and reduce what we have learned to bounded essentials to some degree. If we did not, we would be swamped with particularities and bereft of meaning, our judgement would be forestalled, our writing would be an unreadable and unthinkable mass of detail devoid of interest even to those about whom we write. But to say that essences and categories are the tools and instruments we must use to perceive, think, and write, much less act, does not mean that we are licensed to use them without reflection or self-consciousness. As Kenneth Burke (1969: 281) remarked, though tools and instruments may appear to 'transcend human purpose . . . they have purpose embedded in their structure and design'. We have to recognize as best we can the purposes built into and encrusted upon the essences and categories we use, and we have to assess as best we can how well those purposes fit our own.

Conclusion

It is worth bringing together some of the issues raised and questions addressed by the chapters in this collection, which revolve around the point that occident and orient and the distinction between them all are shaped by political circumstance.

This circumstance helps explain why the content of those terms and relationships is so fluid. Consider, for example, the Western construction of the West in this collection's first chapters. Through much of the Western use of the phrase 'cargo cult' runs an unspoken Weberian invocation of the occidentalist West as populated by people who select on a rational basis the means that they will use to pursue their ends. For Reed-Danahay, however, the occident is portrayed as the land of overarching social structures. In the gift–commodity model it is autonomous market actors that constitute the West. Finally, in representations of British villages it is cosmopolitans—people in control of their passions, committed to a rational order, and free of allegiance to place. These different attributes are coherent to the extent that they make sense culturally, and it is possible to pull out some underlying common themes. However, doing so would ignore their patent diversity. It seems more plausible to see them as elements of a pool of images. People select one or another element as standing for the West according to their circumstance, which includes both their position relative to Western centres of power and the nature of the thing that they want to distinguish from the West. Of course, because orient and occident generate each other dialectically, the very nature of the thing that they desire to distinguish from the West is in part a product of that pool of images.

Politics also shapes the valuation of the West. Those who see themselves as close to the centre of the West, as they understand it, would probably find congenial a flattering occidentalism. Equally, however, there are those who see themselves as distant from that centre and who want no part of it. This political rejection of the West through a negative occidentalism is apparent particularly in the case of the advocates of *tambu*, though it appears as well among the adherents of *kastom* mentioned earlier in this Introduction. But matters are more complex than this neat dualism allows. For instance, while the Japanese reject the occidentalized West of the *gaijin*, increasingly they see themselves as surpassing the West economically. This is not, then, a rejection by those who are peripheral to the centres of world power and wealth. Instead, it is a rejection by those who see themselves as severing the link between those centres and the West. Moreover, among those clearly less powerful than the West, the Zulus that Thornton describes are as far from Western centres as the *tambu*-using Tolai and Duke of York Islanders, yet they constructed an image of the West with strong positive elements. In between are some of the Sri Lankans Spencer analyses. They neither rejected nor embraced the West outright, but saw in it things of worth and things to be scorned.

These Sri Lankan intellectuals point to another complication, that distance from the West need not be a matter of geographical space. Colombo may be a long way from London, but for these writers the latter touched upon the former and so influenced it in important ways. They saw that some of these influences were baleful, but others were beneficial. Conversely, some Afro-centrics who indisputably live in the geographic West construe it negatively. This is especially striking among those who adhere to 'melanism' (e.g. Barnes 1988; Finch 1990; King 1990; Welsing 1991). Melanists see occidentals as inadequate people who have shamelessly taken and debased the wisdom and virtues of Africa. It is interesting to see how that melanist rhetoric echoes the advocates of *tambu*, *kastom*, and *kerekere*. It does so when it occidentalizes the modern West as inhumanly mechanistic and impersonal, in contrast to an orientalized Africa of human empathy and creativity. In its way, this also resembles an orientalism that Herzfeld mentions in his chapter, in which some Greeks see Japan in particular, and countries of the Far East more generally, as a land of rigid conformity that steals Western ideas, while the West is seen as the land of individual expression, spontaneity, and creativity.

The importance of politics is brought home even more clearly when we remember that it does not just shape the content of 'the West', but helps determine whether that entity even exists as more than a simple geographical marker. Arguments in the United States in favour of multiculturalism, for example, move at times beyond a concern to trace the contribution of different groups to American life, and instead appear to dissolve the country into a space where different groups live their separate lives (see Asante 1991; Ravitch 1990, 1991). Likewise, in the battleground that is English literature, the reconstruction of the canon tends at times

Alice always said our marriage was like "two corner pieces." You know, from a jigsaw puzzle. Anyone could see we fit together. Easy-peasy. Janice liked her immediately. She said we clicked.

I think about this walking to and from work, wondering if I could fit people together based on the pain that their dermals project. Everyone looks like lopsided shadows. Each hole is a little different. Some are older and smooth; some are new and jagged. Some curve, like giant commas. Pain-pauses in anguished lives.

Even little kids wear holes over their hearts. From what? Grief over dead pets? Broken homes? Worse?

I don't like to think about it.

At night, in the dark, I can't see people's holes. But the dermals on their temples still glow. Like electric fireflies. Or neon eyes.

⋅•◆•⋅

Janice uncovers a soupy casserole she brought over and takes out my plates.

"You're not eating enough, bro."

"Hey, do you remember when I read your diaries?"

"Oh god, I was so pissed!" she laughs, sitting down.

"You didn't want anyone to know what you were feeling. You know, privacy and stuff."

"Oooh," she nods, "this is about you getting a dermal. But I was a teenager! And it was better after you knew how I felt. And it was better after Dad knew too. Remember how he made us see that therapist? Wasn't it better after that?"

"I guess so."

"No sense in bottling things up," she says, dishing out a glob of casserole on my plate.

"But back then... you shared stuff with people who already knew you. Who already loved you."

"Except the therapist."

"Yeah, well. But it was more... *personal* back then. You know?"

She sighs and pushes a noodle around on her plate. "I'm just saying that it feels good when you get the e-Pat. You can own your pain."

"Show it off, you mean?"

to turn instead into its dissolution, with different literary histories and traditions for different sets of people. However, while the more extreme critics of multiculturalism may foresee the collapse of the West as a conceptual or even a social entity, it seems more likely that there will be the sort of implicit reconstruction that Lindstrom describes. That is, the emergence of a new universalism that will, on close inspection, look like universal Westernism that generates in turn a new set of alien orientals. Or it may result in little more than the celebration of diversity of tastes and styles that is so marked a feature of Western consumer capitalism. People would be different, but their differences would be constrained by and expressed in a common frame (Wilk 1995).

Political factors account for another point brought out in this collection. The occidentalized West is an imagined entity that, in its memorable clarity, obscures the vast areas of Western life that conflict with its vision, as Creighton notes in her discussion of Japanese occidentalism. Indeed, this echoes an element of Said's criticism of Orientalism, that it obscures vast areas of life in the Middle East that conflict with its vision. I need to stress here, however, that this need not be any crude and unprincipled selectivity in perception. Consider the Western anthropologists studying societies in Melanesia, whom I describe in my chapter on gift and commodity systems. The people and societies they confronted really were different from urban America, Britain, and Australia, home to most of those researchers. It should be neither a surprise nor a cause for censure that those anthropologists sought to explain that difference or that they sought to do so by developing and invoking a set of principles that accounted for what they saw, or even that those principles defined some of what they saw as more important and worthy of attention, and some as less. It is difficult to imagine how people could conduct research, much less live their daily lives, in any other way. And, to continue the example, if such selective perception is unexceptionable for Western anthropologists studying closely the societies of Melanesia that they confront in their field-work, it is even more unexceptionable for their understanding of the taken-for-granted Western societies from which they came.

In other words, the sheer existence of essentialist rendering and selective perception is likely to be routine. Pointing out that existence is not very revealing. Even pointing out that it causes errors and misperceptions, though worthwhile, is not very exciting, for these are inevitable. Instead, it is necessary to do what this collection tries, to begin to show how that essentialist and selective vision arises, how it reflects people's social and political situations, and how it affects their lives and works.

I will conclude by returning to an issue I raised at the beginning of this Introduction. I said there that recent criticisms of anthropology have focused on the ways that anthropologists construe and present the societies they study. Many of the points made by critics are valid. However, the weight of their argument ultimately is likely to generate a misleading picture of the problems the discipline faces. This is because their criticism focuses on the relationship between anthropologists and the people they study, a relationship that, they argue, is opaque and problematic. However, in their far-ranging critiques of the discipline they are silent about the relationship between anthropology and the West, which suggests that they see that relationship as transparent and straightforward, or at least not worthy of attention. However, as many of the chapters in this collection show, this is not the case. The West that many anthropologists seem to carry around in their heads is as partial and distorted as the critics claim is the case with anthropological renderings of the alien.

There are many reasons for this anthropological occidentalism (I describe some in Carrier 1992*b*). But whatever those reasons, until anthropologists recognize the existence of their occidentalisms and their significance for anthropological orientalism, attempts to improve the ways that anthropologists construct and render the alien are likely to meet with only partial success. One purpose of this collection is to hasten this recognition.

Acknowledgements

I want to thank Achsah Carrier for her help and encouragement while I was writing this chapter, which draws on arguments that are made at greater length in Carrier (1992*a*, 1992*b*). Bernard Ortiz de Montellano helpfully provided useful information on melanist literature. I am also grateful for comments made when I presented parts of this chapter at an anthropology department seminar at Harvard University.

Notes

1 To essentialize a group or region does not require that it be seen as static or simple. It can be construed as going through stages of development or evolution, as Richard Handler (1988: 4–5, 40–3) says occurs in nationalist essentialisms. Equally, it can be essentialized in terms of its complexity and continual change, as Michael Herzfeld (1987: 157–66) argues is the case for Europe.

2 Marshall Sahlins (1993) has raised questions about whether *kerekere* was not in fact an emblematic Fijian custom before the period of extensive colonial

impact. Thomas (1993) in turn has countered Sahlins's objections. Sahlins's paper also contains an important reminder, that many of the arguments that I make and describe in this Introduction have been made before, most notably by Gregory Bateson (e.g. 1958) with his concept of schizmogenesis.

References

ABERCROMBIE, NICHOLAS, HILL, STEPHEN, and TURNER, BRYAN S. (1986). *Sovereign Individuals of Capitalism*. London: Allen & Unwin.

ASANTE, MOLEFI K. (1991). 'Multiculturalism: An Exchange', *American Scholar*, 60: 267–72.

BALSHEM, MARTHA (1991). 'Cancer, Control, and Causality: Talking about Cancer in a Working-Class Community', *American Ethnologist*, 18: 152–72.

BARNES, CAROL (1988). *Melanin: The Chemical Key to Black Greatness*. Houston, Tex.: C. B. Publishers.

BATESON, GREGORY (1958). *Naven*. Stanford, Calif.: Stanford University Press.

BOURDIEU, PIERRE (1977). *Outline of a Theory of Practice*, trans. Richard Nice. Cambridge: Cambridge University Press.

——and PASSERON, JEAN-CLAUDE (1990). *Reproduction in Education, Society and Culture*, 2nd edn., trans. Richard Nice. London: Sage Publications.

BURKE, KENNETH (1969 [1945]). *A Grammar of Motives*. Berkeley, Calif.: University of California Press.

CARRIER, JAMES G. (1987). 'History and Self-Conception in Ponam Society', *Man*, 22: 111–31.

——(1992a). 'Introduction', in J. Carrier (ed.), *History and Tradition in Melanesian Anthropology*. Berkeley, Calif.: University of California Press: 1–37.

——(1992b). 'Occidentalism: The World Turned Upside-Down', *American Ethnologist*, 19: 195–212.

CHEN, XIAOMEI (1992). 'Occidentalism as Counterdiscourse: *He shang* in post-Mao China', *Critical Inquiry*, 18: 686–712.

CLIFFORD, JAMES (1988). *The Predicament of Culture: Twentieth-Century Ethnography, Literature, and Art*. Cambridge, Mass.: Harvard University Press.

DUMONT, LOUIS (1970). *Homo Hierarchicus: The Caste System and its Implications*. Chicago: University of Chicago Press.

——(1977). *From Mandeville to Marx: The Genesis and Triumph of Economic Ideology*. Chicago: University of Chicago Press.

ERRINGTON, FREDERICK K. (1987). 'Reflexivity Deflected: The Festival of Nations as an American Cultural Performance', *American Ethnologist*, 14: 654–67.

——and GEWERTZ, DEBORAH B. (1987). 'Of Unfinished Dialogues and Paper Pigs', *American Ethnologist*, 14: 367–76.

FABIAN, JOHANNES (1983). *Time and the Other: How Anthropology Makes its Object*. New York: Columbia University Press.

FARDON, RICHARD (ed.) (1990). *Localizing Strategies: Regional Traditions of Ethnographic Writing*. Edinburgh: Scottish Academic Press.

FINCH, CHARLES S. (1990). *The African Background to Medical Science*. London: Karnak House.

FITZPATRICK, PETER (1980). *Law and State in Papua New Guinea*. London: Academic Press.

FONER, ERIC, and WEINER, JON (1991). 'Fighting for the West', *Nation* (29 July–5 Aug.): 163–6.

FULLER, CHRIS J. (1989). 'Misconceiving the Grain Heap: A Critique of the Concept of the Indian Jajmani System', in Jonathan Parry and Maurice Bloch (eds.), *Money and the Morality of Exchange*. Cambridge: Cambridge University Press: 33–63.

GEWERTZ, DEBORAH B., and ERRINGTON, FREDERICK K. (1991). *Twisted Histories, Altered Contexts: Representing the Chambri in a World System*. Cambridge: Cambridge University Press.

HANDLER, RICHARD (1988). *Nationalism and the Politics of Culture in Quebec*. Madison, Wis.: University of Wisconsin Press.

HERZFELD, MICHAEL (1987). *Anthropology through the Looking-Glass: Critical Ethnography in the Margins of Europe*. Cambridge: Cambridge University Press.

HIRSCH, ERIC (1990). 'From Bones to Betelnuts: Processes of Ritual Transformation and the Development of "National Culture" in Papua New Guinea', *Man*, 25: 18–34.

KEESING, ROGER (1982). 'Kastom in Melanesia: An Overview', *Mankind*, 13 (special issue): 297–301.

——and JOLLY, MARGARET (1992). 'Epilogue', in James G. Carrier (ed.), *History and Tradition in Melanesian Anthropology*. Berkeley, Calif.: University of California Press: 224–47.

——and TONKINSON, ROBERT (eds.) (1982). 'Reinventing Traditional Culture: The Politics of Kastom in Island Melanesia', *Mankind*, 13 (special issue).

KING, RICHARD (1990). *African Origin of Biological Psychiatry*. Germantown, Tenn.: Seymour Smith.

KUPER, ADAM (1988). *The Invention of Primitive Society*. London: Routledge.

LAWRENCE, PETER (1964). *Road Belong Cargo: A Study of the Cargo Movement in the Southern Madang District, New Guinea*. Manchester: Manchester University Press.

LAWSON, STEPHANIE (1993). 'The Politics of Tradition: Problems for Political Legitimacy and Democracy in the South Pacific', *Pacific Studies*, 16/2: 1–29.

MASON, PETER (1990). *Deconstructing America: Representations of the Other*. London: Routledge.

MILLER, DANIEL (1987). *Material Culture and Mass Consumption*. Oxford: Basil Blackwell.

NADER, LAURA (1989). 'Orientalism, Occidentalism and the Control of Women', *Cultural Dynamics*, 2: 323–55.

PEARCE, ROY HARVEY (1965 [1953]). *Savagism and Civilization: A Study of the Indian and the American Mind*. Baltimore: Johns Hopkins Press.

POLIER, NICOLE, and ROSEBERRY, WILLIAM (1989). 'Tristes Tropes: Postmodern Anthropologists Encounter the Other and Discover Themselves', *Economy and Society*, 18: 245–64.

RAVITCH, DIANE (1990). 'Multiculturalism: E Pluribus Plures', *American Scholar*, 59: 337–54.

——(1991). 'Multiculturalism: An Exchange', *American Scholar*, 60: 267–76.

SAHLINS, MARSHALL (1993). 'Cery Cery Fuckabede', *American Ethnologist*, 20: 848–67.

SAID, EDWARD (1978). *Orientalism*. Harmondsworth: Penguin.

SCHWARTZ, THEODORE (1962). 'The Paliau Movement in the Admiralty Islands, 1946–1954', *Anthropological Papers of the American Museum of Natural History*, 49: 211–421.

SILVERMAN, DEBORA (1986). *Selling Culture: Bloomingdale's, Diana Vreeland, and the New Aristocracy of Taste in Reagan's America*. New York: Pantheon Books.

SMITH, BERNARD (1985). *European Vision and the South Pacific*. (2nd edn.) New Haven, Conn.: Yale University Press.

SMOLLETT, ELEANOR (1993). 'America the Beautiful: Made in Bulgaria', *Anthropology Today*, 9/2: 9–13.

SPENCER, JONATHAN (1989). 'Anthropology as a Kind of Writing', *Man*, 24: 145–64.

——(1990). 'Writing within: Anthropology, Nationalism and Culture in Sri Lanka', *Current Anthropology*, 31: 283–91.

THOMAS, NICHOLAS (1991*a*). 'Anthropology and *Orientalism*', *Anthropology Today*, 7/2: 4–7.

——(1991*b*). *Entangled Objects: Exchange, Material Culture and Colonialism in the Pacific*. Cambridge, Mass.: Harvard University Press.

——(1992*a*). 'The Inversion of Tradition', *American Ethnologist*, 19: 213–32.

——(1992*b*). 'Substantivization and Anthropological Discourse: The Transformation of Practices into Institutions in Neotraditional Pacific Societies', in James G. Carrier (ed.), *History and Tradition in Melanesian Anthropology*. Berkeley, Calif.: University of California Press: 64–85.

——(1993). 'Beggars Can Be Choosers', *American Ethnologist*, 20: 868–76.

TUCKER, ROBERT C. (ed.) (1978). *The Marx–Engels Reader*. (2nd edn.) New York: W. W. Norton.

WELSING, FRANCES CRESS (1991). *The Isis Papers*. Chicago: Third World Press.

WILK, RICHARD (1995). 'Learning to be Local in Belize', in Daniel Miller (ed.), *Worlds Apart: Modernity through the Prism of the Local*. London: Routledge: forthcoming.

1

Cargoism and Occidentalism

Lamont Lindstrom

Paul Nizan in *Aden, Arabie*, his travelogue of disillusionment, wrote gloomily that 'The Orient reproduces the Occident and is a commentary on it' (1987: 110). Although Nizan had in mind wretched attempts of European *colons* to replicate life back home, his disappointment in the similarities between Orient and Occident says something about the gravity of expectation that surrounds this boundary. Nizan travelled to *Arabie* seeking difference but he discovered only more of the same—and that in an odiously intensified form. The Orient is a corrosive commentary on the Occident: 'The liquid has been decanted and only the essence is left; everything that diluted the solution has evaporated' (1987: 110).

Edward Said, in a more recent, more sophisticated argument, has also suggested that the Orient exists in part as an Occidental commentary. Had Nizan succeeded in locating in Arabie some Oriental mystery, that contrast too would have been fraudulent—a mirage of Nizan's own desires for exotica and change. Said thus takes to task the body of expectation, knowledge, and practice that impelled Nizan to make his pilgrimage from Occident to Orient, inviting him to presume that he was in fact stepping over a fundamental boundary. Said calls all this a discourse, and labels this discourse Orientalism:

Orientalism can be discussed and analyzed as the corporate institution for dealing with the Orient—dealing with it by making statements about it, authorizing views of it, describing it, by teaching it, settling it, ruling over it: in short, Orientalism as a Western style for dominating, restructuring, and having authority over the Orient. . . . [W]ithout examining Orientalism as a discourse one cannot possibly understand the enormously systematic discipline by which European culture was able to manage—and even produce—the Orient. (1978: 3)

Orientalism produces the Orient but also reveals and is a commentary on Occidental institutions, styles, and interests. The Orient, and Orientalism, necessarily presume an Occident and a parallel if sometimes less clearly spoken discourse of Occidentalism. Nizan's mirrored Occident, in this regard, appears one of decayed capitalism; Said's is one of modernist surveillance and management, a system of colonialist control.

James Carrier has argued that each of these discursive domains is 'understood in reified, essentialist terms, and each is defined by its difference from the other element of the opposed pair' (1992*b*: 196). Within this sort of classificatory dualism, orientalist discourse automatically provides commentary on occidentalism. The Orient that Nizan experienced unavoidably reflected and reproduced his Occident. To come to grips with our orientalism, therefore, we also have to be able to discern our more shadowed occidentalism (Carrier 1992*b*: 199).

The orient appears opposed to the occident in several well-known stances (see Carrier 1992*b*; Mason 1990: 52–3, 124–7; Said 1978: 58–9). It may reflect as reversed image, a looking-glass wonderland. It may serve within evolutionary or dialectical models as the primitive, the ancient, or the grandfather. Equally, it may be the savage, the child, or the younger brother. It may be female to an occidental male. It might be nature to occidental culture; or sinful heathen to God's elect. Or it may lurk as radical other, a territory that is totally alien to the self.

Orientalist discourse elaborates upon these various registers of difference that separate occident and orient. Carrier (1992*b*) reviews the several ways in which difference itself attracts anthropologist and non-anthropologist (e.g. Paul Nizan) alike, and also the proclivity and the danger of essentializing such difference. Essentialization of either orient or occident

can lead to an exaggerated and even false sense of difference. Difference itself can become the determining, though perhaps unspoken, characteristic of alien societies, so that signs of similarity become embarrassments, to be ignored or explained away in terms that maintain the purity of Us and Them. (1992*b*: 203)

Said, also wary of essentialized difference, deconstructs Orientalism purposely to erase the boundary between Orient and Occident—a boundary which hides the diversity that exists among all those labelled Orientals and, at a different level, obscures our common humanity (1978: 328).

At first glance, thus, we appear to construct a discourse of the occident—and our constructions are sometimes elaborated but typically unspoken—in terms of these several registers of difference that make us unlike the orient. We essentialize ourselves versus the other, driven as we are by dualistic classificatory devices common within Western patterns of thought, and driven, as well, by a range of economic and political interests (see Kuklick 1991). I suggest in this chapter, however, that the story is often more complex than one of duelling essentialisms. The boundary between occident and orient is porous along much of its reach. Occidentalism/orientalism, as a doubled discourse, occasionally admits similarity and common humanity into its story as well as marked differences.[1]

To investigate one strand of occidentalist discourse and the sorts of difference and similarity it allows, I turn to one minor version of orientalism—to stories of the Melanesian cargo cult. I dip into a stream of nearly fifty years of cargo cult writing, a literature that I would like to call 'Cargoism'.[2] Actually, Cargoist authors have themselves already invented the term 'Cargoism', applying it to the sort of mentality that they suspect lies behind island preoccupations with cargo cult (see Harding 1967). I borrow the term to refer to the bounteous archive of cargo cult texts, also applying it to the sort of orientalist—and occidentalist—mentality that I suspect lies behind our own preoccupations with cargo cult.

Cargoist literature, limited to one of the more obscure fringes of the orient—the Melanesian islands—and to one minor sort of religio-political convulsion—a strategy to acquire Western commodities through ritual action—testifies to some of the more complex forms that occidentalist discourse takes. Seemingly, tales of oriental (read Melanesian) cargo cultists are at once tales of occidental non-cargo cultists. A story-line that they are not like us, and we not like them, however, is much too simple. Tales of the cargo cult, rather, narrate a 'fluidity' in the other (Carrier, Introduction, this volume) but also a fluidity in the self. The cargo cult is at once exotic and familiar; the cargo cultist is both other and self.

Some terms[3]

Carrier (1992*b*: 198), taking note of power differentials within the world system of the past several centuries that influence the relative capacities of different peoples to define and describe one another, proposed the terms 'ethno-orientalism' and 'ethno-occidentalism'. These terms label discourses about the self, in the former case, and discourses about the West, in the latter, that orientals themselves have devised in parallel with our orientalism and occidentalism. For purposes of this chapter, I would like to ignore the slant of the historical playing field and use, instead, the term auto-orientalism to refer to self-discourse among orientals. In this scheme, thus, occidentalism is discourse among orientals about the West. What Carrier and others have called occidentalism, I will call auto-occidentalism—the self-discourse of Westerners (and this term should replace my use of occidentalism, above). This terminology allows me several additional labels that are important for a reading of cargo cult tales. These include internal-orientalism (or, in this case, internal-Cargoism) (the location of the orient (here, cargo cultists) at home); auto-Cargoism (an adoption of Cargoist discourse by Melanesians to talk about themselves); sympathetic-Cargoism (Western constructions of the Melanesian that permit a measure of similarity between self and other); pseudo-occidentalism (or presumptions about what the oriental may be saying about the occident); and assimilative-Cargoism (the erasure of boundaries so that stories of the oriental/Cargo other explicitly transform into stories of the self). The Cargoist archive is packed with internal-orientalist, sympathetic-orientalist, pseudo-occidentalist, and assimilative-orientalist elements that blur and even erase the boundary and the differences that separate us and them.

Cargoism

The discourse of cargo cults provides a curiously spectacular story of both occidentalism and auto-occidentalism. On the one hand, here are stories that characterize a Melanesian other in terms of a set of essentialized differences—stories that at the same time evoke an opposed non-cargo-cultist self. Cargoism, in this regard, is necessarily also a genre of auto-occidentalism. But, on the other hand, here are people seemingly engaged in mimetic ritual behaviour to obtain wealth and manufactured goods. In aping Western manners and ends, they display a range of Melanesian constructions of the occidental. As Roy Wagner (1981: 31) and others have pointed out, the cargo cult prophet's occidentalist truths about wealthy Europeans and their cargo parallel the anthropologist's orientalist truths about cultic Melanesians and their ritual. Cargoism, at first glance, consists of our auto-occidental analyses of Pacific Islanders' own occidentalism.

It is easy to tease essentialized dualism from Cargoist writing—to locate the boundaries that divide us from them. The first appearance in print of the term 'cargo cult' occurred in November 1945, in the colonial news magazine *Pacific Islands Monthly*. An Australian, Norman M. Bird, who during the just-concluded Pacific War had been active in the New Guinea Volunteer Rifles (an irregular company of armed settlers), was dismayed by crumbling colonial and racial certainties. He wrote:

Stemming directly from religious teaching of equality, and its resulting sense of injustice, is what is generally known as 'Vailala Madness,' or 'Cargo Cult.' . . . By his very nature the New Guinea native is peculiarly susceptible to these 'cults' . . .

[H]e will emerge, as he is, a primitive savage with all a primitive savage's in-
stincts. The New Guinea native is not unreliable. He is worse—he is unpredictable. The result of an organized uprising of these armed savages could be the
massacre of Europeans in these islands. (Bird 1945: 69–70)

These racial oppositions are old acquaintances. The native is cultic,
susceptible to madness, primitive, savage, unpredictable, childlike, dangerous, and a killer. Such description works through unspoken comparison: the native is all of these things relative to the White Man who is
religious yet rational, civilized, predictable, adult, and kills only when
proper. This comparison need not be explicitly made in the text itself
because it is always already understood. Each of these points of implied
comparison sustains an auto-occidentalist claim, as many critics of
orientalism have observed. Such comparison 'is at one and the same time
a discourse on self and a discourse on the other, involving the process of
"negative self-definition", by which self is defined in terms of what it is
not, namely, the other' (Mason 1990: 90–1).

When the term 'cargo cult' passed from the colonial community into
the hands of anthropologists in the late 1940s and 1950s (see Lindstrom
1993), a more sophisticated, less racist, process of 'negative self-definition'
emerged, although considerable comparative crudeness could still occur.
The 1972 *Dictionary of Anthropology*, for example, defined cargo cult as a

Millenary movement among native peoples believing that the imminent arrival of
spirits from the dead [*sic*], bringing quantities of the Europeans' goods for the
loyal believers, would precede the coming of the millennium . . . Modern cargo
cults are found chiefly in New Guinea and Melanesia, e.g. the Solomon Is.: those
places, in fact, where the people have recently and suddenly emerged from a
primitive way of life, and missed all the gradual steps in developing their civilizations. They generally take the following form: a leader tells his followers to
expect great shipments of modern luxury goods, clothing, guns and food. In
anticipation they build an airstrip or great warehouse; although the goods should
have come to them long ago the British (or whatever the colonial power) have
diverted them for their own use. Therefore the cargo cults are generally anti-
government and disruptive, and cause much concern with the authorities. They
have developed since World War II, and since then become increasingly more
common. They are often quite illogical and the leaders frequently urge the destruction of money. (Davies 1972: 44–5)

In this text, the Cargoist themes of Melanesian irrationality, rebellion,
primitiveness, disrespect for money, and reactive rather than creative
action continue to delineate the occidental, who sits in cargo cult's shadow,
who is none of this.

"God, don't be such a dick."

"Remember Facebook?" I ask. "The dermals remind me of that. You know, putting it all out there..."

"Social media was like the Model-T for the implants. This is different. What, you think I'm over-sharing? You think..." She stabs at her casserole and frowns. "Honestly, how can people's pain make you so uncomfortable, when you're the nicest guy I know?"

I shrug.

She puts her hand over her black hole, just under her stomach. And I suddenly feel cruel. She was going to name the baby after our favorite aunt.

"Look, when you get the e-Pat, you *claim* your pain," she says. "It's like saying 'Fuck it.' You're showing the world, but it's not showing off. It's *memorializing*. You've been through so much from losing Alice. Don't you want a tribute to her loss?"

Doctor Green used to be my pediatrician. He still looks into my ears and makes me say "ah."

"Mmm," he nods when he hears my request. "Everybody's got them now. We do the low-incomes for free, and visit all the schools. Reminds me of the old Fitbit craze, when folks went crazy over heart rates and calories. Kind of gadgety, you know?"

"Do you think e-Pats are harmful?"

"Oh no, no. They're just projectors from neural receptors." He rubs something on my temple, preparing it. "Besides, who am I to argue with world peace?"

"My sister says that seeing everyone's pain makes people less selfish. More inward than outward."

"Mmm, and I do remember the outward. Rhinoplasties, chin implants, pec implants, this side's gotta match that side, plump that out, poof this out ... fillers, Botox, Brotox for the fellows." He chuckles. "Yes, this is better. Uglier, but better."

Another doctor walks down the hallway. His white lab coat seems to disappear into a black hole around his middle. In fact, his whole torso is almost completely black, like a crack running right through him.

More sensitive anthropological observers of cargo cults, however, quickly abandoned coarse oppositions between mad cultic savages and civilized and logical Europeans. Anthropologists, of course, make it their business to force the seemingly irrational to make sense in its own terms. Cultural understanding of this sort, in which the other's terms are discovered and then used to explain, reduces but does not eliminate the bounds of difference. We are like Melanesians in that we act according to the lights of our culture; but we are unlike Melanesians because those terms differ.

Peter Lawrence's early analysis of the Yali Movement, described most fully in *Road Belong Cargo*, introduced this cultural rationalist approach to cults. Lawrence began by making seemingly irrational Melanesian desires for cargo make sense. He argued that cultists desire European material goods because of the cultural significance they understand these goods to have. Islanders have 'the desire for the material culture of the European, and hence for economic and social equality with him' (Lawrence 1954: 1, 3). 'For them the cargo has become the symbol of the political power of the Europeans, and this power they feel they must combat' (1954: 20). European goods acquired their peculiar charge given the traditional importance of wealth within Melanesian society:

[M]aterial wealth, apart from its primary utility, had a secondary and perhaps greater value as the symbol of social relationships. Its existence enabled cooperation between, and its abundance conferred prestige on, both individuals and groups. (Lawrence 1964: 28–9)

Seemingly extreme desires for cargo are actually rational in Melanesian cultural terms. Under colonialism, Melanesians encountered new sorts of wealth that they had to acknowledge and attempt to control in order to have any chance to create moral relationships of equality and amity with Europeans.

Having rationalized cargo in Melanesian terms, anthropologists moved onwards to make sense of cult. Whereas Mr Bird's Cargoism took the raw cult to be a mad reaction to powerful Europeans, culturally informed Cargoism instead tried to read the cult to discern its meanings. Anthropologists proposed two such interpretations. The first admitted the cult's status as religious reaction to powerful outsiders, but found this religiosity functional and logical given political conditions. The second went further and normalized the cult as an ordinary, even admirable example of Melanesian creativity and cultural imagination (see e.g. Rimoldi 1971: 88).

The first reading asserted that Melanesian reactions to European domination ordinarily would have taken a political form; but European surveillance and suppression of Melanesian society was such that opposition to the colonial system had to disguise itself in a religious, cultic garb. As soon as European interference declined, however, people would abandon cults for rational economic co-operatives and political parties (Worsley 1957: 255). Furthermore, cults articulated a resistance to ruling ideologies as well as to colonial authority (1957: 225), and they functioned to overcome indigenous social divisions and to 'weld previously hostile and separate groups together into a new unity' in opposition to European colonialists (Worsley 1957: 228). The leaders of the novel social unities looked skyward for a broader sort of political legitimacy that they now required:

By projecting his message on to the supernatural plane, [a prophet] clearly demonstrates that his authority comes from a higher sphere, and that it transcends the narrow province of local gods and spirits associated with particular clans, tribes or villages. (1957: 237)

Cultic religiosity, here, worked as an ideological glue that pasted together sometimes hostile local groups, smoothing over their differences for the coming struggle with the common colonialist enemy. This, for Peter Worsley, helped answer the question, 'why do the movements take a religious form?' (1957: 236).

Anthropological Cargoism's second reading of cults situated these more deeply within Melanesian culture. Cults are creative rather than merely reactionary responses to the difficult circumstances of the European presence. In fact, cultic social organization is normal in Melanesia. Cults are not desperate reactions of people pushed around by powerful Europeans; rather, they are dynamic endeavours that are indigenous within Melanesian society: 'Let us be sure of this. Nothing in the interpenetration of Melanesian life by Europeanism *of itself* entails or need lead to cultistic conduct. The impulse to cult can come only from the "within" of Melanesian life' (Stanner 1958: 19).

Lawrence (1954, 1964), especially, helped nativize cult by plumbing that Melanesian 'within'. The first chapter of his *Road Belong Cargo*, 'The Native Cosmic Order' (1964: 9–33), presented summary analyses of Melanesian religion, epistemology, leadership, and notions of time.

First, Melanesian religion is 'above all a technology' (McAuley 1961: 18, quoted in Lawrence 1964: 29). Melanesians overlook, thus, our Western discriminations between religion/economy and ritual/technology. Their economic practice includes significant ritualistic elements; their religious vocation demands a practical benefit. Melanesians ordinarily seek economic advantage through ritual action.

Second, Melanesian epistemology presumes that knowledge is revealed and the wise have been inspired. The Melanesians do not believe in individual creativity: 'Except in minor matters, they dismissed the principle of human intellectual discovery' (Lawrence 1964: 30). Melanesian social activists, thus, are always prophets in that they must present and legitimize their designs for new order as ancestral revelations. Prophetic dreams, mass hysteria, and cultic trance are normal devices of social change in Melanesia, not reactionary.

Third, the Melanesian leadership type, the big man, parallels the cult prophet. Melanesian polities favour cults:

Leadership depended on personal pre-eminence in important activities, but secular skill alone was inadequate. What counted was mastery of ritual by which men could ensure success. The leaders were men who 'really knew' and who could direct the activities of others—those who did not 'really know'—to the best advantage. (Lawrence 1964: 31)

Cults are just a variety of routine Melanesian politicking that has been coloured by the colonial encounter. Cargo is an especially promising new field for enterprising men: 'Such individuals might once have bent their talents towards becoming headmen, but now that the office has lapsed the cargo motive supplies an alternative means of achieving social distinction' (Hogbin 1958: 219–20). Ordinary Melanesian politics runs along cultic lines. Big men and prophets, as leaders, share similar political interests and strategies.

Finally, Melanesian notions of episodic time expect social change to be abrupt, disjunctive, and total. A local sense of lineal, progressive time does not exist. Change is disjunctive: 'This episodic conception of history and change is not restricted to the past but provides a model for change in the future as well: coming change must also be total, drastic, and radical' (McDowell 1988: 124). Melanesians normally organize cults when they seek to change their lives. 'What we call "cult" or "movement" is nothing less than the ordinary form of ritual and interpretive innovation in Melanesian societies' (Wagner 1979: 164).

This sort of cultural translation both rationalized and nativized the Melanesian cult. Like 'cargo', which does not mean cargo, 'cult' does not mean cult. The cult is not—or not just—an aberrant ritualized reaction to a powerful European presence. It is, rather, a normal, creative Melanesian institution of cultural dynamism and change. Melanesian economy runs on ritual. Melanesian social planning passes as revelation. Melanesian leaders are prophetic. Melanesian time is episodic. Melanesian change is sudden. Cults are culturally constructive. Melanesian desire for European wealth is ordinary, and not excessive or strange, given the importance of goods and of reciprocal exchange within traditional social relations. Likewise, anthropology normalized Melanesian reliance on cults in terms of island political structures, epistemology, and notions of time. Anthropological Cargoism concluded, therefore, that: 'Cargo cult is just a name we give to Melanesian culture when its usually covert interpretations of the world around us emerge into the open' (Wagner, quoted in Counts 1972: 374). In sum: 'It would not be far amiss, in fact, to speak of [Melanesian contact culture] as a *cargo culture*' (Schwartz 1976: 170).

Anthropology's culturally informed Cargoism produced a more refined set of oriental/occidental oppositions; and this reading of cargo cults cast, as its shadow, a more culturally informed auto–occidentalism. Difference is no longer so simple as Mr Bird's savage versus civilized, or irrational against rational. Instead, the Melanesian and the European are both rational in their own terms—only the terms of this rationality differ. Melanesians have a rationality—a cargo culture—that encourages the ritual pursuit of material goods. Occidentals, on the other hand, possess a different sort of culture that better apprehends material reality.

Our technologically effective rationality, in fact, creates that wealth which cultic Melanesians desire. We permit individual creativity; they must rely instead on inspiration to explain new ideas and information. We believe in steady progress; they in temporal disjunctions and sudden change. We have politicians and social planning; they have prophets and prophecy. In our society, the spheres of economics, politics, and religion are clearly demarcated so that we recognize the difference between capital, profit, salary, donations, bribes, purchases, gifts, tithing, and the like. We have differentiated parties, corporations, and churches; they make do with general purpose cults. Over there, economics, politics, and religion all blur together so that the circulation of material goods constitutes the crux of Melanesian social order in total. We are, in sum, complex and changing; they are simple and static (see Gewertz and Errington 1991).

Because anthropological Cargoism makes the cargo cult make sense in Melanesian terms, the eye of orientalist comparison (whether explicit or implicit) focuses on culture. Yes, cargo cults are sensible and comprehensible given Melanesian culture and the logic it permits, but because the goods never arrive island rationality is deficient when compared to ours.[4] Acting sensibly in their own terms, historically, left Melanesians vulnerable to political and economic exploitation against which their only response has been inefficient cultic ritual. Acting sensibly in our terms has allowed us to exploit and to laugh off and explain away as either silly or tragic their Cargoist protests about that exploitation.

Cargoist discourse explains away Melanesian desire for cargo and cultic organization by making sense of this desire and this organization in cultural terms; it also sketches and colours in a counter-image of a more rational occidental culture. Our rationality actually lets us possess the cargo that they only dream about. We understand cultic Melanesians; they do not understand us. Our task, then, is to school and enculturate them in our more efficient ways of thinking, our technology, and our notions of progress and development. Only then will the cargo cult fade away. Only then will the oriental find reason.

We know our culture as reasonable and effective because we stand on the right side of the boundary that Cargoism traces. But this boundary is a shifty one. Cargoism's cover story is that Melanesians have cargo culture; and, unlike them, we do not. However, our Cargoist discourse has migrated to the islands so that some Melanesians now talk about themselves as cargo cultists. And, on this side of the line, it appears that some of us have been infected with cargo culture after all.

Auto-Cargoism

Said (1978: 322) deplored the hegemonic effects of Orientalism wherein the discourse washes back so that its subjects come to think and talk of themselves as 'Orientals'. Cargoism, too, has come home to Melanesia as islanders have learned from anthropologists that they have a cargo culture. A self-application of the term 'cargo cultist' requires adroit negotiations of identity. The expression draws obvious boundaries between Melanesians and outsiders, but also delineates differences within island communities themselves.

The term's conspicuous presence in commonplace representations of Melanesia demands of islanders that they confront the cargo cult. The independence of Papua New Guinea (1975), the Solomon Islands (1978), and Vanuatu (1980) saw a general revaluation of island tradition (*kastom*) throughout the region, and an increased production of political statements of 'Melanesianism'. New political élites evoked shared culture and tradition to foster sentiments of national unity and national distinctiveness *vis-à-vis* Europeans. Perforce, cargo cult was pulled along by some of this charged Melanesianist discourse: if we islanders are cargo cultists, then cargo cults must be good.

The species of Cargoist text that described cargo cultism as a sort of proto-nationalism helped here. Melanesian cultists, in this view, were akin to freedom fighters. Cults were honourable ways to resist domination: '[O]ne of the frequent features of the cults is that they united previously separate social groups. This, in fact, if allowed to develop, was exactly the social change needed to combat the whites' (Waiko 1973: 419; see also Hannet 1970: 25; Kerpi 1975). Moreover, an honourably traditional cargo culture may be useful after independence, too. 'Cargo cults can and have contributed to [national] development in a broader sense' (Ferea 1984: 1). The cargo cult heritage of the new nation 'instills confidence, pride, and initiative which had been taken away by the white man' (Pokawin 1984: 79). Cargo cults are a form of noble resistance to the world system; and cargo prophets are nationalist heroes. 'There is nothing sinful, heretical, or mad about [cargo cultism]; it was quite normal and acceptable' (Opeba 1987: 62).

Auto-Cargoism, however, more typically has borrowed the invidious discourse's darker judgements of cults. Cargo cultists, rugged proto-nationalists as they are, have the bad habit of maintaining their opposition to centralized political authority even after national independence has been secured. In such cases, auto-Cargoism performs a discursive about-face. Freedom-fighting cult nationalists can rapidly mutate into obnoxious cabals bent on subverting the new state. Cultists are sinful, heretical, mad, abnormal, and unacceptable within a new world of modern rationality. Auto-Cargoism serves as a useful slander. Leaders of Vanuatu's ruling political party, for example, explained away unseemly local resistance on Tanna Island to their rule in terms of cargo cultural delusion (Weightman and Lini 1980: 183–5). In Papua New Guinea, politicians at the national and provincial levels have also decried their rivals as simple cultists: 'A firm stand will be taken against organizations in the North Solomons which "smack of cargo cults." The warning came yesterday from the North Solomons Premier, Dr. Alexis Sarie' (*Post-Courier* 1976: 3).

Auto-Cargoism also serves political élites by excusing failed economic development programmes (Buck 1989: 168). Theoretically, economic development will finish off the cargo cult. In practice, though, cargo cult snuffs out development despite the honest efforts of national leaders:

New Ireland politician Mr. Noel Levi has urged the Lihir Island people to abandon any 'cargo cult-type' beliefs . . . 'I can tell you that achievement comes only from hard work and co-operation between yourselves,' Mr. Levi told the people at Londolovit, Lihir, during a recent flying visit. (*Post-Courier* 1980: 13)

Melanesian auto-Cargoists borrow this orientalist discourse and put it to use, alternatively accusing one another of being too cultist (too Melanesian) or of being not cultist enough (too European). The hegemony or, if this is too strong, the allure of Cargoism, however, works both sides of the occidental/oriental frontier. Occidentals also admit strains of cargo culture in their midst. And we might suppose that, despite Cargoism's original functions to apprehend Melanesian cultists, the West is nowadays the discourse's chief target.

Internal-Cargoism

Smelling cargo cults within the self fades the boundary between oriental and occidental. Some of us, it turns out, are like them after all. Cargoism, as a form of orientalism, proposes that the known object is vulnerable to scrutiny; it implies ability to dominate it, to have authority over it (Said 1978: 6, 95). But equally important are Cargoism's effects within the West—its claims to know/control not so much the other as ourselves (Lindstrom 1990; see Introduction, this volume). An internal-Cargoism on this side of the frontier parallels Melanesian auto-Cargoism in its local political impact.

Peter Mason, in an analysis of the function of the American other within Europe, noted 'the reactive process by which the popular classes of the European continent came to be tarred with the same brush as the Amerindian peoples (the "Indianisation" of Europe)' (1990: 56, see also 60–3). Internal-Cargoism, too, like internal-Indians, is part of the confining girdle of discourse that circumscribes the normal and the expected at home. Melanesians, while abused for being cultists (and Orientals for being Oriental), are supposed—are known—to be such. This condemnation is multiplied many times if a self (not an other) challenges the occident's politically and culturally authoritative rationality and truth. Concern to know and thus dominate orientals by means of a regulatory discourse is also an apparatus for an internal disciplining of the self (or of some of ourselves).

An extension of the term cargo cult beyond Melanesia demands its simplification to three core features. Cargo cults, first, enunciate a desire for wealth of some sort. Second, cargo cults entail collective behaviour. Cultists need not be formally organized into obvious groups, but application of the term at least implies widespread, public involvement in irregular ritual and belief. This is something more dangerous to occidental rationality and character than some individual waywardness. There must be notable, popular manifestations for an observer to deploy the label 'cult'. Third, cargo cultic behaviour and belief look for supernatural means to achieve collective ends.

This third feature is the live element of cargo cult, underwriting its extension beyond Melanesia and its infiltration back into the West. The distilled essence of cargo cult is an unworkable relationship between rational ends and irrational means. Cargoist discourse easily paraphrases supernatural, ritual means as irrational or illogical at the same time as it reads desire for increased wealth or political sovereignty as rational. The object of cultic desire, whether this is money, industrially manufactured goods, or freedom from oppression, demands less explanation, for occidentals, than does the ritual, magical practice of its fulfilment. Cargo, in the West, has long made better sense than cult.

A miscellany of Western attempts for collective benefit coupled with strategies that auto–occidentalism deems irrational have attracted the label cargo cult. Such labelling occasionally evokes tragedy, playing upon the melancholy future of unfulfilled desire. But most often, cargo cult labelling highlights the irrationality of practice rather than sorry futures. The closer cargo cult comes to the self, the more the tone of such extended usage slides from melancholy to mockery.

Employments of cargo cult to label one's own poor may still suggest tragedy. This is a local version of Lihir Island and other Third World development schemes revealed in the end as nothing but cargo cult (see e.g. *The Economist* 1991: 20). The poor, our internal orientals, are yet distant enough that the combination of noble economic goals with unwise and ineffective means can evoke a discursive melancholy rather than derision. Newspaper columnist William Raspberry, for example, criticized American social welfare policy that teaches the poor, 'like New Guinea's "cargo cultists," to become mere clients' (1986: A9). Raspberry cited the work of John McKnight, a Northwestern University professor who has located cargo cults erupting in the neighbourhoods of Chicago: 'There are many people in Chicago today who are waiting for a Saturn [automobile] plant to drop down. They are waiting for a parachute load of transistors to come and save us. It's a tragic mistake' (McKnight, quoted in Chandler 1985: 203).

Whereas McKnight's Chicago cargo cultists merely wait tragically, searching their economic skies, Douglas Dean (1970) located a more dangerous mob in Kansas City. Here, he suggested, 'a large "cargo cult" exists within the minority black culture' (1970: 156). Blacks who reject dominant occidental culture, 'preferring not to assimilate and consequently lose identity are forming a "Cargo Cult" of their own, demanding economic equality and cultural separatism' (1970: 163). This is cargo cult tragedy with an apocalyptic edge to it: '[T]he next evolving stage may be a cry for revolution' (Dean 1970: 165). Clearly, although Dean might defend his use of cargo cult as the neutral language of social scientific analysis, his extension of the term to label economic boycotts, black capitalism, shop-lifting, and the Black Power movement at large not only highlighted the comic irrationality of such strategies but deprecated by orientalizing them as well.

Cargo cults continue to erupt in more places than just Chicago and Kansas City. The collapse of communist governments in the former Soviet Union and Eastern Europe, and associated attempts to cultivate capitalist economies, have precipitated cargo cults all over Europe. The East fervidly waits, in ultimate tragedy of course, upon the cargo of the West. The *Manchester Guardian Weekly* reported that 'the new Soviet religion is the cargo cult' (Walker 1989: 21). The *Spectator* headlined Poland's 'Cargo Cult Candidate', Stanislaw Tyminski, who promised 'wealth, high salaries, and instant happiness' (Applebaum 1990: 12).

And Western Europeans, too, are going cargo cultist as fast as their Eastern cousins. A gross cargo shrine has newly risen from the plains of central France: 'Euro Disney is a multi-layered, £2.2 billion cargo cult where nostalgia for the cinematic America that never was joins hands with consumer fanaticism' (Webster 1992: 7). And the Japanese likewise, canny businessmen though they are, 'have developed a cargo-cult mentality about Western pop culture' (McDonell 1991: 41). Sony and Matsushita corporations spent fanatically to acquire Hollywood movie studios that will never repay their investments.

The internal-Cargoist story is deployed against wayward claims that menace auto-occidentalist normality. Western culture itself, so these texts suggest, is at stake as cargo cults erupt all around. And as cargo cults close in upon us, they appear less and less tragic, and more and more crazy. Computer users, bewitched by flashy software, 'practically fall over like cargo-cult natives hypnotized by shiny metal' (Dvorak and Somerson 1992: 128). The president of the California Institute of Technology took pains to alert his school's graduates to the dangers of 'cargo cult science' (Feynman 1974: 10). This bad science consists of 'educational and psychological studies [that] . . . follow all the apparent precepts and forms of scientific investigation, but they're missing something essential, because the planes don't land' (1974: 11). Polish candidate Tyminski is a 'genuine religious maniac' (Applebaum 1990: 12). Schemes to build a 'Science

City' in South Australia are really only a cargo bad dream—an 'irrational megaproject', 'high-tech fantasy', a 'flight from reality' (Harwood 1991).

Internal cargo cultists are foolish and irrational, sometimes dangerously so. The flexibility of boundary between Western technologic and Melanesian ritual rationalities, however, functions to protect constructions of normal occidental culture and mentality. Those whose actions challenge these constructions can be shoved over the line into cargo cult madness.

Sympathetic-Cargoism

If internal-Cargoism suggests that some of us, at least, are like Melanesians in our either silly or tragic lack of economic rationality and a poor grounding in occidental logic, other Cargoist texts go further to suggest that some of them are like us. Anthropological Cargoism as a whole, which preaches that cargo cults need be understood culturally in terms of the local rationality, presumes that both Europeans and Melanesians, in fact, do act rationally even though they possess disparate premisses about the world. Cargoists who frame cults within universalist theories of human progress, human nature, or human mentality also presume cross-cultural universals that erode the occidental/oriental boundary (see Carrier 1992*b*: 203–4). These erosions range from gross assertions that cargo cults result from base but universal human emotions of envy and greed (see Mair 1948: 67; *Pacific Islands Monthly* 1958: 59) to refined evolutionary and developmental models.

The latter include Marxist historical materialists along with Christian universalists. Worsley, for example, classified cargo cult as merely a form of millenarian movement that has 'found support at all levels of society at one time or another' (1957: 225). These movements are routine responses everywhere to specific sets of unequal political circumstances. Christian Cargoists likewise interpret cargo cults as local vehicles for universal human expectations of salvation (Steinbauer 1979: 158) or for the service of universal moral and psychological needs. Kenelm Burridge, for instance, made sense of cults in terms of a general human desire to 'sustain in the moral world a vision of synthesis with what is divine' (1960: 279): Melanesian cultists, like us, 'want to be men in much the same way as white men seem to them to be men: competent, independent individuals capable, through conflicts of choice, of ordering their own lives in their own way' (1960: p. xxi).

Sympathetic-Cargoism of this sort presumes certain basic human commonalities among Europeans and Melanesians, between Burridge's

"Syria," Doctor Green says, "back in the twenty-tens, when we were fighting ISIS. Crossed over the Aegean as a refugee kid; lost most of his family."

My doctor's white coat is complete and his body is unblemished—no darkness anywhere. For a moment I'm relieved I've met someone who has lived a painless life, but then I notice his temple is bare.

"Hey, you don't wear one?"

"Phhssh, I'm old. I've lost so much, I bet I'd be nothing but just two eyes." He waggles his bushy eyebrows.

He finishes pushing something cold on my forehead, then looks at my vitals on his tablet.

"All right, here you go," he stands me up. "Ready?"

He faces me toward a full-length mirror, says something about synapses, dendrites, memory and serotonin, but I'm suddenly worried that I won't have anything to project. Worried that my grief is just a droplet compared to everyone else's. Oh god, what if nothing shows up?

There's a slight buzz in my brain, like a little bee. I remember the smell of Alice, her soft hands, her laugh. The bee-buzzing soon quiets, and the dermal on my temple glows.

It projects downward: making a fist-shaped black hole on my chest. It looks like my heart has been shot out.

"Alice," I murmur. "My wife."

<hr />

"Congratulations!" Janice shrieks through the vid-chat. "It looks great!"

"I don't know..."

"It's beautiful. Look at how jagged that one edge is."

I finger the projection, feeling my shirt but seeing only the darkness. "I guess we're all walking wounded."

"That's the point. I know you think it's just a fad, but next year most insurance companies will discount for them. Less stress, fewer mental health claims, happier hearts..."

"Misery loves company."

"Seriously, it works like a vaccine. It's for community health."

"It's depressing."

white men and his cultists. Both are rational in their own terms; both possess the range of human emotions; both are engaged in universal processes of societal evolution; both are potentially children of God; both struggle with identical moral predicaments. Sympathetic-Cargoism still presumes, however, one significant gap between self and other. Within its social, historical, moral, or biological unities, it situates the Melanesian other as less evolved, less complex, a younger brother who struggles behind.

Mason noted similar poses in Norse sagas that record Viking encounters with North American Indians. In these stories, the encounter with the other

has two forms. In the first, unfamiliar human beings are denied their humanity—they become monstrous. In the second, they are assimilated to the self which perceives them: since the Norsemen were outlaws . . . the people whom they encounter are assigned the same status—and killed. (1990: 98)

The oriental is assimilated to the self—but not to the whole self (see Carrier 1992*a*: 15). The cargo cultist is like an earlier or junior version of an occidental. The cargo cultist, like us, may be rational, but his or her logic is less efficient in apprehending the structures and forces of the material world. The cargo cultist, like us, is envious and greedy, but these emotions derange us less given our higher state of psychological, cognitive, and moral development. The cargo cultist resorts to typical human millenarianism, but this response recalls the European Middle Ages (Worsley 1957: 226). The cargo cultist shares our political goals, but must resort to religion rather than real politics given a lower stage of societal evolution and simpler economic infrastructure. The cargo cultist struggles with basic moral issues, but there our philosophy has gone before. The cargo cultist might be saved, but first must follow our lead to Jesus.

If internal-Cargoism suggests that some Westerners may betray the occident by slipping into cargo culture's dreamland of dangerous desire, sympathetic-Cargoism narrows the divide somewhat. It admits that Melanesians are to a degree like us. This cultic orient is not, therefore, as Said (1978: 96) suggested, 'absolutely different . . . from the West'. Instead, a gradient difference persists in the pose of the oriental as a sort of junior occidental.

Pseudo-occidentalism

Another strand of Cargoism also admits similarity between orient and occident, although in somewhat roundabout fashion. These are Cargoist texts that purport to describe Melanesian views of Europeans. However, instead of reliably translating the occidentalism of Melanesians—their understandings of the West that are in part incorporated within cult symbol and ritual—these accounts are patent guesses, built of stereotypes and wishful thinking. This is a sort of pseudo-occidentalism, or our assumptions about what islanders are saying about us. Pseudo-occidentalism is more typically produced by journalists and travel writers who stumble upon cargo cults than it is by anthropologists who must attempt to observe their discipline's dictate to study the native point of view.

Pseudo-occidentalism works by imagining a Melanesian story about occidentals, the truth of which it denies, but only half-heartedly. Pseudo-occidentalism typically proposes that Melanesians view the West as either overpoweringly good or overpoweringly bad. Occidentals thus tell stories about themselves using an oriental's voice. But since the oriental now appears to share and speak the truth about the West, this diminishes the boundary that separates us.

Anthropological Cargoists have been most willing to explain cults as reactions to colonialist exploitation, although others too have adopted the theme that natives view Europeans as political and economic exploiters. Mr Bird's introductory Cargoist text built on this motif:

> A native, infected with the disorder, states that he has been visited by a relative long dead, who stated that a great number of ships loaded with 'cargo' had been sent by the ancestor of the native for the benefit of the natives of a particular village or area. But the white man, being very cunning, knows how to intercept these ships and takes the 'cargo' for his own use. (1945: 69)

Mr Bird both denied and implicitly accepted the accusation he heard the native making. The Melanesian view of the European was perverted and incorrect; a form of madness. Yet, in his madness, the native spoke European truths.

Pseudo-occidentalism, of this critical sort, begins with a European suspicion that cultists perceive them to be powerful exploiters. In early colonial accounts of Tanna Island's John Frum movement, for example, British District Agent Alexander Rentoul reported that protesting Islanders organized their John Frum ('Broom') movement 'to sweep (or "broom") the white people off the island of Tanna—Tanna for the Tannese was their slogan. I believe that this movement did originate in this way, and was first prompted by dissatisfaction with the Missions' (1949: 31). Rentoul admitted the accusation of unsatisfactory occidentals that he heard the

Tannese to enunciate, but went on to disavow its accuracy. He argued
that islanders misconceive Europeans to be exploiting them. What they
need, he suggested, is a crash course in moral and technological education
to understand in occidental terms the truth of what European missionaries, administrators, and traders are really like. His refutation of the role
of European exploiter, though, is only half-hearted as it does not question
taken-for-granted European powers. A subsequent District Agent on Tanna
ended his own prescription for a cargo cult cure with the suggestion that
'there is a need for economic and political institutions which will give the
Tannese a sense of having some say in their own destiny' (Barrow 1951:
382). The Tannese, so it appears, tell the truth about power, but need
further education in European motives.

The doubled claims about the self carried within pseudo-occidentalist
texts are more obvious in a second, more positive sort of story. Cargoists
have much preferred the role of cargo god to that of colonial exploiter. In
these stories, the imagined cultist deifies rather than impugns the mighty
occident. One pseudo-occidentalist text from the pages of the American
tabloid *Weekly World News*, for example, was headlined 'Wacky Tribe
Thinks Ex-prez LBJ Is a God!':

A Stone Age tribe of cave dwellers in the rugged and remote Bismarck Mountains
of central Papua New Guinea worships a former U.S. president as a god-king,
reports the stunned leader of a recent anthropological expedition to the area. A
faded and wrinkled color photograph of Lyndon B. Johnson hangs garlanded with
flowers in the mammoth, cathedral-like cave of the primitive tribe's high priest
. . . 'Once or twice a week, the entire tribe actually stages a torchlight procession
to the cavern and carries overflowing baskets of orchids and yam-like vegetables
as offerings to their god-king.' The photograph, approximately 11 inches by 14
inches, shows the beaming 1960s-era chief executive frolicking with his pet beagles
on the White House lawn, playfully tugging at one of his pets' ears . . . the tribe
has been venerating LBJ as its 'holy, wise and generous' deity for about 20 years
. . . The high priest told the anthropologists that an ancient tribal legend pre-
dicted that a pale-faced god with large, protruding ears and his long-eared hounds
would descend from heaven—from nearby Mt. Wilhelm, which towers above the
clouds at 14,793 feet—to shower blessings on the simple savages and help them
form a good society. (O'Neill 1988: 29)

Parallel pseudo-occidentalist texts purportedly describe the beliefs
of John Frum movement supporters on Tanna Island, who have remained fixated upon god-like Americans since their Second World War
experiences:

[T]he 60,000 islanders of Vanuatu watched in awe as half a million American soldiers—white and black, friendly and, by island standards, fabulously rich—passed through the sleepy colonial backwater on their way to war. . . . The men would drink the intoxicating juice of the kava root and raise the American flag in the field between the village huts and sing out strong for paradise. . . . 'The promised land is still coming,' says Chief Won. 'America will bring it. John Frum said so.' . . . 'When the Americans come again to this place, John Frum will come too,' says the chief. 'John said our brothers are in America. They will come and help us. They are our friends'. (Ashbrook 1986: 2)

The west Pacific is dotted with crude wooden crosses painted red in honor of the G.I. who became god in the influential 'cargo cult' known as the John Frum movement. . . . [O]ne branch of the widespread cult reveres, as a sacred relic of the mysterious white messiah, an old United States Army field jacket with sergeants stripes and the red cross of the Medical Corps on the sleeves. (*New York Times* 1970: 7; see also Hamilton 1983: 1)

The US has a special place in the hearts of the cultists who believe in John Frum, the king of America, whose return will not only bring a time of unprecedented wealth, but will also rid the islanders of the demanding ways of foreigners, especially Europeans. (Glines 1991: 86)

These stories suggest a Tannese vision of America as fabulously rich, friendly, a white messiah, brotherly, and a supporter of freedom and independence from colonial powers. An underlying comic tone pokes fun at these island beliefs, but only half-heartedly denies them. The Tannese may exaggerate in their native way, but they none the less *do* understand that America really is, as everyone knows, fabulously rich, friendly, brotherly, and a supporter of freedom for native peoples from wicked European colonialists.

The cultist who accuses Europeans of exploitation gets at the truth of the matter, even though he may overstate the case and misunderstand the motivations and constraints of European political and economic institutions. Everyone admits that occidentals routinely overpower orientals. The cultist who worships GI deities clearly goes too far but he, too, realizes the essential truth. Everyone knows that Americans are gods, or at least are so relative to orientals. Apparent Melanesian readings of occidentals merge with our own. And it is gratifying that they, too, share these important understandings about us. Pseudo–occidentalism is a matter of taking one's own conceits and bouncing these off Melanesians. These stories imply, however, a certain unitary perspective among orientals and occidentals. Even simple Melanesian cultists can recognize us as we are.

Assimilative-Cargoism

The several sorts of Cargoism surveyed so far erode but do not entirely erase the occidental/oriental frontier. Internal-Cargoism maintains that some, but only some, of us are like Melanesians; sympathetic-Cargoism affirms that Melanesians are like occidentals, but of a junior grade; pseudo-occidentalism suggests that Melanesians can share our understandings about occidentals and orientals, although in an exaggerated or incomplete form. One final form of Cargoism, however, eliminates the frontier; here, the occidental floods across the erased borderlands and assimilates with the oriental. These stories recount that most of us nowadays, or even all of us—and not just the internally defective—are like orientals. This orientalization of the self may push a defunct occident into the past, as something now lost in a devolving Western civilization. Or, in a fearful twist, erstwhile orientals (typically the Japanese) become today the real occidentals while we slip into their former oriental posture. With assimilative-Cargoist stories, the boundary that ensured Said's radical difference and absolute separation between occident and orient collapses. This erasure is perhaps not surprising, given increasingly co-ordinated world economic and political structures. Real economic, communicative, and political boundaries separating occident and orient, in addition to discursive constructions, have narrowed considerably.

The cargo cult, once innocuously located in faraway Melanesia, now infects the West. Cargo cults, nowadays, occur everywhere. Australia, that outpost of the occident which neighbours Melanesia most closely, not surprisingly is already badly infected with cultic mentality, according to more than one native Cargoist:

Our so-called 'revolution of rising expectations' was cargo cult writ larger and on a more gigantic scale of irrationality. Our extravagant lives, our flash cars and houses with their swimming pools, our pathetic faith in the fraud of education—near-morons force-fed with university degrees in the delusion that they will secure employment—who ever paused to ask whether all this was either rational or affordable? Our national symbol of cargo cult is Canberra's repulsive and extravagant Parliament House. I saw its prototype in 1943, in an outbreak of cargo cult on the Rai Coast, not far from Madang [New Guinea]. (Ryan 1992)

And America too, once the proud land of cargo, is today instead the home of cargo cult. Ruben F. Mettler, a one-time chairman and chief executive officer of TRW Inc., decried 'the cargo cult mentality in America':

Like South Pacific Islanders who thought that talking into little boxes made the planes come, the U.S. is responding to its problems with magic rituals instead of rational planning and hard work. . . . We urgently need to recognize and remove the unexamined assumptions and myths underlying so much of our contemporary thinking. (1980: 22)

Americans everywhere today find that 'economic pain drives us to cargo cults' (Cockburn 1992: M1); we delude ourselves about the economic rationality of overgrown business schemes, such as Minnesota's Mall of America. Cargo cult mentality—our unexamined assumption and myth— now threatens the future of the occident. Melanesia's cargo cult culture has moved half-way around the globe to transform into America's cargo cult culture—or was it the other way around?

Joseph Conforti (1989) discovered, in American schools, that our native cargo cult ideology has now beaten down an enfeebled Protestant ethic. We really believe, nowadays, that fortune depends on episodic luck, animated by ritualistic strategy, rather than in the old truths of steady, progressive effort and hard work. We nurture both our cargo desires and our faith in ritual and magical practice, kneeling daily at the altar of television. Advertisements

most clearly reflect a cargo cult orientation, in that the advertised product is presented as representing the simple catalyst that would bring about the desired state of affairs. At some point the lines between traditional reality and fantasy seem to fade into an emergent amalgam, a new reality. If this new reality is not yet a fully formed cargo cult, it may at least be understood as constituting a cargo cult orientation. (1989: 5)

Trappist monk Thomas Merton, too, had earlier already sniffed out our cargo cult orientation and mentality:

Man wants to go through the Cargo Cult experience and does so repeatedly. Not only the natives of New Guinea, the Solomon islands, the New Hebrides, and South Africa, but the blacks, the young Chinese, the white Westerners—every-one—all of us find the Cargo experience, in whatever form, vitally important. (1979: 86)

We all are engulfed in a 'tidal wave of Cargo mentality, whether primitive or highly sophisticated, that is sweeping the world in all directions' (1979: 86). The stigmata of our cargo cult culture include fabulous consumer advertising, ritualistic buying and consuming, the adoration of the new, and repudiation of the old (Merton 1979: 83–4).

We have become, in fact, the natives: '[A] true understanding of the Cargo mentality can tell us much about ourselves' (Merton 1979: 83). We are, at last, ourselves nativized by the erosive forces of modernity:

We may in fact be experiencing the impact of the accretions of the West upon the West, the impact of America on Americans, and this experience defines a situation of alienation! It is an alienation of Westerners from the West and of Americans from America. . . . [W]e are experiencing the descent of America into the reality of the myth . . . The cargo cultist in his strange and bizarre behaviour, his Vailala madness, in his myth-dream had probably outlined a modality of modernity. (Long 1974: 413–14)

Assimilative-Cargoism makes cultists, orientals, of us all. The occident fails to reproduce itself. The workings of its rationality and its practice subvert themselves. Alienated from our own occidentalness, we assimilate into the orient. Vailala Madness is our post-modern future. In Westernizing the native we have nativized ourselves.

Assimilative-Cargoism comes from two directions. Some Cargoists (e.g. CEO Ruben Mettler) lament the loss of our occidentalist essentials. We have regressed to the level of the orient, adopting their deficient rationality, inadequate technological means, and emotional extravagance. This is an apocalyptic version of internal-Cargoism wherein the once encapsulated oriental aspects of the self have metastasized to infect the entire occidental body.

But other Cargoists (e.g. Merton and Long) suggest instead that Americans, Australians, and Melanesians alike are now equally netted within the same global economic structures. This is a latter-day version of sympathetic-Cargoism wherein occidental and oriental together have attained a climactic stage in our universal development. Any differences that once may have separated us are scrubbed away by our shared predicament.

In both versions of assimilative-Cargoism, the narrative screens that once deflected cargo cult stories out into Melanesia come down. The truth stands revealed: people everywhere, occidentals and orientals alike, are native cargo cultists. Anthropology argues that the cargo cult is reasonable in the terms of Melanesian culture; but now it also makes good sense in terms of our own. Cargo cult's logic feeds on a construction of a universalized desire that cuts through orient and occident both.

The essence of desire

A principal criticism of orientalist discourse is that this promises to describe the other but, in fact, delivers only more stories about the self. Orientalism is more telling as a 'sign of European–Atlantic power over the Orient than it is as a veridic discourse about the Orient' (Said 1978: 6). We return to Nizan's experience of the Orient as merely a facsimile, a shadow that only comments on the occident.

Cargoist texts, too, clearly tell European stories at least as much as they do Melanesian. Internal-Cargoism, sympathetic-Cargoism, pseudo-occidentalism, and assimilative-Cargoism all wash out Cargoism's categorical boundaries. Progressing through these several layers of Cargoism, the occidental and the oriental step closer and closer until they converge in climactic assimilative-Cargoism. If, in simple Cargoism, European dreams are projected into Melanesian characters, in assimilative-Cargoism, the fact that occidentals are cargo cultists too need no longer be occluded.

This Cargoist denouement reveals an even more powerful level of essentialization that the discourse accomplishes. Cargo texts do more than accent an occidental rationality of technological achievement in counterpoint to inefficient oriental ritualism. Cargoism accepts as normal a certain sort of desire within the hearts of occidentals and orientals alike.

Whatever else they may tell us, Cargoist texts are allegories of desire (see Lindstrom 1993). Thematically, cultists desire wealth, dignity, freedom and independence, and the like. Cargo stories present these lists of desired objects or states of being as normal, pan-human focuses of aspiration. But, more furtively, Cargoism also essentializes desire itself—whatever the exact object of human longing. It suggests that desire itself, and a desire in a particular mood, are normal. Cargoism thus universalizes a manner of desire that is perhaps peculiar to capitalist society, characteristic of the late-modern Western psyche.

Cargoism's desire has an inescapable character. It is unremitting despite (or because of) the fact that it is never fully satisfied. Orientals/occidentals alike can never stop desiring despite the fact that cargo fails to arrive. Cargo stories testify to a truth that desire never ceases. These stories construct, promulgate, and defend constructions of an economic man who must live with unlimited wants but limited means. This sort of unending but pleasurable desire, according to Colin Campbell, emerged in eighteenth-century European religious concerns to display both sensitiveness and sensibility.[5] Such concerns generated a 'romantic ethic' in which desire itself became more highly valued than its gratification: '[T]he desiring mode constitutes a state of enjoyable discomfort, and . . . wanting rather than having is the main focus of pleasure-seeking' (Campbell 1987: 86).

If cargo texts evoke a poetics of desire, then I think we understand why the cargo cult seems at once so strange, yet so familiar; so emblematic of the alien Melanesian other, but also so characteristic of ourselves. Cargo stories are economic parables. Elsewhere (Lindstrom 1993), I have suggested their kinship with Western tales of romance. In the romance, people await love as fervidly and often as tragically as Melanesians seek cargo. Both cargo and love stories together are reflexes of a powerful, underlying master discourse about desire. These are stories of unrequited love, of loving too much, of cargo that never arrives, of madness. Despite the fact that the planes do not land, and love will in the end disappoint, we may never stop desiring/loving. In cargo texts our needs are unlimited. We may pretend that we seek finitude, real love, the arrival of the cargo ships, the ultimate end of desire, but we dream and act oppositely. Our truth is that we must keep on searching for cargo/love because even true love never satisfies desire. We desire desire, more than cargo; we love love, more than sweethearts.

Cargo stories narrate 'man's radical inability to find anything to satisfy him' (Lemaire 1977: 163). They tell of an essential human condition that fixates us on constantly frustrated desire—infinite desire that serves both psychological and market economies. We can never get enough. Love of commodities must remain unrequited. If we could possess everything we desire, just as if we could find true love, our psychological economy would grind to a halt. From this perspective, we are all cargo cultists in that we wait eternally for an end to desire that will not end. The Melanesian cultist merely reads our lines.

Cargoism, as an orientalist discourse, does indeed set up a rational, technologically competent, and far-thinking European who stands partly in the shadow of a textually foregrounded irrational Melanesian cultist. But Cargoist discourse effaces as much as it traces the frontier between occident and orient. It blurs cultural, geographic, and racial distinctions to insist instead that a human desire that is never satisfied and never-ending is the normal, truthful experience of humankind everywhere. In the end, Cargoism universalizes the cargo cult as a natural human predicament.

The discursive construction of universal human essentials of this sort is, in its way, even more pernicious and dangerous than the particular orientalist or occidentalist variety. The latter, at least, leave open a way out—even if that alternative is oriental and devalued. The construction of desire of one particular sort as a normal, human universal within the occident and orient alike leaves fewer clues, within the discourse, that an alternative to cargo cults, economic man, and romantic love might somewhere or sometime exist.

Notes

1 This does not imply, however, that an enriched, more complex occidentalism gets any closer to the truth of the self or the other.
2 Parts of this chapter draw upon *Cargo Cult: Strange Stories of Desire from Melanesia and beyond* (Lindstrom 1993).
3 Although my argument locates erasures of the boundaries between orient/occident, East/West, oriental/occidental, and orientalism/occidentalism, as I proceed I shall none the less have to maintain the essence of these categories as categories, as a manner of speaking, along with an essentialist 'cargo cult' and 'Cargoism' as well. Readers may supply their own quotation marks (see Carrier 1992*b*: 206–7).
4 Of relevance here is the extensive debate within anthropology and philosophy about cross-cultural rationality that turns upon, among other conundrums, the Nuer statement that 'twins are birds' (see e.g. Wilson 1970).
5 Marshall Sahlins (1972: 2) proposed that a differently constructed, limited and graspable desire once characterized hunting and gathering societies; that 'it was not until culture neared the height of its material achievements that it erected a shrine to the Unattainable: Infinite Needs' (1972: 39).

References

APPLEBAUM, ANNE (1990). 'The Cargo Cult Candidate', *Spectator* (8 Dec.): 12.

ASHBROOK, TOM (1986). 'Tanna Islanders Still Waiting for John Frum', *Boston Globe* (23 Oct.): 2.

BARROW, G. L. (1951). 'The Story of Jonfrum', *Corona*, 3: 379–82.

BIRD, NORMAN M. (1945). 'Is there Danger of a Post-war Flare-up among New Guinea Natives?' *Pacific Islands Monthly*, 16/4 (Nov.): 69–70.

BUCK, PEM DAVIDSON (1989). 'Cargo-Cult Discourse: Myth and the Rationalization of Labor Relations in Papua New Guinea', *Dialectical Anthropology*, 13: 157–71.

BURRIDGE, KENELM (1960). *Mambu: A Study of Melanesian Cargo Movements and their Social and Ideological Background*. London: Methuen.

CAMPBELL, COLIN (1987). *The Romantic Ethic and the Spirit of Modern Consumerism*. Oxford: Basil Blackwell.

CARRIER, JAMES G. (1992*a*). 'Introduction', in J. Carrier (ed.), *History and Tradition in Melanesian Anthropology*. Berkeley, Calif.: University of California Press: 1–37.

——(1992*b*). 'Occidentalism: The World Turned Upside-Down', *American Ethnologist*, 19: 195–212.

CHANDLER, CHRISTOPHER (1985). 'Chicago Interview: John McKnight', *Chicago*, 34/11: 202–7.

COCKBURN, ALEXANDER (1992). 'Economic Pain Drives Us to Cargo Cults', *Los Angeles Times* (1 Nov.): M1.

"It's *affirming*," she says. "What's wrong with that?"

"You mean, aside from the fact that it makes me feel naked?" For a moment I can't find the words. Then I sigh. "I don't know. I guess I'm thinking about puzzle pieces."

"Puzzles?"

"Yeah. Alice always said we fit together. But what if I see a woman walking down the street, and her pain looks just like mine? Her projection matches mine perfectly? What would that *mean*?"

"That would be great! You could talk; have something in common. That happens, you know. Pain-pairings. The Japanese call it *kumiki*, like those little interlocking boxes? Oh, there was just a movie about..."

"I gotta run." I log-off.

At work, everyone notices my new dermal. I get a few claps on the back. Some hugs. My boss says, "I met your wife at our Christmas party last year. Fine girl. So sorry for your loss."

The new intern looks at my chest in sympathy and waves a beautiful, black-holed wrist. Smiling, she heads over.

I run to the men's room in a panic. This was a mistake.

I lean over the sink. I put my hand on my new ink-dark hole, feeling only my cotton shirt.

There's a knock on the restroom door.

"You okay in there? The first day is the hardest," she says. Her voice is young and soft. I imagine she's nice, that I'd probably like her, and that terrifies me even more.

"Um, yeah. I'll be out in a minute." I run some water.

"I tried to kill myself," she whispers.

"Oh. Uh, geez. I'm sorry...my wife. Cancer."

I hear her lean against the restroom door. "You want to talk about it over a cup of coffee?"

"Uh, I've got a lot of work today."

What I *really* want to say is that I don't want to know what happened to her. And I think this new world peace is a fluke—it's not because of the damn dermals, and it's not going to last. We're all going to be just as numb to everyone else as we ever have been. We're all going

CONFORTI, JOSEPH M. (1989). 'The Cargo Cult and the Protestant Ethic as Conflicting Ideologies: Implications for Education', *Urban Review*, 21: 1–14.

COUNTS, DOROTHY E. (1972). 'The Kaliai and the Story: Development and Frustration in New Britain', *Human Organization*, 31: 373–83.

DAVIES, D. (1972). *A Dictionary of Anthropology*. New York: Crane, Russak & Co.

DEAN, DOUGLAS H. (1970). 'Economic Sources of Transcultural Conflict in Kansas City, Kansas', *Kansas Journal of Sociology*, 6: 156–68.

DVORAK, JOHN, and SOMERSON, PAUL (1992). 'Why Can't Business Apps Be More Like Us—Efficient and Cool!' *PC Computing*, 12/5: 128, 130.

Economist (1991). 'The New Cargo Cults: Don't Forget the Pioneers', *The Economist* (4 May): 20.

FEREA, WILLIAM B. (ed.) (1984). 'Cargo Cults and Development in Melanesia', unpublished MS. Port Moresby: University of Papua New Guinea.

FEYNMAN, RICHARD P. (1974). 'Cargo Cult Science', *Engineering and Science*, 37/7: 10–13.

GEWERTZ, DEBORAH B., and ERRINGTON, FREDERICK K. (1991). 'We Think, Therefore They Are? On Occidentalizing the World', *Anthropological Quarterly*, 64: 80–91.

GLINES, C. V. (1991). 'The Cargo Cults', *Air Force Magazine*, 74/1: 84–7.

HAMILTON, JOHN (1983). 'The Cargo-Cult Chief and the Letters from a God', *Brisbane Courier-Mail* (1 Dec.): 1–2.

HANNET, LEO (1970). 'Disillusionment with the Priesthood', *Kovave*, 2/1: 22–8.

HARDING, THOMAS (1967). 'A History of Cargoism in Sio, North-east New Guinea', *Oceania*, 38: 1–23.

HARWOOD, JOHN (1991). 'Technopolis in Australia: The Rise of a Millennial Cargo Cult', *Ecologist*, 21/5: 214–19.

HOGBIN, H. IAN (1958). *Social Change*. London: Watts.

KERPI, KAMA (1975). 'Cargo', *Kovave*, 5/1: 30–6.

KUKLICK, HENRIKA (1991). *The Savage within: The Social History of British Anthropology, 1885–1945*. Cambridge: Cambridge University Press.

LAWRENCE, PETER (1954). 'Cargo Cult and Religious Beliefs among the Garia', *International Archives of Ethnography*, 47: 1–20.

——(1964). *Road Belong Cargo: A Study of the Cargo Movement in the Southern Madang District, New Guinea*. Manchester: Manchester University Press.

LEMAIRE, ANIKA (1977). *Jacques Lacan*. London: Routledge & Kegan Paul.

LINDSTROM, LAMONT (1990). 'Knowledge of Cargo, Knowledge of Cult: Truth and Power on Tanna, Vanuatu', in Garry W. Trompf (ed.), *Cargo Cults and Millenarian Movements*. Berlin: Mouton de Gruyter: 239–61.

——(1993). *Cargo Cult: Strange Stories of Desire from Melanesia and beyond*. Honolulu: University of Hawaii Press.

LONG, CHARLES H. (1974). 'Cargo Cults as Cultural Historical Phenomena', *Journal of the American Academy of Religion*, 47: 403–14.

McAuley, J. P. (1961). 'My New Guinea', *Quadrant*, 9: 15–27.

McDonell, Terry (1991). 'The Japanese Cargo Cult', *Esquire*, 116/4: 41.

McDowell, Nancy (1988). 'A Note on Cargo Cults and the Cultural Construction of Change', *Pacific Studies*, 11: 121–34.

Mair, Lucy (1948). *Australia in New Guinea*. London: Christophers.

Mason, Peter (1990). *Deconstructing America: Representations of the Other*. London: Routledge.

Merton, Thomas (1979). *Love and Living*. New York: Farrar, Straus, Giroux.

Mettler, Ruben F. (1980). 'The Cargo Cult Mentality in America', *Business Week* (22 Sept.): 22.

New York Times (1970). 'On a Pacific Island, They Wait for the G.I. Who Became a God', *New York Times* (19 Apr.): 7.

Nizan, Paul (1987). *Aden, Arabie*. New York: Columbia University Press.

O'Neill, Chuck (1988). 'Wacky Tribe Thinks Ex-prez LBJ Is a God!' *Weekly World News* (6 Dec.): 29.

Opeba, Willington Jojoga (1987). 'Melanesian Cult Movements as Traditional Religious and Ritual Responses to Change', in Garry W. Trompf (ed.), *The Gospel is Not Western: Black Theologies from the Southwest Pacific*. Maryknoll, NY: Orbis Books: 49–66.

Pacific Islands Monthly (1958). 'Many "Still Believe" in Cargo Cult: The Cargo Cult Won't Die Quietly in the Pacific', *Pacific Islands Monthly*, 61/2 (Feb.): 40.

Pokawin, Stephen (1984). 'Cargo Cults and Development', in William B. Ferea (ed.), 'Cargo Cults and Development in Melanesia', unpublished MS. Port Moresby: University of Papua New Guinea: 73–82.

Post-Courier [Papua New Guinea] (1976). 'Clamp down on Cults', *Post-Courier* (30 Sept.): 3.

——(1980). 'Levi Warns of Cargo "Delusion"', *Post-Courier* (27 May): 13.

Raspberry, William (1986). 'Tapping the Poor's Capacity to Produce', *Tulsa World* (7 Jan.): 11.

Rentoul, Alexander (1949). ' "John Frum": Origin of New Hebrides Movement', *Pacific Islands Monthly*, 19/6 (Jan.): 31.

Rimoldi, M. R. (1971). 'The Hahalis Welfare Society of Buka, New Guinea', Ph.D. dissertation (Dept. of Anthropology, Australian National University, Canberra).

Ryan, Peter (1992). 'New Symbols for Same Old Cargo Cult', *Age* (26 Sept.): 2.

Sahlins, Marshall (1972). *Stone Age Economics*. Chicago: Aldine Atherton.

Said, Edward W. (1978). *Orientalism*. New York: Vintage Books.

Schwartz, Theodore (1976). 'The Cargo Cult: A Melanesian Type Response to Change', in George Devos (ed.), *Responses to Change: Society, Culture, and Personality*. New York: A. Van Nostrand Co.: 157–206.

Stanner, W. E. H. (1958). 'On the Interpretation of Cargo Cults', *Oceania*, 29: 1–25.

STEINBAUER, FRIEDRICH (1979). *Melanesian Cargo Cults: New Salvation Movements in the South Pacific*. St Lucia: University of Queensland Press.

WAGNER, ROY (1979). 'The Talk of Koriki: A Daribi Contact Cult', *Social Research*, 46: 140–65.

——(1981). *The Invention of Culture*. (Rev. edn.) Chicago: University of Chicago Press.

WAIKO, JOHN (1973). 'European–Melanesian Contact in Melanesian Tradition and Literature', in Roland J. May (ed.), *Priorities in Melanesian Development*. Canberra: Australian National University: 417–28.

WALKER, MARTIN (1989). 'The Cult of Russia's New Rich', *Manchester Guardian Weekly* (19 Nov.): 21–2.

WEBSTER, PAUL (1992). 'Hi-tech Mickey: Overpriced, over the Top, and over Here', *Manchester Guardian Weekly* (19 Apr.): 7.

WEIGHTMAN, B., and LINI, H. (eds.) (1980). *Vanuatu: Twenty-Wan Tingting Long Taem Blong Independens*. Suva: Institute of Pacific Studies, University of the South Pacific.

WILSON, BRYAN R. (ed.) (1970). *Rationality*. New York: Harper & Row.

WORSLEY, PETER (1957). *The Trumpet Shall Sound: A Study of 'Cargo' Cults in Melanesia*. London: Macgibbon & Kee.

2

The Kabyle and the French: Occidentalism in Bourdieu's Theory of Practice

Deborah Reed-Danahay

The division of labour between those who study the West and those who study the Rest is rarely so strikingly found to reside within the work of a single person as it does in the case of Pierre Bourdieu. Bourdieu has done ethnographic research among the Kabyle peoples of Algeria, but has also contributed to the sociological analysis of Western Europe (most notably, by studying those renowned producers of High Culture—the French bourgeoisie). For several decades, Bourdieu has been developing an influential theory of the relationship between culture and power, through an examination of cultural practices and 'common-sense' understandings of the world. His approach, particularly with the concept of 'habitus' (the internalized predispositions of one's social group), claims to privilege neither structure nor individual agency in social analysis, and, indeed, seeks to break down such dualisms (Bourdieu and Wacquant 1992: 178–9). My argument in this chapter will be that Bourdieu has none the less used, and thereby perpetuated, a different kind of dualism in his work.

I shall compare two of Bourdieu's most famous books, produced at approximately the same moment in his career, and suggest that they illustrate the use of a paired occidentalism and orientalism in their analyses of French and Kabyle society. My discussion will centre on the texts of *Reproduction in Education, Society and Culture*, co-written with Jean-Claude Passeron and based upon a sociological study of secondary education in France, and *Outline of a Theory of Practice*, drawn from ethnographic research among the Kabyle peoples of Algeria. These books are significant in establishing Bourdieu's career and, as Richard Jenkins has recently written, it was through them that he 'acquired his international reputation—as a social theorist, an ethnographer of Algeria and a sociological observer of Modern France' (Jenkins 1993: 617). The French version of *Reproduction* was first published in 1970 and that of *Outline* in

1972; both appeared in English translation in 1977. Although rarely read together, due to the scholarly division of labour which has relegated *Outline* primarily to anthropological circles and *Reproduction* to those of sociology, these two books form a pair. They established important themes and modes of analysis which continue to influence Bourdieu's work and its uses by other scholars. By analysing them side by side, I hope to show that Bourdieu's writings on French education and on rural Algeria have more in common than is usually assumed, and to revise previous inter-pretations of their relation to one another.

In my analysis, I shall refer to the English version of each book. The main text of *Reproduction* was not altered significantly in translation, and the recent 1990 English edition to which I refer adds only a new intro-duction by Bourdieu. The English version of *Outline*, it must be noted, is not identical with the earlier French version, and reflects some changes in Bourdieu's thinking. As Derek Robbins notes (1991: 81), however, the French version of *Outline* is itself a revision of earlier field-work reports. A newer book, *Le Sens pratique* (1980), recently translated into English as *The Logic of Practice* (1990), constituted a further reworking of the Alge-rian materials. Rather than embark on a search for kernels of the 'essence' of Bourdieu's thinking, it is more fruitful to recognize that he is constantly revising and returning to earlier themes in his work. I have decided, therefore, to consider the English versions of both *Outline* and *Reproduction* as comparable examples of Bourdieu's theoretical ideas as introduced to English-speaking scholars in 1977, rather than as definitive statements of his thought. The scope of Bourdieu's work does not permit easy generalizations, and my 'archaeology' of his thought in this chapter is, thus, focused primarily on a particular phase during the 1970s.

Reading Bourdieu

Previous analyses of Bourdieu's work have struggled to make sense of the relationship between his work in Algeria and in France. This has usually led to conflicting interpretations of his work and its development. An-thropologists rarely turn to Bourdieu's work on French education, al-though it was for a long time his most famous. This is undoubtedly due to the relative neglect of European societies and of relations of power by a discipline historically concerned with cultural understandings of the other. Most anthropologists first knew Bourdieu primarily through *Out-line of a Theory of Practice* (1977), and have viewed him as part of a trend concerned with processes of social agency and practice (Ortner 1984).[1] In an influential discussion of current theory in anthropology, George Marcus and Michael Fischer, for example, situate Bourdieu as a practice theorist concerned with 'the production of cultural meaning and symbols, as a central practice or process in social action' (Marcus and Fischer 1986: 85).

Sociologists have rarely been drawn to Bourdieu's studies of an obscure population in rural Algeria, and are more familiar with his studies of French education and class culture. One of Bourdieu's critics in this field, Paul Willis, has argued, in contrast to Marcus and Fischer, that the notion of 'cultural production' is absent from Bourdieu's work. Willis associates Bourdieu with a vulgar 'social reproduction', and writes, 'for all the richness of the Bourdieuan system . . . agency, struggle, and variety have been banished from history' (Willis 1981: 55).

Few English-speaking readers of Bourdieu's work are familiar with both his 'sociological' and more 'ethnological' writings, and most appear unaware of such conflicting appraisals of his work. The growing literature on Bourdieu increasingly treats both the Algerian and French research (e.g. Robbins 1991; Harker, Maher, and Wilkes 1990; Jenkins 1992; Calhoun, LiPuma, and Postone 1993). For the most part, however, this literature neglects to explain adequately the relationship between the Algerian and French research.

Loïc J. D. Wacquant (1993), in a recent commentary on 'fragmented readings' of Bourdieu by an American audience, argues that Bourdieu's sociological and anthropological writings complement each other in positive ways, and that the failure to see this is mostly due to the readership. Wacquant notes that there are two sources of problems in the interpretation of Bourdieu's work: that of consumption (the readership) and that of production (writing and publication by Bourdieu himself). After a somewhat cursory nod to problems with production—in that Bourdieu never clearly articulates an overall synthesis of his sociological and anthropological work—Wacquant's focus is on the intellectual 'ethnocentrism' associated with the consumption of Bourdieu's work. Wacquant's defence of Bourdieu rests on an argument that Bourdieu's efforts to transcend both disciplinary boundaries and the usual theoretical categories are missed by American scholars, who are too entrenched in their own cultural and academic world-views.

Although Wacquant's argument that disciplinary boundaries are responsible for many misunderstandings of Bourdieu's work is valid, I believe that he has too easily dismissed the role of the side of production (as he calls it) in interpretations of Bourdieu. Why is it, for instance, that Bourdieu chose to focus his attention on practice in his research among the Kabyles, and on the structural basis of power in his work on education in France? Is it not possible that the fragmentation of the work itself has led to fragmented readings? As I argue in this chapter, the key to an understanding of this fragmentation lies in Bourdieu's use of an essentialized dualism of 'modern' and 'traditional' societies.

The difficulties for readers in reconciling the Algerian and French research emphases are aptly illustrated in two early attempts at a synthesis of his work. Stephen Foster (1986) and Richard Harker (1984; Harker, Maher, and Wilkes 1990) both attribute the apparent discrepancy between the research and writings on France and on Algeria to a chronological shift reflecting Bourdieu's intellectual development. Because of their different starting-points, however, these interpretations of Bourdieu's thought contradict each other. Foster, an anthropologist, suggests a development from concerns with agency to those with structural domination. Harker, an educational sociologist, suggests the opposite—a move from a concern with structure to a concern with process.

Foster (1986) creates a narrative of Bourdieu's career trajectory wherein ethnographic research in Algeria was followed by a turn back toward France (informed by the Algerian context). Foster also suggests that Bourdieu underwent an intellectual shift from concern with practice in Algeria to concern with reproduction in France. He writes that 'after writing *Outline of a Theory of Practice*, Bourdieu followed the route already taken by returning colonists and Algerian migrant workers, and began to investigate the question of social reproduction at home in France' (Foster 1986: 105–6). He then suggests that Bourdieu's ensuing 'analysis of symbolic domination, social and cultural reproduction, and modern power in France . . . illuminates the structure of colonialism from the side of the dominant society' (1986: 108). The fact that *Reproduction* was published two years before *Outline* is, apparently, overlooked by Foster.

A different interpretation of Bourdieu's thought is offered by Harker (1984; Harker, Maher, and Wilkes 1990). In stark contrast to that of Foster, Harker's chronology posits a Bourdieu whose 'early' educational writings in France were followed by more 'sophisticated' research on practice in Algeria. Wishing to defend Bourdieu against criticisms, such as that of Willis, that his theory of educational reproduction is overly deterministic, Harker suggests that Bourdieu has since redeemed himself through a more practice-oriented approach in later Algerian research. Harker writes:

A careful reading of Bourdieu's ethnographic work adds a dimension not readily discernible from the earlier educational writing. It provides a foundation for a theory of practice which incorporates social change and human agency, as well as an examination of the structural limits within which they must work. (Harker, Maher, and Wilkes 1990: 102)

From Foster, we hear that the work in Algeria preceded the work in France; from Harker, that the study of reproduction in French society came before the work on practice in Algeria. To some degree, these diverse conclusions reflect the difficulties involved in pinpointing a transition from Algeria to France, or from ethnology to sociology, in Bourdieu's work. He conducted research in both Algeria and rural France in 1959–60, even though his earliest Algerian research did occur a few years before that (Robbins 1991: 29). Another problem in assessing the development of Bourdieu's work for English-speaking researchers is the order of translation of his writing. However, as I have already noted, *Reproduction* and *Outline* were published within two years of each other in France and both appeared in English the same year. Bourdieu has continued to work on both the Algerian and French materials, rather than abandoning one in favour of the other. He has often returned to issues from his research in Algeria (e.g. Bourdieu 1980). Moreover, his interest in French education has continued, with *Homo Academicus* in 1984, followed by *La Noblesse d'état* in 1989. There has, thus, been a continued juxtaposition between 'modern' and 'traditional' societies in Bourdieu's work. Whereas Bourdieu posits a linear transition from one type of society to the other, however, his own work cannot be interpreted with a linear model.

It is the dualism between 'modern' and 'traditional' societies, rather than a chronologically based shift in Bourdieu's orientation, that explains the relationship between *Outline* and *Reproduction*. Bourdieu's assumptions about the different bases for social action in two types of society have oriented his research emphases. As he makes clear in *Outline*, Bourdieu views literacy as the main distinguishing feature between traditional and modern societies, and links different forms of power and domination to literate and non-literate social formations. In France, therefore, Bourdieu turned to the institutional, standardized forms of reproducing culture in a literate society—associated with the school. In Kabylia, he turned to kin-based, local-level forms of social and cultural reproduction—those surrounding the dwelling or house. This dualism essentializes European culture (the occident) as one of standardization and impersonal social relations.

Despite Bourdieu's own claims against false dichotomies, *Outline* and *Reproduction* repeatedly make use of an essentialized typology of 'traditional' and 'modern' societies. Bourdieu describes France as an example of a 'modern', 'literate', 'class–based', 'differentiated' society, and Kabylia as an example of 'traditional', 'nonliterate', 'classless', and 'undifferentiated' society. Traditional societies are characterized, for Bourdieu, by personal relations of power in which social practice and agency are both evident and effective in social reproduction; modern societies, by impersonal relations of power in which social reproduction is accomplished through a denial of social practice and agency. In his descriptions of both French and Algerian society, Bourdieu makes use of a form of occidentalism— 'the essentialistic rendering of the West by Westerners' (Carrier 1992: 199). Bourdieu's model reifies categories of the occident (associated with the present and future) vs. the orient (associated with the past). Although it is common for this contrast to be utilized as categories of 'us' vs. 'them' (Todorov 1989), Bourdieu generally avoids associating himself with an us–as–occident perspective. For Bourdieu, there are two 'thems': modern people and traditional people; and he sets himself apart as the detached sociologist.

Bourdieu practises and reproduces dualistic thinking in spite of himself. He denies both a romanticized orientalism and a hegemonic occidentalism, but substitutes for these an argument that our salvation lies in scientific sociological inquiry (a 'sociology of sociology'), which has the possibility of going beyond common-sense understandings of the world.[2] In *Reproduction* Bourdieu criticized Margaret Mead, and other cultural anthropologists, for the utopian vision 'that institutionalized education, unlike traditional education, constitutes a "mechanism of change", capable of "creating discontinuities" and "building a new world"' (Bourdieu and Passeron 1990: 65; see also Gewertz and Errington 1991, on Mead). In *Outline* he likewise argued against utopian visions of 'traditional' societies, as when he ridiculed ' "participant" anthropology' for, among other things, often being 'inspired by nostalgia for the agrarian paradises, the principle of all conservative ideologies' (Bourdieu 1977: 115). Much empirical research, Bourdieu recently laments, 'continues to address questions that are more frequently the product of "scholarly common sense" than of serious scientific thinking' (Bourdieu and Wacquant 1992: 175). This is a point which he takes up in much detail in his analysis of developments in French higher education after the events of May 1968 (Bourdieu 1984).

Bourdieu has said in defence of his work that his method has been to 'make the mundane exotic and the exotic mundane, in order to render explicit what in both cases is taken for granted' (Bourdieu and Wacquant 1992: 68). He has, he claims, self-consciously played with and thereby called into question the dichotomy between 'foreign' and 'familiar' (Bourdieu and Wacquant 1992: 163). And yet, I argue here, in his descriptions he has depended upon essentialized categories of the mundane and the exotic, modern and traditional, even when inverting these categories.

The French and their schools

Reproduction, to which I will now turn, presents a sociological analysis of modern power relations as they operate through schools in France. Rural Kabyle society rests in the shadows of this analysis, as a contrasting image.

Bourdieu's research and writings about France have consistently dealt with the interplay between family-based systems of socialization and formal educational systems in the construction of class hierarchies, although his research has primarily targeted the school, rather than families. According to Bourdieu, 'the earliest phase of upbringing [in the family] . . . produces a primary habitus, characteristic of a group or class, which is the basis for the subsequent formation of any other habitus' (Bourdieu and Passeron 1990: 42).

In *Reproduction in Education, Society and Culture*, Bourdieu's best-known book, Bourdieu and Passeron outline the ways in which the French educational system participates in bourgeois forms of cultural domination. The culture of the French school closely resembles that of the class culture ('habitus') of the bourgeoisie, Bourdieu insists, which explains the school success of bourgeois children. The school has assumed part of the bourgeois family's role in cultural and social transmission to its heirs, and now serves to reproduce the class interests of the bourgeoisie. Schooling transmits the symbolic, rather than purely material, capital of the bourgeoisie to future generations, thereby assuring their dominant position in society. Such symbolic or cultural capital entails 'cultural goods' (Bourdieu and Passeron 1990: 30), which include linguistic styles, values, interests, and tastes.

Bourdieu and Passeron argue that the educational failure of lower-class children and the success of middle- and upper-class children appear to be 'natural' processes, rather than the result of a selection and exclusion which favours the dominant classes. This occurs through symbolic violence, and a 'masking' of reality, whereby the role of the school in domination and the reproduction of class hierarchies is misrecognized as such and its legitimacy taken for granted. The success of the bourgeoisie becomes associated with natural talent (seen as a 'gift'), while the lower to look the same, with black holes and hearts, and so what? I want to say that I could have been a better husband, and that I could have been a cool uncle. And what kind of world are we going to live in? How will there still be art and expression and hope and secret diaries when you're freakin' wearing *it* every single freakin' day?

"Should I come in?"

"No! I'm fine."

I slump against the cold, tiled wall. Defeated. What I'm *really* afraid of is the empty side of the bed, of forgetting Alice.

When I hear the intern's heels click-click down the hallway, I make my escape. I run into the coffee cart guy with his black-throated gash.

"Sorry!" I yell back as I sprint full speed to the elevators.

What if I wake up one morning and the hole over my heart is a different shape? Smaller. Less jagged. What if I've slept in the middle of the bed? Or ...

"Quit showing me! Quit showing me!" I scream to everyone.

"Are you all right?" I hear, but all I can see are blobs of black. Someone is calling HR.

What if I can't get over this? What if my hole starts to grow? Could I fall into myself?

I shove someone else aside. A waste bin goes skittering. I punch a potted palm and dirt scatters,

Finally, I throw myself on the elevator's down button. It beeps its cheerful, terrible chirp, and when the doors open up, they're ready to swallow me whole.

educational and occupational outcomes of subordinate classes take on the appearance of a natural failure due to lack of talent. Lower-class children misrecognize the objective structures of power and symbolic violence which operate at school through the devaluation of their own cultural capital and the legitimization of bourgeois forms of capital. They, therefore, internalize their own failures and choose low-skilled careers—which ultimately leads to the reproduction of class hierarchies. As bourgeois children, in turn, succeed in school and acquire educational credentials and diplomas, they gain institutional legitimacy for their class positions.

Reproduction is a classic study of cultural legitimacy and hegemony, and of the mechanisms through which schools and teachers are invested with and transmit power and authority. Its focus is on standardized, structural mechanisms of inculcation in educational institutions. The first half of the text is formally written, like a treatise of logic, with an ordered numbering of paragraphs. Bourdieu and his co-author adopt a distant, authoritative voice, lending an aura of timelessness and scientific truth to their pronouncements. Michel de Certeau's observation about Bourdieu's rhetoric, that his 'subtle descriptions of Bearnian or Kabylian tactics often give way to violently imposed truths' (1984: 59), is especially apt in *Reproduction*. There are no specific social actors in the analysis, and acronyms for various structural principles operating in educational processes (like pedagogic work (PW) and pedagogic authority (PA)) form the basis of the discussion. The text is buttressed by allusion to previous statistical analyses and limited classroom observations. Teachers become 'pedagogic agents', while the students themselves, and their behaviours, are largely ignored in the analysis, as are day-to-day classroom events.

A major premiss of *Reproduction* is that the French educational system is similar to a traditional society in its self-perpetuating system of cultural and social reproduction. In *Reproduction*, Bourdieu writes of the 'quasi-perfect reproduction of culture in a traditional society' (Bourdieu and Passeron 1990: 9), and of 'the inertia of educational institutions, whose essential function always leads them to self-reproduce as unchanged as possible, like traditional societies' (1990: 32). The authority of the school is compared to the legitimacy of leadership in traditional societies, in which there is an 'undifferentiated and therefore indisputable and undisputed social authority' (1990: 29). Bourdieu and Passeron describe the symbolic violence of the school's authority as 'long-term' and 'in contrast to the authority of political power [in modern societies], which is always confronted with the problem of its own perpetuation (succession)' (1990: 33).

Schools are essentially conservative, traditional institutions, Bourdieu argues, aimed at self-preservation and replication. As in his earlier work, *Les Héritiers* (Bourdieu and Passeron 1964), Bourdieu uses non-Western ethnography in *Reproduction* to jolt the reader with parallels between schools and traditional societies. Evoking Malinowski to critique teacher attitudes, Bourdieu humorously writes that 'as in the Kula cycle, where the armshells always go round in one direction and the necklaces in the other, all the wit and wisdom go from teachers to students and all the dullness and crudity from students to teachers' (Bourdieu and Passeron 1990: 112). Bourdieu also notes the shared similarity of the school and the Catholic Church to traditional cultures. With a touch of irony, he likens teachers to priests in their ability to convince their publics that their failures are their own fault (1990: 112–13), and compares educational processes to those of baptism and confirmation (1990: 36–7). These somewhat facetious, rhetorical comparisons between 'traditional' and 'modern' societies operate in conjunction with more serious and self-consciously theoretical formulations.

Bourdieu sees resemblances between the social conservatism and systems of authority in schools and traditional societies. However, he describes the school's mode of pedagogy, or inculcation, as very modern because it depends upon impersonal social relationships. Bourdieu thereby distinguishes between traditional schools (which reproduce the dominant culture in a 'differentiated' society like France) and traditional pedagogy (which uses implicit means of instruction in traditional, 'undifferentiated' societies like Kabylia). Bourdieu sets up a continuum from traditional (implicit) to modern (explicit) forms of pedagogy, which produce the internalization of the habitus, describing these two forms in the following terms:

- *Implicit pedagogy* is 'the mode of inculcation producing a habitus by the unconscious inculcation of principles which manifest themselves only in their practical state, within the practice that is imposed' (Bourdieu and Passeron 1990: 47) and
- *explicit pedagogy* is 'the mode of inculcation producing a habitus by the inculcation, methodologically organized as such, of articulated and even formalized principles' (1990: 47).

Bourdieu adds that 'implicit pedagogy is doubtless the most efficient way of transmitting traditional, undifferentiated, "total" knowledge' (1990: 47). As he writes:

In the case of implicit pedagogy or inculcation, the master transmits unconsciously, through exemplary conduct, principles he has never mastered consciously, to a receiver who internalizes them unconsciously. In the limiting case,
seen in traditional societies, the whole group and the whole environment—that is,
the system of the material conditions of existence, insofar as they are endowed
with the symbolic significance which gives them a power of imposition—exert an
anonymous, diffuse PA [pedagogic authority] without specialized agents or speci-
fied moments (e.g. the forming of the Christian habitus in the Middle Ages,
through the catechism of the calendar of feasts and the ordering of everyday
space, or the devotional 'book' of symbolic objects). (1990: 48)

Bourdieu's intent in employing this dichotomy between explicit and
implicit pedagogy becomes clearer when he links the explicit pedagogy
of the school to 'a greater degree of verbalization and classificatory
conceptualization' (Bourdieu and Passeron 1990: 49). Moreover, he describes the bourgeoisie as those 'whose material conditions of existence
allow them to stand more completely aside from practice, in other words
to "neutralize" in imagination or reflection the vital urgencies which
thrust a pragmatic disposition on the dominated classes' (1990: 48–9).
Here, Bourdieu is saying that the French school depends upon explicit
principles of inculcation, for which the bourgeoisie is already well prepared. In contrast, members of the subordinate classes are, according to
Bourdieu, more traditional and less detached from practice.

Bourdieu equates the working classes and peasants in France with
members of traditional societies, all of whom, he argues, tend to socialize
their children through implicit, practice-oriented modes of inculcation.
They are, thus, distinguished from the dominant members of French
society, who rely upon explicit modes of inculcation and the discursive
elaboration of principles. In this formulation, Bourdieu is drawing upon
a linguistic model that resembles Basil Bernstein's (1977) theory of elaborated and restricted codes associated with social class.[3]

In attempting to critique the school and its relationship to class reproduction among the bourgeoisie, Bourdieu appeals to an essentialized
dualism between 'traditional' and 'modern' teaching and learning. He
also opposes traditional and modern forms of power and social reproduction. In this way, Bourdieu can make the seemingly contradictory argument
that a school can work to reproduce society in a traditional manner (i.e.
unchanging), yet transmit knowledge and power through modern means
(i.e. explicit inculcation). His use of the terms 'traditional' and 'modern'
are shifting, but consistently set up a dichotomy between a cluster of
social relations and processes associated with the past and those associated

with the present and future. Bourdieu even refers to 'the happy uncon-sciousness' of implicit pedagogy (Bourdieu and Passeron 1990: 62), giving it a timeless simplicity lost to modern peoples.

In the next few pages, I will turn to the essentialized portraits of occident and orient articulated in Bourdieu's ethnographic writings on Algeria. De Certeau has suggested that Bourdieu had to go to Algeria in order to describe France. The role of literacy in the mode of domination operating in schools is implied in *Reproduction*, but it is only in relation to what de Certeau (1984: 52) calls 'the inverse' of the school, the Kabyle house, that the importance of literacy to Bourdieu in characterizing the West becomes clear.

The Kabyle and their houses

Although based upon ethnographic research among the Kabyle peoples, *Outline of a Theory of Practice* is as much a criticism of scholarly practice as it is a study of the Kabyle. The Kabyle remain somewhat ill-defined both spatially and temporally in the analysis, as if the specific historical location of the subject of study were irrelevant. We are not, for example, given their precise geographical conditions, population size, history, or political organization. It seems enough, for Bourdieu, that we know the Kabyle as a pre-industrial, 'traditional' peasant society—the assumption being, one gathers, that this label speaks for itself. This lack of historical specificity in Bourdieu's descriptions of the Kabyle in *Outline* is, I argue, connected to his more general programme of a critique of Western soci-ety and of the educational and academic institutions which arise from, support, and reproduce class hierarchies. For Bourdieu, the Kabyle serve as a model of (or also, perhaps, in Geertzian terms, for) traditional society as a counterpart to modern society. They are the orient to our occident.

In *Outline*, Bourdieu finds fault with both objectivist approaches to culture, like structuralism, and more subjectivist approaches, like ethnomethodology. Bourdieu uses the book to caution against the codifi-cation of human behaviour in terms of rules characteristic of structural-ism (a product of those forms of knowledge and social organization he associates with literacy). On the other hand, he also condemns reliance upon 'common-sense' understandings of the world voiced by informants, who, he argues, 'misrecognize' those objective conditions of existence only truly apparent to the sociologist.

Talk of rules, a euphemized form of legalism, is never more fallacious than when applied to the most homogeneous societies (or the least codified areas of differentiated societies) where most practices, including those seemingly more ritualized, can be abandoned to the orchestrated improvisations of common dispositions. (Bourdieu 1977: 17)

Bourdieu's turn away from structuralism toward an attention to social practices is, consequently, more apparent in his work on rural France and in Kabylia because he views these societies as fundamentally different from modern societies.

One of the most famous sections in *Outline* is Bourdieu's analysis of the Kabyle house, which is a vital part of his theory of practice. The analysis of the Kabyle house has appeared in several other publications (Bourdieu 1970, 1973, 1980), and was also included in the original French version of *Outline*. An abbreviated version of this analysis appears in the English text (1977: 90–1). In Bourdieu's discussion of the Kabyle dwelling in *Outline*, one can see a passage from structural analysis to a more practice-oriented approach. Bourdieu begins with a very structuralist-sounding description, influenced by Bachelard as well as Lévi-Strauss. He shows how the interior space of the dwelling inverts public uses and meanings of space, generates proverbs, and expresses basic principles of the Kabyle sexual division of labour. Bourdieu goes beyond this, however, to suggest the ways in which individuals absorb body hexis (gestures and postures) and cultural knowledge as they live in and through the space of the house. Kabyle children, in particular, Bourdieu suggests, acquire a habitus in relation to the house. As he or she learns, for example, how to enter the house properly and decipher the gendered locations for activities within it, a Kabyle child constructs a sexual identity—'the major element in its social identity' (1977: 93).[4]

Bourdieu uses the absence of literacy among the 'traditional' Kabyle to distance them from 'modern' society. He draws an explicit contrast between the French school and the Kabyle dwelling in *Outline*, writing:

In a social formation in which the absence of the symbolic-product-conserving techniques associated with literacy retards the objectification of symbolic and particularly cultural capital, inhabited space—and above all the house—is the principal locus for the objectification of the generative schemes. (1977: 89)

Bourdieu also makes a metaphorical connection between the house and a book, stating that ' "the book" from which the children [in Kabylia] learn their vision of the world is read with the body'—that is, through space (1977: 90). Bourdieu argues that both the Kabyle house and the French school ensure cultural and social reproduction. The ways in which literate and non-literate, undifferentiated and differentiated, modern and traditional societies reproduce themselves differ, however, according to his theory.

It is in relation to his discussion of the Kabyle dwelling that one finds Bourdieu's clearest statement of the process of inculcation, vital to cultural and social reproduction, which underlies his theory of the habitus. Bourdieu defines and brings into clearer focus the mechanisms of power in French education by describing their opposite in Kabyle socialization processes.

So long as the work of education is not clearly institutionalized as a specific, autonomous practice, and it is a whole group and a whole symbolically structured environment, without specialized agents or specific moments, which exerts an anonymous, pervasive pedagogic action, the essential part of the modus operandi which defines practical mastery is transmitted in practice, in its practical state, without attaining the level of discourse. The child imitates not 'models' but other people's actions. . . . [I]n verbal products such as proverbs, sayings, maxims, songs, riddles, or games; in objects, such as tools, the house, or the village; or again, in practices such as contests of honour, gift exchanges, rites, etc., the material which the Kabyle child has in practice, which means, that in all this endlessly redundant material, he has no difficulty in grasping the rationale of what are clearly series and in making it his own in the form of a principle generating conduct organized in accordance with the same rationale. (Bourdieu 1977: 87–8)

The way in which *Outline* articulates an essentialized occidentalism is most strikingly seen in the final chapter, subtitled 'Basis for a Theory of Symbolic Power'. This chapter is closely linked to Book I of *Reproduction*, called 'Foundations of a Theory of Symbolic Violence'. Bourdieu explicitly uses a dichotomy between modern and traditional societies, defined through the presence or absence of literacy, in this final chapter of *Outline*. For Bourdieu, the important aspect of literacy is that it 'enables a society to accumulate culture' (Bourdieu 1977: 187) through objectification and the creation of codified texts. Since it is 'the degree of objectification of the accumulated social capital' (1977: 184) which forms the basis of different modes of domination, modern, literate societies have different systems of power relations from those of traditional, non-literate societies. Bourdieu writes in *Outline* that the French school carries the process of objectification associated with literacy to even greater heights, claiming that 'the objectification efforts of literacy are nothing in comparison with those produced by the educational system' (1977: 187). For Bourdieu, academic qualifications stand in a similar relation to cultural capital as does money to economic capital. He argues that such qualifications ensure that statuses remain distinct from the individuals who occupy them. As a consequence of this objectification of academic credentials and titles, 'relations of power and domination no longer exist directly between individuals; they are set up in pure objectivity between institutions' (Bourdieu 1977: 187).

Bourdieu contrasts 'ancient Kabylia' to modern European societies, in a move which denies any coevalness between the two (Fabian 1983). Ancient Kabylia is a society having 'no self-regulating market (in Karl Polanyi's sense), no educational system, no juridical apparatus, and no state' (Bourdieu 1977: 183). Bourdieu characterizes two forms of social relations and power, and associates these with 'traditional' and 'modern' societies.

- *Non-literate/traditional societies* are 'social universes in which relations of domination are made, unmade, and remade in and by the interactions between persons' (Bourdieu 1977: 184); whereas
- *literate/modern societies* are 'social formations in which, mediated by objective, institutionalized mechanisms, such as those producing and guaranteeing the distribution of "titles" (title of nobility, deeds of possession, academic degrees, etc.), relations of domination have the opacity and permanence of things and escape the grasp of individual consciousness and power' (1977: 184).

- A *non-literate/traditional* society is one with 'social relations which, not containing within themselves the principle of their own reproduction, must be kept up through nothing less than a process of continuous creation' (Bourdieu 1977: 189); but a
- *literate/modern* society is viewed as 'a social world which, containing within itself the principle of its own continuation, frees agents from the endless work of creating and restoring social relations' (Bourdieu 1977: 189).

Bourdieu offers an evolutionary scheme of modes of domination—from personal, to direct (slavery), to impersonal (capitalist). In the precapitalist phase, there was a need for 'gentle, hidden exploitation' (Bourdieu 1977: 192), where a euphemization of power combined overt and symbolic forms of violence. During the phase of early capitalism and slavery, direct forms of domination were most common. According to Bourdieu, we have returned to 'symbolic violence' in the present era, because 'wealth, the ultimate basis of power, can exert power, and exert it durably, only in the form of symbolic capital' (Bourdieu 1977: 195). Bourdieu essentializes Kabyle society as one based upon personal relations of power. He essentializes France as its opposite—a society in which impersonal, 'symbolic' forms of violence arise in tandem with literacy and are augmented by schools.

French forms of occidentalism

Although Bourdieu's aim in his analyses of French institutions has been to critique abuses of power in the West, his over-reliance upon the dualism between 'modern' and 'traditional' societies, particularly as illustrated in the two books under consideration here, has led to the neglect of important questions. Bourdieu draws comparisons in both *Outline* and *Reproduction* between the structure of social relations in state institutions in France and the practice of kinship-based social relations in the remote Algerian region of Kabylia. National institutions are made to seem irrelevant to the study of the Kabyle, however, while they are given a central role in Bourdieu's studies of France. At the same time, day-to-day symbolic behaviours, which form the core of Bourdieu's analysis of the Kabyle, receive scant attention in *Reproduction*.

Bourdieu's work on French education in *Reproduction* reified the import of centralized power in France and downplayed negotiations and resistances to the state. When studying education among his urban compatriots, Bourdieu did not focus the same amount of attention on everyday practice and ethnographic detail as he did in his studies of either the Kabyle (Bourdieu 1977, 1980) or the French peasants of Béarn (Bourdieu 1962, 1972). His focus on Kabylia as a 'traditional' society, a form of orientalism, resulted in studies of social and familial practices among the Kabyle, to the neglect of national institutions and local–national interactions in that setting (cf. Herzfeld 1987). That there were colonial schools in Kabylia during Bourdieu's research there is not apparent in his work, and the presence of Koranic schools receives scant mention. Questions about the role of colonial education among the Kabyle, and comparisons between French schools and Algerian schools, remain unanswered (cf. Amrouche 1988 on Kabyle education).

The dualism between structure and agency, against which Bourdieu has argued so strongly, is not unrelated to the dualism between 'traditional' and 'modern' in his work. The notion of structure is more visible in his writings on French society, while that of practice is accented in his ethnographic research among the traditional Kabyle. It is this contrast which has prompted such varied interpretations among anthropological and sociological readers. Some readers, in defence of Bourdieu, claim that it is only by reading both the French and Algerian work that one can gain an adequate understanding of his transcendence of the dualism of structure and practice. Earlier in this chapter I summarized Wacquant's (1993) recent argument to this effect. However, the question remains as to why Bourdieu chose to fragment his work in this fashion.

The tension between structure and agency in Bourdieu's thought is part of a wider dialogue concerning the cultural and historical bases of such notions as social determinism and free will, as well as the very Western, capitalist origins of individualism. Bourdieu has seemingly inverted this argument in his work by stressing the lack of individual agency among those dominant in the West, while at the same time stressing the possibilities for social manipulation by individuals in a non-Western context (i.e. the Kabyle). Whereas he provided a delicious analysis of the nuances, particularly in tempo, surrounding gift exchange among the Kabyle in *Outline*, Bourdieu's discussion of 'gifts' among the French in *Reproduction* focused on their cultural concept of natural talent, as structurally defined and class-determined, with no room or need for social creation.[5] Bourdieu's analysis of the uses of time by French professors to heighten their reputations, in *Homo Academicus* (1988), illustrates his growing concern with social practice (particularly among the bourgeoisie) in France. However, this more recent book is primarily an analysis of the relationship between social origins and eventual position in the social field of French academia, wherein individual behaviour is seen as tightly orchestrated by habitus.

What should one make of this dichotomy between traditional and modern, Kabyle and French, in the two books under consideration here? Could Bourdieu even suggest this dualism in the same terms if he had looked at national or colonial institutions (including schools) among the Kabyle and at French practices in everyday life (including households)? It is only because he chose to focus so narrowly on French institutional arrangements in schools, rather than on children and families as social agents, that Bourdieu could ignore social manipulation among the French in schools. And it is only because he has ignored the state in his analysis of Kabyle social life that Bourdieu could set it up to be an inversion of France.

Bourdieu's clear-cut dichotomizing between societies with schools and literacy and those without is called into question by several recent approaches to the history and theory of education. Harvey Graff has commented on the tendency to divide the world into literate and non-literate societies, which Jack Goody (1977: 146) has called the 'Grand Dichotomy', whereby 'men and women of the book project their presumed advantages and disadvantages on others' (Graff 1987: 382). Graff adds that 'one of the dichotomies that need to be transcended is the relationship of literacy to modernization' (1987: 385). The work of Graff (1979, 1987), Goody (1977, 1986), and François Furet and Jacques Ozouf (1982), among others, offers modes of rethinking assumptions about the effects of literacy as well as its origins. In France, for example, literacy spread in rural communities alongside, but not always directly in, schools. Before state schooling was enforced as mandatory, peasants voluntarily attended illegal schools in the French countryside as a means to acquire literacy skills. The relationship between education and literacy in the history of France, is, therefore, complicated, and literacy cannot be viewed as synonymous with formal education (Furet and Ozouf 1982).

Running almost parallel to the 'modern' vs. 'traditional' opposition in Bourdieu's work is his implied dichotomy between socialization and education. Bourdieu's notion of the learner among the Kabyle allows for more social agency than does his notion of the learner in France; but in both, the learner is essentially passive in the acquisition of habitus. In Kabylia, the child acquires a habitus through bodily movements and a total environment rather than through deliberate instruction. In France, according to Bourdieu, all learning beyond the family takes place in standardized, determined ways, with specialized agents of teaching and a formal curriculum.

This type of dichotomy has been challenged by recent studies in learning and cognition. Although influenced by Bourdieu's theory of social practice as articulated in *Outline*, Jean Lave and Étienne Wenger have detailed a theory of learning that avoids dualisms concerning modern vs. traditional modes. They challenge the view that schooling is 'a more effective and advanced institution for educational transmission than (supposedly) previous forms such as apprenticeship' (Lave and Wenger 1991: 61), and argue that all learning (not merely in so-called 'traditional' societies) is a form of social practice and of cultural construction. With examples ranging from Alcoholics Anonymous in the USA to apprentice midwives in Mexico, Lave and Wenger dismantle the very essentialisms of the West that pervade Bourdieu's research on France. Moreover, F. Niyi Akinnaso (1992) has argued that the deliberate instruction associated with schooling is not a singularly Western institution, thereby encouraging us to move beyond static modern vs. traditional paradigms.

In this early work, Bourdieu essentialized France as a place where people do not engage in cultural creation or negotiate power, because the

codification and objectification of its institutions obviates such social practices. My own ethnographic research on schooling in rural France (Reed-
Danahay 1995; Reed-Danahay and Anderson-Levitt 1991), albeit inspired
by Bourdieu, shows that parents, children, and teachers are involved in
the negotiation and manipulation of cultural meanings and social forms in
French schools, and are not, as Bourdieu suggests, freed 'from the endless
work of creating and restoring social relations' (1977: 189).

Some clues to the seeming paradox of Bourdieu's selective vision of
French and Algerian societies can be gleaned from a historical perspective
on the relationship between these two nations. Bourdieu's work on France
and Algeria is informed by a long history of colonialism and by the
Algerian war of independence, which was under way during his earliest
research. One could easily substitute France and Algeria for Europe and
the Orient in this passage from Edward Said (1978: 1–2):

The Orient is not only adjacent to Europe; it is also the place of Europe's greatest
and richest and oldest colonies . . . and one of its deepest and most recurring
images of the Other. In addition, the Orient has helped to define Europe (or the
West) as its contrasting image, idea, personality, experience.

Bourdieu's critique of the French educational system is informed by
this contrast between Occident and Orient. The history of French education and the history of French colonialism are not as distinct as one might
assume. The early architects of French schools had the same 'civilizing'
mission in mind for French peasants as the colonialists did for their
subjects. Jules Ferry, the celebrated Minister of Education who oversaw
the institution of universal public primary education in France at the turn
of the century, was also the great imperialist who accelerated French
dominion over Algeria early in the twentieth century (Furet 1985).

Bourdieu's own work can be read as an attempt to criticize this history
of cultural domination through a condemnation of French schooling and
its symbolic violence. The French educational system embodies the long-
standing efforts of the centralized state to homogenize diversity and create cultural unity. The Kabyle represent, in Bourdieu's work, the exotic
other threatened by a similar process, but at some remove. In conducting
research on French education and on rural Algeria, Bourdieu is expressing two facets of the tension in all nation-states, which is heightened in
French culture, between unity and diversity, domination and resistance.
However, he locates possibilities for resistance through practice, in studies of Algerian peasants rather than French students or teachers.

Algeria cannot, however, be essentialized categorically as the Orient to France's Occident. Lisa Lowe usefully cautions against essentializing the very dualism of orientalism/occidentalism as we critique the essentializing and ultimately hegemonic work of concepts of the West and the Rest. She writes:

The binary opposition of Occident and Orient is thus a misleading perception which serves to suppress the specific heterogeneities, inconstancies, and slippages of each individual notion. This heterogeneity is borne out most simply in the different meanings of 'the Orient' over time.... Notions such as 'French culture', 'the British Empire', and 'European nations' are likewise replete with ambiguity, conflicts, and nonequivalences. (Lowe 1991: 7)

Parts of France, particularly in the south, are sometimes located in the same cultural region, the 'Mediterranean', as is Algeria. The Mediterranean is a region which 'threatens to expose fuzziness in our categories' and holds an ambiguous place in Eurocentric thought—'European or oriental, familiar or exotic?' (Herzfeld 1987: 15–16; see also Herzfeld, this volume). I first encountered Bourdieu, labelled as a Mediterraneanist (rather than a sociologist or ethnographer), early in my studies of European peasant society. Bourdieu's (1965) was an influential voice in the construction of the discourse on 'honour' in Mediterraneanist scholarship,[6] which helped to define the Mediterranean as a cultural area. Before I learned of his educational writings, I considered Bourdieu's studies of rural France and Algeria as parallel analyses of societies in a similar cultural region. Both types of society were studied by specialists in the field of 'peasant studies', concerned with the other in Western societies. As other contributors to this volume who focus on Europe suggest, the concept of the occidental is a shifting one, ever adapting to changing political and social conditions (Herzfeld, Nadel-Klein, Lindstrom, this volume).

Although I have not elaborated upon Bourdieu's extensive writings on rural France in this essay, when he situates the Béarnaise peasants in relation to dominant French society he uses a pairing of occidentalism and orientalism similar to that seen in his Algerian work. Moreover, it is most probably due to occidentalist thinking among scholars that Bourdieu's writings on Algerian peasants are more widely read than those on French peasants. It is when Bourdieu's writings on France reinforce stereotypes of French society as centralized and bureaucratic (i.e. those on education) that they receive most recognition.

Conclusions

This look at occidentalisms in Bourdieu's two books *Reproduction* and *Outline* raises questions concerning how anthropologists might avoid essentialisms when constructing 'cultural critiques' of their own societies. In order to highlight the ways in which élites reproduce their own class cultures and position in French society, Bourdieu has essentialized the role of institutions in France and the practices of kin-based social groups elsewhere. He presented France as a place where power is impersonal and where schools have taken over family roles in socialization. This model, however, depends directly upon an assumption that a different system exists in Kabylia, one with personal and direct forms of power, and implicit, practical forms of socialization within the family. Bourdieu's occidentalisms in France were twinned with orientalist conceptions of the Kabyle. He thereby underplayed the role of the state for the Kabyles and of day-to-day symbolic behaviour among the French. Despite his disdain for 'utopian visions', Bourdieu presented Kabylia as an ideal model of the traditional with which to rethink our own modern forms of symbolic violence and class culture (see also Robbins 1991: 171).

Reproduction has been extremely influential in the critical study of education, and has helped unpack the relationship between education and social class (Apple 1979; Lareau 1989). At the same time, however, it ignored some of the everyday practices of French parents and children, especially those of the dominated classes, and has contributed to hegemonic views of French education as bureaucratic, standardized, and uniform. *Outline*, in contrast, offered a model for new emphases on social practice in everyday life. Bourdieu left the task of integrating the study of institutional power with the study of everyday practice for future work.

Most critics of occidentalism and orientalism target the use of this dualism to promote and elevate Western values and institutions. My argument here is not to suggest that Bourdieu intends to celebrate the West. Rather, it has been to show how Bourdieu's work, particularly the earlier phase described here, used an essentialized vision of the West to criticize modern forms of symbolic violence.[7] Bourdieu has often argued that the only way truly to understand social life is to undertake a 'scientific' approach, which goes beyond 'common-sense' understandings. The ways in which Bourdieu's own view of French institutions is informed by French 'common-sense' understandings remain unacknowledged by Bourdieu and contribute to his unreflexive use of occidentalisms in the two texts under consideration in this chapter. Michael Herzfeld takes up this point when he comments that 'Bourdieu has confused the ideology of his own milieu with its practices' (Herzfeld 1987: 83).

In formulating critical perspectives on our own societies, Western anthropologists should turn a more reflexive gaze toward our models of idealized cultural arrangements. This would permit us to become increasingly aware of the ways in which our own common-sense understandings of the world are reflected in our theoretical discourse, an important concern voiced by Bourdieu himself. More importantly, it would shed light on the ways in which the common-sense/scientific dichotomy is related to occidentalist/orientalist perspectives. When Bourdieu upholds an 'objective',[8] 'scientific' view of either French or Algerian society, he is relying upon the very codification and impersonal use of power which he seeks to analyse. Comparative cultural perspectives not informed by a search for the exotic or traditional, which imply their mundane and modern complements, but by a more balanced view of historical interconnections and global cultures, will lead to a more reflexive view of our essentialisms when they are aimed both at home and elsewhere.

Acknowledgements

Many of the ideas in this chapter have developed from research I conducted during my participation in the 1990 NEH Summer Seminar on 'Poetics and Social Life', under the direction of Michael Herzfeld, at Indiana University. An earlier version of this chapter, not directly informed by the concept of occidentalism, was presented at the 1991 AAA meetings.

Notes

1 Some noteworthy exceptions to this are Michael Herzfeld (1987) and Joan Vincent (1990).

2 Jenkins (1992: 95–6) argues that Bourdieu has not transcended the subjectivism–objectivism dichotomy he seeks to remedy in his work, due to his own attempt to constitute empirical reality as objective.

3 The affinities between Bourdieu's and Bernstein's work have yet to be fully explored in the literature. Bourdieu himself notes them (see, in particular, Bourdieu 1982: 39), and they have been addressed by Michael Apple (1979), Henri Giroux (1983: 96–8), and Robbins (1991: 7–8). See Bernstein (1977) for his theories of class domination and language.

4 The role of sexual identity in the habitus, usually associated with social class, is an intriguing topic Bourdieu never fully enunciates. See, however, Jane Cowan (1990) for an attempt to link habitus and gender.

5 See Carrier (this volume) for an analysis of 'the gift' in Maussian thought. The gift as natural talent in France is related to the notion of the commodity in Mauss—a form of inherited symbolic capital in Bourdieu's terms.

6 I thank Michael Herzfeld for reminding me of this important piece of Bourdieu's history.

7 In doing so, Bourdieu illustrates a point made in the Introduction to this volume, that essentializations can be used to reflect critically on the West (see also Rosaldo 1989: 82).

8 I thank Michael Herzfeld for encouraging me to think about this issue in relation to Bourdieu. See also Reed-Danahay (1993) for a more detailed argument about theory and ethnography in France.

References

AKINNASO, F. NIYI (1992). 'Schooling, Language, and Knowledge in Literate and Nonliterate Societies', *Comparative Studies in Society and History*, 34: 68–109.

AMROUCHE, FADHMA A. M. (1988). *My Life Story: The Autobiography of a Berber Woman*, trans. Dorothy S. Blair. London: The Women's Press.

APPLE, MICHAEL W. (1979). *Ideology and Curriculum*. London: Routledge & Kegan Paul.

BERNSTEIN, BASIL (1977). *Codes, Class, and Control*. New York: Schocken Books.

BOURDIEU, PIERRE (1962). *'Célibat et condition paysanne'*, *Études rurales*, 5–6: 32–136.

——(1965). 'The Sentiment of Honour in Kabyle Society', trans. P. Sherrard, in John G. Peristiany (ed.), *In Honour and Shame: The Values of Mediterranean Society*. London: Weidenfeld & Nicolson: 191–241.

——(1970). *'La Maison kabyle ou le monde renverse'*, in Jean Pouillon and Pierre Maranda (eds.), *Échanges et communications: mélanges offerts à Claude Lévi-Strauss à l'occasion de son 60ème anniversaire*. Paris: Mouton: 739–58.

——(1972). *'Les Stratégies matrimoniales dans le système de reproduction'*, *Annales*, 4–5: 1105–27.

——(1973). 'The Berber House or the World Reversed', in Mary Douglas (ed.), *Rules and Meanings: The Anthropology of Everyday Knowledge*. Harmondsworth: Penguin Books: 98–110.

——(1977). *Outline of a Theory of Practice*, trans. Richard Nice. Cambridge: Cambridge University Press.

——(1980). *Le Sens pratique*. Paris: Éditions de Minuit.

——(1982). *Ce que parler veut dire*. Paris: Fayard.

——(1984). *Distinction: A Social Critique of the Judgement of Taste*, trans. Richard Nice. Cambridge, Mass.: Harvard University Press.

——(1988). *Homo Academicus*, trans. Peter Collier. Stanford, Calif.: Stanford University Press.

——(1989). *La Noblesse d'état: grand corps et grandes écoles*. Paris: Éditions de Minuit.

——(1990). *The Logic of Practice*, trans. Richard Nice. Stanford, Calif.: Stanford University Press.

——and PASSERON, JEAN-CLAUDE (1964). *Les Héritiers, les étudiants, et la culture*. Paris: Éditions de Minuit. (English edn.: *The Inheritors: French Students and their Relation to Culture*, trans. Richard Nice. Chicago: University of Chicago Press, 1979.)

————(1990). *Reproduction in Education, Society and Culture*, 2nd edn., trans. Richard Nice. London: Sage Publications.

——and WACQUANT, LOÏC J. D. (1992). *An Invitation to Reflexive Sociology*. Chicago: University of Chicago Press.

CALHOUN, CRAIG, LIPUMA, EDWARD, and POSTONE, MOISHE (eds.) (1993). *Bourdieu: Critical Perspectives*. Chicago: University of Chicago Press.

CARRIER, JAMES G. (1992). 'Occidentalism: The World Turned Upside-Down', *American Ethnologist*, 19: 195–212.

CERTEAU, MICHEL DE (1984). *The Practice of Everyday Life*, trans. S. Rendall. Berkeley, Calif.: University of California Press.

COWAN, JANE (1990). *Dance and the Body Politic in Northern Greece*. Princeton, NJ: Princeton University Press.

FABIAN, JOHANNES (1983). *Time and the Other: How Anthropology Makes its Object*. New York: Columbia University Press.

FOSTER, STEPHEN W. (1986). 'Reading Pierre Bourdieu', *Cultural Anthropology*, 1: 103–9.

FURET, FRANÇOIS (ed.) (1985). *Jules Ferry: fondateur de la République*. Paris: Éditions de l'École des Hautes Études en Sciences Sociales.

——and OZOUF, JACQUES (1982). *Reading and Writing: Literacy from Calvin to Jules Ferry*. Cambridge: Cambridge University Press.

GEWERTZ, DEBORAH B., and ERRINGTON, FREDERICK K. (1991). 'We Think, Therefore They Are? On Occidentalizing the World', *Anthropological Quarterly*, 64: 68–91.

GIROUX, HENRI (1983). *Theory and Resistance in Education*. South Hadley, Mass.: Bergin & Garvey.

GOODY, JACK (1977). *The Domestication of the Savage Mind*. Cambridge: Cambridge University Press.

——(1986). *The Logic of Writing and the Organization of Society*. Cambridge: Cambridge University Press.

GRAFF, HARVEY J. (1979). *The Literacy Myth: Literacy and Social Structure in the Nineteenth Century City*. New York: Academic Press.

——(1987). *The Legacies of Literacy: Continuities and Contradictions in Western Culture and Society*. Bloomington, Ind.: Indiana University Press.

HARKER, RICHARD (1984). 'On Reproduction, Habitus and Education', *British Journal of Sociology of Education*, 5: 117–27.

HARKER, RICHARD, MAHER, CHELAN, and WILKES, CHRIS (eds.) (1990). *An Introduction to the Work of Pierre Bourdieu*. London: Macmillan.

HERZFELD, MICHAEL (1987). *Anthropology through the Looking-Glass: Critical Ethnography in the Margins of Europe*. Cambridge: Cambridge University Press.

JENKINS, RICHARD (1992). *Pierre Bourdieu*. London: Routledge.

——(1993). 'Review of Pierre Bourdieu, *The Logic of Practice*', *Man*, 28: 617–18.

LAREAU, ANNETTE (1989). *Home Advantage: Social Class and Parental Intervention in Elementary Education*. London: Falmer Press.

LAVE, JEAN, and WENGER, ÉTIENNE (1991). *Situated Learning: Legitimate Peripheral Participation*. Cambridge: Cambridge University Press.

LOWE, LISA (1991). *Critical Terrains: French and British Orientalisms*. Ithaca, NY: Cornell University Press.

MARCUS, GEORGE E., and FISCHER, MICHAEL M. J. (1986). *Anthropology as Cultural Critique*. Chicago: University of Chicago Press.

ORTNER, SHERRY (1984). 'Theory in Anthropology since the Sixties', *Comparative Studies in Society and History*, 26: 126–66.

REED-DANAHAY, DEBORAH (1993). 'Talking about Resistance: Ethnography and Theory in Rural France', *Anthropological Quarterly*, 66: 221–9.

——(1995). *Les Notres: Schooling, Identity, and Resistance in Rural France*. Cambridge: Cambridge University Press.

——and ANDERSON-LEVITT, KATHRYN M. (1991). 'Backward Countryside, Troubled City: French Teachers' Images of Rural and Working-Class Families', *American Ethnologist*, 18: 546–64.

ROBBINS, DEREK (1991). *The Work of Pierre Bourdieu*. Boulder, Col.: Westview Press.

ROSALDO, RENATO (1989). *Culture and Truth: The Remaking of Social Analysis*. Boston: Beacon Press.

SAID, EDWARD (1978). *Orientalism*. New York: Pantheon Books.

TODOROV, TZVETAN (1989). *Nous et les autres: la réflexion française sur la diversité*. Paris: Éditions Seuil.

VINCENT, JOAN (1990). *Anthropology and Politics: Visions, Traditions, and Trends*. Tucson, Ariz.: University of Arizona Press.

WACQUANT, LOÏC J. D. (1993). 'Bourdieu in America: Notes on the Transatlantic Importation of Social Theory', in Craig Calhoun, Edward LiPuma, and Moishe Postone (eds.), *Bourdieu: Critical Perspectives*. Chicago: University of Chicago Press: 235–62.

WILLIS, PAUL (1981). 'Cultural Production Is Different from Cultural Reproduction Is Different from Social Reproduction Is Different from Reproduction', *Interchange*, 12: 48–67.

3

Maussian Occidentalism: Gift and Commodity Systems

James G. Carrier

In *Orientalism*, Edward Said criticizes what he calls the 'textual attitude' (1978: 92) in Oriental studies, the reliance on texts to define what is authentic and worthy of attention. One corollary of this attitude is that the past and the present collapse into each other in a timeless essence. Said puts it thus:

[A]n observation about a tenth-century Arab poet multiplied itself into a policy towards (and about) the Oriental mentality in Egypt, Iraq, or Arabia. Similarly, a verse from the Koran would be considered the best evidence of an ineradicable Muslim sensuality. (1978: 96)

But what is critical sauce for the Muslim Oriental goose is likewise critical sauce for the capitalist Occidental gander. The same timeless, textual essentialism exists in some influential anthropological treatments of the West. In these, the capitalist West *is* autonomous possessive individuals. To rephrase Said, I put it thus:

[A]n observation about seventeenth-century English political philosophers multiplied itself into a policy towards (and about) the commodity mentality in England or the United States. Similarly, a passage from Locke would be considered the best evidence of an ineradicable Western individuality.

Like all polemics, and like all essentialisms, this simplifies a complex reality. But I have found it useful for thinking about the ways that academics render social identities and relations in the West. I want to approach this issue by looking at common interpretations and invocations of the West as the land of impersonal transactions and the market. This construction of the West is rooted deeply in anthropology and sociology, and it has affected researchers working in many areas. However, its appearance is striking in Melanesian ethnography, where it springs in part from the distinction between gifts and commodities laid out in the work of Marcel Mauss, particularly his essay *The Gift*, but also his essay on the concept of the self (Mauss 1985).

While Mauss has long been important among Melanesianists, his influence grew markedly in the early 1980s, following the publication of C. A. Gregory's (1980, 1982) work on gift and commodity systems. However, it is important to remember that the Maussian model I describe here is only an exemplar of a more diffuse framework that draws on many sources, such as Marx (in the case of Gregory) and Steve Barnett and Martin Silverman (1979) in the case of Marilyn Strathern (1985*b*; 1988), whom I discuss at length later in this chapter. Other sources include Locke (see Strathern 1985*a*) and the theory of possessive individualism that is laid out by C. B. Macpherson (1962). Thus, although I refer to a Maussian model, it must be remembered that I use that model only as a convenient illustration of a more pervasive dualism that sees Melanesian societies as gift systems and Western societies as commodity systems. Further, I do not claim that the model I sketch represents a thorough, nuanced rendering of what Mauss wrote. That is why I call that model 'Maussian', rather than 'Mauss's'.

After sketching the core of the Maussian model I address three issues. The first is the way the model distorts and simplifies a complex Western reality. This Maussian occidentalism supports and is associated with the Maussian orientalism of the society of the gift. The second issue I address is the way that this orientalism affects anthropological renderings of village societies in Melanesia. As I will show, researchers use evidence shaped by the model to reflect on the difference between the West and the Rest, and so regenerate the very essentialisms that it contains. In Melanesia, the Maussian model comes full circle. Finally, I consider some of the reasons Maussian occidentalism is so attractive.

Gifts and commodities

The popular core of the Maussian model is the distinction between gifts and commodities, terms that can be applied to the social identity of objects, to forms of transactions, and to sorts of societies (see generally Carrier 1991). At one extreme are gift societies, dominated by kinship relations and groups that define individuals and their relations with and obligations to each other. In transactions in these societies, objects are inalienably associated with the giver, the recipient, and the relationship that defines and binds them. Consequently, objects and people are seen as defined by their locations in a web of social relationships. At the other extreme are the commodity systems of the modern West. Here, people are not defined by kin relationships and groups, but are independent individuals who transact freely with each other. In transactions in these societies, objects are alienated commodities, separate from the giver and the recipient. Consequently, objects and people are defined by their autonomous identities.

In gift societies, the gift embodies all aspects of social life. In such societies 'all kinds of institutions are given expression at one and the same time—religious, judicial, and moral, . . . likewise economic' (Mauss 1990: 3). This view is common among anthropologists studying societies in Melanesia. Thus, in their cross-cultural analysis of Highlands New Guinea societies, Paula Rubel and Abraham Rosman (1978: 320) conclude that 'the structure of ceremonial exchange also organizes behaviour in other cultural domains, which is why it can be singled out as the dominant sphere'. This view is so widespread that one influential writer could say that 'exchange itself is the central dynamic' of Melanesian social organization (Whitehead 1986: 80) without feeling the need to argue the point.

The essence of modern Western commodity societies is alienation. People in Western societies are alienated from the people and the objects around them. Equally, transactions there are fragmented, both because transactors are alienated from each other and because the realm of transaction has become isolated from the rest of social life. As Mauss (1990: 46, 47) puts it, these are the societies 'of purely individual contract, of the market where money circulates, of sale proper, and above all of the notion of price reckoned in coinage', of the 'strict distinction' between 'things and persons'.

I said that this model of the distinction between societies of the gift and of the commodity is common in anthropology, and especially among Melanesianists, and that the model draws selectively on many sources without necessarily being true to any of them. Certainly it simplifies Mauss's own rendering of the West somewhat, for he states at a number of points that gift relations do exist in Western industrial societies. Thus, in the introduction to *The Gift* he says that gift relations 'still function in our own societies, in unchanging fashion'. However, he does go on to say that these relations are 'hidden, below the surface' (1990: 4). This uncertainty recurs, as when he says that 'societies immediately preceding our own' have 'traces' of gift systems (1990: 47). Likewise, he refers to the 'victory of rationalism and mercantilism' in the West (1990: 76; but also see the contrary points he makes on the same page). Mauss describes the existence of gifts in the West at greatest length in the book's conclusion. However, many of his illustrations are reports of decaying practices among French peasantry or of laws that are not enforced (1990: 66–7, 154 n. 5).

A BEGINNER'S GUIDE TO GOODBYE SEX

Joaquin Fernandez

THE SERIES OF TEXT MESSAGES YOU RECEIVE, WHEN READ ALL at once, will break your heart. This is why you must read them constantly. This is why you must steal moments from your day and sneak furtive, hungry glances to your phone at your desk while your co-workers mill about and pretend not to notice. You will not make it easy for them.

You will drink too much because you are a cliché and because your friends have missed you while you were eating brunch and going for walks and making love in the afternoon. Your friends will be there for you and you will feel bad and you will buy the next round. Good for you. You will wake alone in the bed you shared and your head will scream and throb. Your phone will offer no news from her and as the days pass you will have less and less of an opinion on this. Good for you.

That Sunday morning her hair was up and her shorts were short and she smelled like rain and fake cinnamon. She came up behind you and her smooth and flawless thighs rubbed pleasant and cloying

Where he asserts the existence of gift relations in more central parts of modern society, the uncertainty is clearest and most poignant. Often he seems to be straining to see signs of a resurgence of gift relations in reforms that are always 'laboriously in gestation' but have not yet borne fruit (e.g. 1990: 67–8, 78).

In the model that I have sketched, gift and commodity systems are inseparable. They define each other dialectically, in that they are generated as opposites of each other. Nicholas Thomas raises this point when he questions 'whether . . . the gift is anything other than the inversion of the commodity' (Thomas 1991: 15; see also Biersack 1991, and her invocation of Kirby 1989). Gift societies show the embeddedness of economic activities in a web of social relations that is significant precisely because, in the modern West, the economy supposedly is no longer so embedded.

I want now to address an issue anthropologists rarely consider, the occidentalism of the Maussian model. I shall do so by suggesting ways in which its rendering of the West as the land of commodity systems populated by what Abercrombie, Hill, and Turner (1986) call the *Sovereign Individuals of Capitalism* is likely to hide as much as it reveals.

Commodity systems

Certainly the modern West contains an elaborate system of alienated market transactions. However, the Maussian model occidentalizes the West by using the sheer existence of this system, however elaborate, as the basis for an essentialist typification of the whole of Western society that requires that 'we ignore exchanges and productive activities concerned with non-commodities' (Davis 1973: 166; see Friedland and Robertson 1990). I will question this typification by showing the sorts of relations and areas of social life that it calls upon us to ignore.

The most obvious of these areas is the family. While relations within the family are influenced by capitalist employment relations outside it (e.g. Lamphere 1986), influence has not meant displacement. Instead, people conceive of household relations in ways that resemble Mauss's gift relations. As David Schneider (1980: 46) summarizes the beliefs of the Americans he studied, family relations are based on the enduring bonds of love that are themselves based on shared biogenetic substance, and the transactions within the family are expressions of those relations, rather than of the alienation of the market.

Likewise, many people in their marriages see themselves not as individuals, but as 'moral persons' (Parry 1986: 456; see Mauss 1985), defined by their positions in a structure of social relations that encompasses them. For such people, building a marriage entails creating such communal identities. For example, in their study of newly married couples, Penny Mansfield and Jean Collard (1988: 113, 151) found this underlay much of what people said about their joint efforts to set up a home, and it appeared as well when working husbands came to see their work in terms of their obligation to contribute to their marriage. Even among settled married couples, people often experience the things they do as part of the creation and maintenance of a group and a communal existence. As one woman described her housework to Peter Willmott and Michael Young (1960: 132):

I often feel at the end of the day that all my efforts have been of no avail. I remember all the polishing and cleaning, washing and ironing, that will have to be done all over again, and like many other housewives I wish that my life could be a bit more exciting sometimes. But when the evening fire glows, when the house becomes a home, then it seems to me that this is perhaps the path to true happiness.

Although mundane family transactions may not have the visibility of large-scale, public transactions in the market, they are important for the survival of family members as individuals and for the survival of the family as a group. The mothers that Diana Barker (1972) describes who cooked and kept house for their children, like those that Peter Corrigan (1989) describes who bought clothing for their children, are giving labour and objects that are necessary for their recipients' survival and for the regeneration of relations within the household, just as they are expressions of the moral and religious values of the giver, and the values and indeed the judicial rules of the society at large. The importance of these transactions as embodiments of social relations is apparent when the giver refuses to give or the recipient to accept, the sort of circumstance described by Rhian Ellis (1983) in her analysis of meals in the violent breakdown of marriage.

Appropriately, many of the objects transacted in such relationships are not alienated commodities. Mihaly Csikszentmihalyi and Eugene Rochberg-Halton, who studied the ways Americans think of valued objects, say (1981: 86) that people's talk about objects is marked by the theme of 'kinship; of the ties that bind people to each other—that provide continuity in one's life and across generations', a theme that was marked by the intensity of the way people talked: 'It is the cumulative effect of hearing people talk about their parents, spouses, and children, the depth of their emotion in doing so, that is impressive.' As one woman explained what it meant to have a quilt that her relatives had made and given: 'It means my whole family, that we all enjoy receiving these things . . . And if somebody makes it and puts so much time in it, to me it's love that's been put into the object' (1981: 143, ellipses in original). Because such objects embody the relationship of giver and recipient, they cannot be discarded freely in the way that commodities can. This is illustrated by the way a householder explained to Csikszentmihalyi and Rochberg-Halton (1981: 66, emphasis added) the reason why the painting was there above the sofa. 'My parents gave it . . . to us. They saw the empty space above the sofa and one day they brought us this picture to fill it. *It's not my style, but they gave it to us so I keep it.*'

It is not just within households that people carry out transactions of economic significance within durable, personal relationships. In his study of a residential area in Toronto, Barry Wellman found substantial giving and getting among friends, relatives, and neighbours (e.g. Wellman and Wortley 1990). The resources that people transact in these relationships can be substantial. Those who dig a friend's garden, who look after a neighbour's child every other day, who help a relative repair a house, are engaged in transactions that affect the subsistence of the recipient and provide things that would cost significant amounts of money if purchased in commercial transactions. Likewise, Edwina Uehara (1990) studied poor mothers in Chicago who had recently lost their paying jobs and were facing financial crisis. She found that many of these women received substantial amounts of money, services, and material objects from neighbours, friends, and kin. Whether it was a Thanksgiving turkey, rent money, or a bag of groceries, and whether it was given without being asked, loaned freely and without much concern for repayment, or only loaned grudgingly, these things had a significant impact on these women's basic subsistence. Together, these studies demonstrate that the separation of economic from social relations, the disembedding of economy from society, does not appear to be all that clear.

Even outside these more clearly social relationships, commodity relations are not all-pervasive. This is apparent, and perhaps to be anticipated, in the black economy. An example is the petty dealing of stolen goods in London's East End, which may seem a colourful distraction from real commerce, but is important socially and economically for those involved. Here, transactions are not the impersonal exchange of material equivalents. Instead, as Gerald Mars describes it, frequently the thing given is seen as a 'favour'. It 'has to be repaid, but only when the opportunity arises and only with whatever comes to hand. And "whatever is at hand" may not be material at all.' These transactions, then, entail diffuse, open-ended personal obligations, with the consequence that the 'goods that were given have been dematerialized and the transaction has been personalized' (Mars 1982: 173). While these transactions are important for people's economic survival, transactors often do not seek maximum economic advantage, and in fact 'money is only a part, and rarely the most important part' of these deals (Mars 1982: 171; see also Henry 1976).

This is because such dealings are not impersonal. Instead, they are usually between people who are linked through ties of kinship, neighbourhood, and extensive personal experience, people for whom these transactions are part of the development and maintenance of social relations with others. And it is this that makes these transactions obligatory in a way that gift transactions are, but legal market transactions are not. People need to offer to transact in order to maintain their social reputations as fully competent members of the community. Indeed, one of the points that Dick Hobbs makes in his study of the East End is that people there who are entrepreneurs, ready to buy and sell anything, cannot be understood in terms of commodity logic, as rational actors in an impersonal market. Instead, they are enacting a moral value.

For example, when Barry was approached by Vince and offered several hundred yards of high-quality stolen carpet, Barry was not interested, yet promised to attempt to find a buyer. Barry could have refused to buy the carpet and left it at that; however it was important that Vince's entrepreneurial abilities be acknowledged, thereby reaffirming the mechanisms and language of exchange as a core organizational device of the indigenous order. (Hobbs 1989: 142)

Here, commodity logic is not some residual propensity to truck and barter that finds expression when it is liberated from social constraint. Rather, it is a social value that binds and obligates potential transactors to each other. It is a way that people maintain personal identities that reflect as much adherence to a set of moral values about 'doing the business' (Hobbs 1989) as they do the desire to maintain personal repute or secure the economic means of survival. And beyond this, the entrepreneurial pose, ever ready to do a deal, helps people identify themselves as 'trusted insiders as against the threatening outside' (Mars 1982: 175), and so maintain the distinctive social and cultural identity of the group itself.

More mundane and more pervasive than shady deals struck in pubs in the East End is retail trade. This is the realm of supermarkets full of anonymous commodities and customers and cheerily impersonal staff (Carrier 1990). However, even here many people buy and sell as part of enduring personal relations. This is apparent in the widespread use of credit in small shops until at least the middle of the twentieth century (e.g. Johnson 1985: ch. 6). This credit was as much a social as a financial relationship. It was based on the decision to enter into a personal relationship of trust, and shopkeeper and customer were expected to support each other in good times as well as bad.

This is most obvious from the perspective of the customers, who expected that the shopkeeper would not simply give credit, but would carry them through bad times: through bouts of illness, injury, or unemployment, through strikes or bad harvests, through times of extraordinary expenses like medical bills or funeral costs. In short, they expected the shopkeeper to trust them to repay when times got better. Equally, the shopkeeper expected the customer to be loyal to the shop, buying there when times were good and purchases could be paid for in cash, even though a more impersonal store near by might have the same goods for less. In such a relationship, buying a tin of milk was not the impersonal exchange of equivalents, but was the recreation of a durable personal relationship, harking back to previous transactions and anticipating future ones. This appears to have been marked commonly by the fact that customers never quite paid off their debt, the small balance remaining marking the continuation of the relationship of trust between shopkeeper and customer. This is illustrated by what Gerald Mars (1982: 173) says of practices from the time of his youth:

[W]hen a trust relationship does break up the debt *has* to be paid off—precisely and immediately. The open-ended transaction is closed, and the method of final settlement reverts to normal market exchange. The transaction is, in effect, depersonalised . . . as it was among working-class families in the north of England where I grew up. The credit account at the local store would be broken through dispute. Then the bill was paid and the family's custom removed to another shop.

One of the reasons that retail trade is distinctive is that it is the point where different forms of transaction intersect, that of the household and that of the firm. This intersection is more pronounced in forms of direct selling. The neighbourhood children who knock on the door to sell Girl Scout cookies, chocolates, or Christmas wrap are carrying out retail trade within a pre-existing set of social relationships between seller and customer. This intersection and overlap appear as well in what John Davis

(1973: 167–71) describes as 'party selling', perhaps most familiar in the United States as the 'Tupperware party'. Such selling takes place within a number of social, as distinct from purely economic, frames. It takes place in a party organized for the purpose; the woman, typically, who organizes the party with the help of a company agent is a 'hostess'; the people she invites are friends and neighbours; those invited are urged to buy in order to help their friend and neighbour. Here too, then, economy and society overlap, and a form of retail trade that supports a number of large corporations does not conform to the cultural understanding of 'the economy' and market exchange.

Durable personal relationships seem to exist as well at times in the heart of capitalism. Ronald Dore's analysis of relations between large firms, primarily in Japan but also in Britain, shows that manufacturing firms and their suppliers, for example, often see themselves as bound by durable obligations in a way that resembles the credit relationship between shopkeeper and customer that I have described. In other words, these firms are not wholly alienated and independent transactors; rather, they are linked in 'social relations . . . [that] take on a moral quality and become regulated by criteria of fairness' (Dore 1983: 479; see also Creighton 1991). Moreover, evidence of these sorts of relatively durable relationships is not restricted to the level of the firm. Studying relations among agents and employees of various American firms, Mark Granovetter found that 'continuing economic relations [between agents of different firms] often become overlaid with social content that carries strong expectations of trust and abstention from opportunism' (Granovetter 1985: 490; see also Gambetta 1988; Prus 1989: ch. 4). Stewart Macaulay (1963) suggests that allegiance to these moral values is one reason why relatively few firms use formal contracts in their dealings with each other.

Further, occidentalist renderings of the West as a commodity system do not seem to apply in any straightforward way to people who work in firms. For example, much of the New England fishing fleet recruits crew and investment capital among family members rather than through impersonal markets, a pattern that has been expanding over the past few decades at the expense of ships organized in terms of commodity relations (Doeringer, Moss, and Terkla 1986). David Halle (1984: 5–6) found that the American blue-collar chemical workers he studied were frequently linked to their co-workers not just by virtue of common ties to their employer but by kin and affinal ties with one another. Here Halle confirms in the context of American working-class life of the 1970s what Young and Willmott (1986: 73–6) argued for English working-class life of the 1950s: when there is competition for work, a person on the job can help a relative get into the firm. In such a situation, co-workers are likely to be kin, and social relations are likely to pervade the impersonal relations that are supposed to exist in the firm. Furthermore, as Margaret Grieco (1987: 37–41) argues, this is not a subversion of economic rationality. Rather, in many circumstances firms prefer to recruit the kin of their existing workers for good commercial relations. Finally, Karen Sacks (1984) shows that employees who normally keep their work and personal lives separate may merge the two when they strike or agitate for changes at work. In this extraordinary circumstance, the hospital workers she studied activated pre-existing social relationships with each other and forged new ones in order to increase their solidarity and resolve.

But even to see work relations among strangers as being impersonal relations between autonomous individuals can be misleading, for transactions among co-workers allow little autonomy in any straightforward sense. Sid the maintenance worker does not freely decide to adjust the machinery of Doris the production worker because Doris will give something valuable in return in the manner of a market transaction. Instead, Sid is the occupant of a position in a structure that defines his relationship with Doris and their obligations toward each other. The fact that Sid and Doris may have decided autonomously to become maintenance and production workers, and may have got their jobs through the impersonal labour market, does not mean that their identities and relationships with each other at work resemble the autonomous individuals who are supposed to populate the commodity realm.

Thus it appears that, in different areas of life in industrial capitalist society, identities, relations, and transactions depart from the commodity model, and instead resemble what exists in gift systems in important ways (though this assertion of resemblance is not an assertion of identity). Impersonal commodity relations and transactions clearly are important in the modern West. But equally important is the distinction between saying that commodity relations are important in the West on the one hand, and on the other casting the West as a society in which commodity relations are so essential that we can ignore the existence of other sorts of relations. To return to a point made earlier, this occidentalism makes sense only when it is juxtaposed with its matching orientalism, the society of the gift. Compared to such societies, the West *is* the society of the commodity—these two essentializations defining and justifying each other dialectically.

Dialectics and selective perception

The effects of this comparative approach can be particularly insidious when our constructions of alien societies become detached from the conception of the West to which they are opposed, and instead become treated as substantive concepts. Thus, in modern anthropology the notion of the society of the gift became detached from its conceptual dialectical opposition to modern Western society. Each became a positive, independent description of a distinct type of society.

These typifications have shaped the ways that anthropologists approach the societies they study, ways that maintain the purity of the categories themselves. So, few anthropologists study gifts in the modern West. Further, those who do so tend to treat them in ways that do not challenge the occidentalized construction of the West (e.g. Cheal 1988; Lévi–Strauss 1969: 56–7). This is manifest in the way researchers tend to see gifts as the gratuitous act of autonomous individuals, a rendering that echoes what Jonathan Parry (1986: 466) calls the 'elaborated ideology of the "pure gift"', the idea that gifts are 'free and unconstrained'. Equally, this is manifest in the way researchers tend to reduce gifts to a relatively peripheral and insignificant realm: formal presents, displays of Christmas cards, and the like. But to restrict gift relations in Western societies to these levels is to ignore the ways that people are enmeshed in gift relationships that are more mundane but of greater economic import.

Equally, these typifications lead anthropologists to ignore commodity relations in village societies. In Melanesia, this means anthropologists commonly ignore the fact that many Melanesians and almost all Melanesian societies depend upon wage labour or commercial production for a good part of their survival. To ignore this is to ignore the ways that village societies articulate with the national economy and the way that articulation shapes village life, not to mention the perspectives of the individuals involved. Margaret Jolly (1992) makes this point in her criticism of Annette Weiner's (esp. 1977) discussion of women's wealth in the Trobriand Islands. Weiner sees women's exchange of their wealth as a token of their unchanging ability to control the cosmic order. Jolly, on the other hand, argues that the growing involvement of Trobriand people with the commodity economy has meant that the exchange of women's wealth takes on new meanings as it has come to be opposed to male involvement in commercial activities and the cash economy.

This orientalism means anthropologists commonly ignore the ways that forms of ceremonial transaction have begun to take on signs of commodity exchange. David Boyd has described an instance of this in the Eastern Highlands province of Papua New Guinea. There, pig distributions have ceased to be just ceremonial gift transactions, but have become as well 'secular, commercialised dance festivals' (Boyd 1985: 325), where the sponsor charges admission at the gate and stallholders sell refreshments. Anthropologists also commonly ignore many of the mundane ways that Melanesians transact in both traditional and modern settings to gain their subsistence. As I have shown elsewhere (Carrier 1992*a*), many of the transactions by which Ponam Islanders, from Manus province in Papua New Guinea, gain their subsistence are not very much like gifts. Some of these take place in a modern institution, the village general store, but even those that occur in more venerable institutions like trade partnerships or local markets do not demonstrate the degree of obligation and mutual identification that characterize the society of the gift.[1]

Obviously, these more commodity-like transactions, relationships, and identities are not invisible to anthropologists in Melanesia. However, they tend to be ignored as inauthentic colonial introductions, or they become relegated to particular schools within the discipline. Transactions that appeared to be of commodities became the special interest only of Marxists (e.g. Godelier 1977), generally peripheral in Melanesian anthropology, or were presumed to appear only in circulation between societies, rather than within them (e.g. Sahlins 1974), and hence to be peripheral to understanding the basic organization and operation of these societies.

The construction of Melanesian societies as gift systems leads to a body of ethnography that is only a partial rendering of Melanesian social life. Further, the partiality of that ethnography is reflected in the more synthetic works that summarize and make use of it. An example of this is Marilyn Strathern's review essay 'Marriage Exchanges: A Melanesian Comment'. The topic itself is unexceptionable, for marriage exchange is important in many Melanesian societies. As Colin Filer (1985) has shown, many Papua New Guineans see contemporary marriage exchange, and particularly brideprice, as part of a complex field of salient economic, social, and political issues, including ethnic identity, family solidarity, divorce, prostitution, domestic violence, wage labour, remittances, and much more. However, like the writers whose work she reviewed, Strathern located marriage exchange in a highly orientalist context. She did so by focusing on a single, albeit complex, issue, 'the role of exchanges in items other than persons when these items are part of or move in conjunction with transactions (such as marriage) conceptualized as exchanges of persons' (Strathern 1984: 42). Further, she ignored the issue of money, an item which pervades marriage exchange and which links that exchange to the wage labour and commodity production where so many Papua New Guineans get their cash.[2]

Thus it appears that influential anthropologists studying Melanesia have elevated the relative salience of gift transactions in the region from a distinguishing characteristic, albeit an important one, to a defining characterization. This in turn generates a key problem identified by the critics of anthropological orientalism, a distorted, exaggerated model of the alien society. The gift transactions that had, quite reasonably, been taken to distinguish life in the Trobriands and the Pacific North-West from life in Paris, London, or Chicago became something very different. They became an absolute, rather than relative, description of a type of society that denies or elides similarities between the village and the West.

The process comes full circle in Melanesia. Not only do the distortions of the initial, dialectical construction of gift and commodity systems become embodied in the ethnography of the region. In addition, anthropologists use that ethnography to reconstruct the initial construction. But they appear to do so unknowingly, for they seem to base their reflections on the empirical evidence of the ethnographic record, which they contrast with their image of the West. Thus, by using evidence shaped by the model, they can construct on what appears as an empirical foundation the very model that generated the distortion in the first place. Again, Marilyn Strathern's work illustrates this process, this time *The Gender of the Gift*.[3]

Drawing on the extensive ethnographic evidence that she invokes to support her argument, Strathern paints a picture of Melanesian societies that contains the core elements of the society of the gift. Melanesians are not autonomous, but 'dividuals', 'the plural and composite site of the relationships that produced them' (1988: 13). And as people are the nexus of social relationships, so are things. A pig or a sweet potato is not a discrete object. Rather, just as a child contains the identity of its parents, so the object 'exists as a specific combination of other identities', the identities of those who produced it (1988: 159). People and things, then, are linked inalienably to their several creators and the social relations of their creation. In somewhat more analytical terms, people and things are not autonomous, but are defined by their position in a structure of identities and relations between identities. Strathern develops this point particularly in her discussion (1984: 148–65) of Lisette Josephides's work (1985) on the Kewa, of the New Guinea Highlands, in which Josephides against your own ridiculous, hairy, chicken legs while you made stuffed French toast. She wanted to tell you something and you had no idea that it was over. You were lost when she began to apologize. You were silent as she mentioned Thailand and her career. You replay the scene until it loses all meaning. Her trepidation becomes malicious; her tears become a taunt. Her success sacrifices the happiness you thought was shared. Bad news, baby: My dreams came true.

For two months, her every movement was an apology you could never accept. The apartment you shared was a long first date, awkward and stale, a winter where no one spoke about the weather. You made love like a romance novel, begging her with your body not to go. She apologized with you in her mouth, hot and hungry and holding back tears. You reached for her like a child afraid to speak, while suppers burned and teakettles whistled, and laundry hid wet in beeping machines.

When her mother arrived, she did the crying for you. She cried while you packed and cleaned and loaded the U-Haul. She cried at dinner, with her daughter's friends from work and the girls from yoga, apologizing and laughing over tiramisu and fried ice cream. She cried in her sleep, almost too quiet to hear. She cried her daughter's tears.

The last time you touch her will feel remarkably like the first. She will be drunk and smiling and full of love for you when she steps out of her dress. You will forget she is leaving because you can still hold her face in your hands. You will forget she is leaving because her lips are soft and wet and inviting. You will forget she is leaving because you are drunk and smiling and full of love for her.

You will have impulses. You will want to yell. You will want to beg. Do these things. You will want to tie her to the bed and hurt her. You will want to kiss and worship every inch of her. Do these things.

Do not cry when you enter her. Do not show anger when you bite her neck. Be tender when you hold her down. Be sweet when you turn her over. Remember every second of her. Catalogue every sound she makes. Commit to memory the flavor of her breast and her thigh and her kiss while it lingers on you. Live a lifetime in these final moments. Rally your strength. Keep your focus. Do not cry when you finish.

When she leaves with her mother for Iowa, you will deflate with exhaustion and relief. You will have been a muscle clenched for months, argued that men appropriate the products of women's labour through the cycle of ceremonial exchange.

Obviously, Strathern was not attempting a neutral, statistical summation of the evidence. Instead, she selected and interpreted the ethnographies she invoked in her argument. But one reason she could invoke such an impressive array of supporting evidence for her points is that the Maussian model has affected so many of the ethnographers who have worked in the region.

However, those less affected see and report a somewhat different picture. For example, in *Entangled Objects* Nicholas Thomas argues that in 'societies to the east and southeast of mainland New Guinea' a number of key types of transactions 'appear to have entailed . . . alienation' (Thomas 1991: 45), so that objects could be divorced from the circumstances of their creation in the way Josephides argued for the Kewa. Again, speaking this time specifically of certain important sorts of exchange goods in Fiji, Thomas says (1991: 65) that 'there is no sense in which the donors retain any control or "lien" over them. Nor is there much sense that there is any significant association of any other kind, any continuing memory of the donor in the thing.' Thomas (1991: 53–4) argues the same point with respect to the identity of people. It may be that a child in a patrilineal society has ties with the mother's kin, but this does not mean that maternal and paternal sides are equally embodied in the child. Instead, the degree of their authority is contingent upon the state of marriage exchange and the political relations between the two groups.

My point is not that Strathern is wrong to assert that Melanesians see people and objects in certain ways, just as my point earlier was not that those who adopt the dialectical model I have described are wrong to assert that Westerners see people and objects in certain ways. Rather, it is that she has not taken the next, and most necessary, step: she has not gone on to consider when and under what circumstances Melanesians see which people and what objects in those ways, just the sort of issue that Maurice Bloch and Jonathan Parry (1989) address. In neglecting to take this step, Strathern casts the whole of Melanesia as a unitary thing, her ' "single" instance' (1988: 341) of gift logic. In other words, she reproduces the model's orientalism by the invocation of evidence itself silently framed in the very terms of that orientalism (an analogous point is in Paine 1969). And in her work, she invokes that orientalism to reproduce its twinned occidentalism. As Melanesia is the inalienable gift and the 'dividual', so the West is the commodity and the 'unitary self, the "possessive individual"' (Strathern 1988: 157).

Roots of the dialectic

I have described the occidentalist renderings of the West in the Maussian model, illustrating both how it distorts the nature of Western societies and how its twinned orientalism distorts the nature of Melanesian societies. Although the model is a fit subject for such an analysis, I said earlier that it is hardly unique. The distinction between societies of the gift and of the commodity is but a slight variation on the distinction between societies of status and contract, *Gemeinschaft* and *Gesellschaft*, affective and instrumental rationality, mechanical and organic solidarity, feudalism and capitalism. This distinction is a coherent and powerful theme in the Western intellectual patrimony. It is embedded deeply in social thought, as well as common sense, and it is hard to escape.

Why, given the evidence that I have provided in this chapter, is the occidentalist rendering of the West held so firmly by Western scholars themselves? Nancy Hartsock suggests some reasons in her criticism (1985) of sociological models of social relations, and especially the predominance of the autonomous actor in these models. Put most simply, she argues that the autonomous actor is a reasonably accurate reflection of the experience of many of those in dominant positions in society (Ouroussoff 1993 illustrates this point and several others in this chapter nicely).

One pertinent dimension on which people can be dominant is that of the market, the home of the autonomous actor. However, Max Weber argued long ago that not all market actors are in a position to act autonomously. The ability to do so is, he said, generally restricted to the dominant, propertied classes, who are not driven to the market by sheer, insistent necessity. The propertyless, however, lack such resources and have no such leisure. They are obliged to transact, and particularly to sell their labour, 'in order barely to subsist' (Weber 1946: 182).

Basil Bernstein's studies of working–class families in Bethnal Green around 1960 (esp. Bernstein 1971; cf. Levine 1985: 198–9) address more directly the degree to which the autonomous actor reflects the perspective and experience of some classes rather than others. The families that Bernstein studied overwhelmingly were involved in the same sorts of occupation and their social and work lives tended to be restricted to their immediate and very densely populated area in Bethnal Green. The result, reminiscent of Durkheim's description of societies of mechanical solidarity, was a high degree of shared experience. This complex of factors produced what Bernstein called a 'positional orientation'. People with such an orientation identified themselves and others in terms of their positions in an over-arching and encompassing web of social relations, reminiscent of Strathern's 'plural and composite site of the relationships that produced them'. Bernstein distinguished this from the 'personal orientation'. This, he said, was characteristic of the more mobile and wealthier members of English middle-class families, who identified themselves and each other as independent entities.[4]

Bernstein's argument finds support in the study by J. Bussey and his colleagues of the giving of presents by people in Bradford, England. The researchers found that higher-class respondents were more likely to account for the giving by saying it was the spontaneous expression of autonomous sentiment, emotion, and affection. Conversely, lower-class respondents were more likely to explain giving by reference to the expectations of others and the dictates of the situation in which they found themselves (Bussey *et al.* 1967: 61, 67). Class differences in orientation toward people are matched by class differences in orientation toward objects. Janet Holland (1981), a colleague of Bernstein's, found that children from middle-class families were more likely to categorize objects on the basis of what they saw as the objects' inherent and trans-situational properties, such as their physical constituents or category membership. Alternatively, working-class children were more likely to categorize in terms of the social context and relationships in which the objects were embedded in those children's lives.

Like Bernstein, Hartsock describes the link between people's experiences and the notion of the autonomous self, but using gender rather than class as an organizing variable. Hartsock says that women generally are compelled to work more than men. Not only do they labour for a wage, the prevailing division of labour by gender in the West means that they also maintain the household and reproduce humanity in their children. In addition to being obliged to work more, the work that women do is different from that of men. Particularly in their domestic labour women are involved in relationships that are more durable and complex, and that are less discretionary, than the 'simple cooperation with others for common goals' (Hartsock 1985: 64) that she says characterizes the work experience of men in the middle classes. As she summarizes her argument, women in their labours experience 'a complex, relational world' rather than one of autonomous individuals, and their interactions with others are not voluntary: '[T]hose in charge of small children have little choice' (1985: 65, 66).

Hartsock's point that men and women vary in their experience and sense of autonomy is echoed in the way that men and women in Western societies are often oriented differently toward the realms of gift and commodity. For instance, kinship, the core area of gift relations in industrial societies, is the province of women rather than men, for it is they who arrange the visits, write the letters, and remember the relationships that those visits and letters mark and maintain (e.g. Firth 1956; Komarovsky 1987; Willmott and Young 1960; Young and Willmott 1986). Similarly, Christmas, probably the most important North American celebration of family and kinship, is largely women's work. They are the ones who draw up the lists, buy the presents, and cook the Christmas dinners (see e.g. Caplow 1984; Cheal 1987).

Given this gender difference, it is not surprising that women appear to think of the objects that surround them differently from the way men do, and do so in a way that situates objects in social relationships. For example, Csikszentmihalyi and Rochberg-Halton (1981: 61) found a consistent pattern of differences, even when husband and wife were talking about the same object. While men tended to talk about significant objects in more egocentric ways, in terms of 'personal accomplishment, or an ideal they strive to achieve', women were more likely to talk in terms of a 'concern for other people' and 'responsibility for maintaining a network of social ties'. (Analogous differences are in Dittmar 1992 and Livingstone 1992.) But to complicate matters, this gender difference depends upon age. It did not appear among the young, who all tended to see objects in terms of sensory pleasure. Equally, it disappeared among the old, who were more uniform in seeing objects in the way that adult women did.

Bernstein and Hartsock both indicate that the autonomous actor is not a fiction. Instead, that actor reflects at least the thinking and probably the experiences of those in particular social locations, which are treated deferentially in Western society and taken to define social identity and relationships in academic understandings of social exchange. Moreover, those in these locations tend to be more powerful than the sets of people whose experiences and identities are likely to depart from the model of the autonomous actor. With this power, people in the dominant locations are better able than others to put forward their experiences and values as definitive of the genius and the essence of the modern West. It is, then, the relatively privileged nature of these positions, values, and experiences, together with the relative power of those in these positions, that help maintain the dominance of the occidentalism that I have described.

Conclusions

In this chapter I have laid out an image of the West that exists in what I have, for convenience, called the Maussian model, and I have introduced evidence to show that this image occidentalizes the West. That is, the model treats certain sorts of cultural and social attributes of the West as embodying the essence of a relatively undifferentiated social entity, Western Society. While I have written of a Maussian model, its occidentalism is a common one, as I have noted. Equally, I have not disputed the importance of commodity relations in the West or gift relations in Melanesia, for example. Certainly they are important, even crucial for understanding these different social systems. However, their centrality is no warrant for treating commodity relations as all that is important in the West or gift relations as all that is important in Melanesia. Rather, these sorts of relations coexist and interact with other sorts of relationships in complex ways that it would be unwise to ignore.

A final note. In discussing the occidentalism of the West as a system of autonomous actors, I presented evidence that indicates that this perception reflects the experiences of certain sorts of people in Western societies. I do not mean this to be another call for the scholarly recognition of 'diversity', for such calls are prone to rest on the same sort of essentializations that I have questioned here. This tendency to essentialism appears in an interesting collection of practical papers (McGoldrick, Pearce, and Giordano 1982) intended to help family therapists deal professionally with people from different cultural backgrounds. While the collection helps dispel the notion of the uniform West of commodity occidentalism, it also reveals a tendency to replace that unity with a set of relatively homogeneous ethnic groups: the Irish, the Jews, the British, and so on, in America. A similar point could be made about Andrew Greeley's work (e.g. Greeley 1989) plotting the differences between the beliefs and values of Protestants and Catholics in the United States.

In place of this sort of diversity of essentialized groups, I would substitute what I think Bernstein was trying to do. He was not concerned to present a picture of Bethnal Green and its residents that stresses some essential 'Bethnal Green-ness'. Rather, he points to a series of social variables that predispose people to think and act in certain ways in certain contexts, variables that take particular forms in particular places at particular times. He is not, in other words, pointing to a diversity of types of people, but to the way that different situations can lead to different ways of thinking and acting. I think it preferable to follow Bernstein's lead, to ask under what circumstances and for what reasons people in Western societies think and act in ways that resemble commodity relations, under what circumstances and for what reasons they think and act in ways that resemble gift relations. If we begin to take these questions seriously, we are more likely to be able to ask the same questions about people elsewhere.

Acknowledgements

I want to thank Achsah Carrier for her help and encouragement while I was writing this chapter. I am also grateful for comments made when I presented parts of this chapter at an anthropology department seminar at Harvard University. Some of the discussion here is drawn from J. Carrier (1992*b*). In different ways, Chris Fuller (1989), Keith Hart (1986), Michael Herzfeld (1987), and Alexandra Ouroussoff (1993) have put forward arguments that parallel those made in this chapter. Some of the arguments and material in this chapter are taken from my *Gifts and Commodities: Exchange and Western Capitalism since 1700* (Carrier 1994).

Notes

1 I omit consideration of the possibility that there will be disagreement among villagers themselves about whether an object or transaction resembles that of a gift or a commodity (see Carrier 1992*a*). Also, although I have described Melanesia here, my points apply more generally. Thus, Daniel Miller (1986) describes a similar mixture of gift and commodity transactions in India.

2 The ethnographies Strathern analyses focus resolutely on village life; Filer's account draws heavily from letters written by urban and peri-urban residents. As Deborah Gewertz and Frederick Errington (1991) demonstrate, combining the urban and the village into a single analysis can be fruitful.

3 Strathern says that she is constructing a hypothetical model, in an effort to use 'the language that belongs to our own [social life] in order to create a contrast internal to it' (1988: 16). Two comments are in order here. First, the need Strathern sees to fall back on such hypothetical models to enable Westerners to understand Melanesian societies presupposes just the radical difference between types of societies that is at issue in this chapter. Second, to say that the book is a kind of thought experiment would seem to make empirical criticism inappropriate. However, the extensive use of ethnographic evidence inevitably gives her work a clear empirical cast, one that comes to the fore in her final chapter. There she summarizes one aspect of the book by saying that she has shown how various Melanesian societies are 'varieties of or versions of a "single" instance. These societies have their conventions in common' (1988: 341).

4 Bernstein's description of positional and personal orientations resembles what Ralph Turner (1976) calls the impulsive and the institutional selves.

References

ABERCROMBIE, NICHOLAS, HILL, STEPHEN, and TURNER, BRYAN S. (1986). *Sovereign Individuals of Capitalism*. London: Allen & Unwin.

BARKER, DIANA L. (1972). 'Young People and their Homes: Spoiling and "Keeping Close" in a South Wales Town', *Sociological Review*, 20: 569–90.

BARNETT, STEVE, and SILVERMAN, MARTIN (1979). 'Separations in Capitalist Societies: Persons, Things, Units and Relations', in S. Barnett and M. Silverman, *Ideology and Everyday Life*. Ann Arbor, Mich.: University of Michigan Press: 39–81.

BERNSTEIN, BASIL (1971). 'A Sociolinguistic Approach to Socialization', in B. Bernstein, *Class, Codes and Control*, vol. i. London: Routledge & Kegan Paul: 143–69.

BIERSACK, ALETTA (1991). 'Thinking Difference: A Review of Marilyn Strathern's *The Gender of the Gift*', *Oceania*, 62: 146–54.

BLOCH, MAURICE, and PARRY, JONATHAN (1989). 'Introduction: Money and the Morality of Exchange', in J. Parry and M. Bloch (eds.), *Money and the Morality of Exchange*. Cambridge: Cambridge University Press: 1–32.

BOYD, DAVID J. (1985). 'The Commercialisation of Ritual in the Eastern Highlands of Papua New Guinea', *Man*, 20: 325–40.

BUSSEY, J., BANKS, S., DARRINGTON, C., DRISCOLL, D., GOULDING, D., LOWES, B., PHILLIPS, R., and TURNER, J. (1967). 'Patterns of Gift Giving: Including a Questionnaire Survey of Bradford Households', B.Sc. (Hons.) thesis (Bradford).

CAPLOW, THEODORE (1984). 'Rule Enforcement without Visible Means: Christmas Gift Giving in Middletown', *American Journal of Sociology*, 89: 1306–23.

CARRIER, JAMES G. (1990). 'Reconciling Commodities and Personal Relations in Industrial Society', *Theory and Society*, 19: 579–98.

——(1991). 'Gifts, Commodities and Social Relations: A Maussian View of Exchange', *Sociological Forum*, 5: 119–36.

——(1992a). 'The Gift in Theory and Practice in Melanesia: A Note on the Centrality of Gift Exchange', *Ethnology*, 31: 186–93.

——(1992b). 'Occidentalism: The World Turned Upside-Down', *American Ethnologist*, 19: 195–212.

——(1994). *Gifts and Commodities: Exchange and Western Capitalism since 1700*. London: Routledge.

CHEAL, DAVID J. (1987). '"Showing Them You Love Them": Gift Giving and the Dialectic of Intimacy', *Sociological Review*, 35: 150–69.

——(1988). *The Gift Economy*. London: Routledge Books.

CORRIGAN, PETER (1989). 'Gender and the Gift: The Case of the Family Clothing Economy', *Sociology*, 23: 513–34.

CREIGHTON, MILLIE R. (1991). 'Maintaining Cultural Boundaries in Retailing: How Japanese Department Stores Domesticate "Things Foreign"', *Modern Asian Studies*, 25: 675–709.

CSIKSZENTMIHALYI, MIHALY, and ROCHBERG-HALTON, EUGENE (1981). *The Meaning of Things: Domestic Symbols and the Self.* New York: Cambridge University Press.

DAVIS, J. (1973). 'Forms and Norms: The Economy of Social Relations', *Man*, 18: 159–76.

DITTMAR, HELGA (1992). *The Social Psychology of Material Possessions: To Have Is to Be.* Hemel Hempstead: Harvester Wheatsheaf.

DOERINGER, PETER B., MOSS, PHILIP I., and TERKLA, DAVID G. (1986). 'Capitalism and Kinship: Do Institutions Matter in the Labor Market?' *Industrial and Labor Relations Review*, 40: 48–60.

DORE, RONALD (1983). 'Goodwill and the Spirit of Market Capitalism', *British Journal of Sociology*, 34: 459–82.

ELLIS, RHIAN (1983). 'The Way to a Man's Heart: Food in the Violent Home', in Anne Murcott (ed.), *The Sociology of Food and Eating*. Aldershot: Gower:164–71.

FILER, COLIN (1985). 'What Is this Thing Called Brideprice?' *Mankind*, 15 (special issue): 163–83.

FIRTH, RAYMOND (ed.) (1956). *Two Studies of Kinship in London*. London: Athlone Press.

FRIEDLAND, ROGER, and ROBERTSON, A. F. (1990). 'Beyond the Marketplace', in R. Friedland and A. F. Robertson (eds.), *Beyond the Marketplace: Rethinking Economy and Society*. New York: Aldine de Gruyter: 1–49.

FULLER, CHRIS J. (1989). 'Misconceiving the Grain Heap: A Critique of the Concept of the Indian Jajmani System', in Jonathan Parry and Maurice Bloch (eds.), *Money and the Morality of Exchange*. Cambridge: Cambridge University Press: 33–63.

GAMBETTA, DIEGO (ed.) (1988). *Trust: Making and Breaking Cooperative Relationships*. Oxford: Basil Blackwell.

GEWERTZ, DEBORAH B., and ERRINGTON, FREDERICK K. (1991). *Twisted Histories, Altered Contexts: Representing the Chambri in a World System*. Cambridge: Cambridge University Press.

GODELIER, MAURICE (1977). 'Salt Money and the Circulation of Commodities among the Baruya of New Guinea', in M. Godelier, *Perspectives in Marxist Anthropology*. Cambridge: Cambridge University Press: 127–51.

GRANOVETTER, MARK (1985). 'Economic Action and Social Structure: The Problem of Embeddedness', *American Journal of Sociology*, 91: 481–510.

GREELEY, ANDREW (1989). 'Protestant and Catholic: Is the Analogical Imagination Extinct?' *American Sociological Review*, 54: 485–502.

GREGORY, C. A. (1980). 'Gifts to Men and Gifts to God: Gift Exchange and Capital Accumulation in Contemporary Papua', *Man*, 15: 626–52.

——(1982). *Gifts and Commodities*. London: Academic Press.

GRIECO, MARGARET (1987). *Keeping It in the Family: Social Networks and Employment Chance*. London: Tavistock.

HALLE, DAVID (1984). *America's Working Man: Work, Home, and Politics among Blue-Collar Property Owners*. Chicago: University of Chicago Press.

HART, KEITH (1986). 'Heads or Tails? Two Sides of the Coin', *Man*, 21: 637–56.

HARTSOCK, NANCY C. N. (1985). 'Exchange Theory: Critique from a Feminist Standpoint', in S. G. McNall (ed.), *Current Perspectives in Social Theory*, vol. vi. Greenwich, Conn.: JAI Press: 57–70.

HENRY, STUART (1976). 'The Other Side of the Fence', *Sociological Review*, 24: 793–806.

HERZFELD, MICHAEL (1987). *Anthropology through the Looking-Glass: Critical Ethnography in the Margins of Europe*. Cambridge: Cambridge University Press.

HOBBS, DICK (1989). *Doing the Business: Entrepreneurship, the Working Class, and Detectives in the East End of London*. Oxford: Oxford University Press.

HOLLAND, JANET (1981). 'Social Class and Changes in Orientation to Meaning', *Sociology*, 15: 1–18.

JOHNSON, PAUL (1985). *Saving and Spending*. Oxford: Clarendon.

JOLLY, MARGARET (1992). 'Banana Leaf Bundles and Skirts: A Pacific Penelope's Web?' in James G. Carrier (ed.), *History and Tradition in Melanesian Anthropology*. Berkeley, Calif.: University of California Press: 38–63.

JOSEPHIDES, LISETTE (1985). *The Production of Inequality: Gender and Exchange among the Kewa*. London: Tavistock.

KIRBY, V. (1989). 'Capitalising Difference: Feminism and Anthropology', *Australian Feminist Studies*, 9: 1–24.

KOMAROVSKY, MIRRA (1987 [1964]). *Blue-Collar Marriage*. (2nd edn.) New Haven, Conn.: Yale University Press.

LAMPHERE, LOUISE (1986). 'From Working Daughters to Working Mothers: Production and Reproduction in an Industrial Community', *American Ethnologist*, 13: 118–30.

LEVINE, DAVID (1985). 'Industrialization and the Proletarian Family in England', *Past and Present*, 107 (May): 168–203.

LÉVI-STRAUSS, CLAUDE (1969). *The Elementary Structures of Kinship*. Boston: Beacon Press.

LIVINGSTONE, SONIA M. (1992). 'The Meaning of Domestic Technologies: A Personal Construct Analysis of Familial Gender Relations', in Roger Silverstone and Eric Hirsch (eds.), *Consuming Technologies: Media and Information in Domestic Spaces*. London: Routledge: 113–30.

MACAULAY, STEWART (1963). 'Non-contractual Relations in Business: A Preliminary Study', *American Sociological Review*, 28: 55–67.

McGOLDRICK, MONICA, PEARCE, JOHN K., and GIORDANO, JOSEPH (eds.) (1982). *Ethnicity and Family Therapy*. New York: Guilford.

MACPHERSON, C. B. (1962). *The Political Theory of Possessive Individualism: Hobbes to Locke*. Oxford: Clarendon Press.

MANSFIELD, PENNY, and COLLARD, JEAN (1988). *The Beginning of the Rest of your Life?* Basingstoke: Macmillan.

MARS, GERALD (1982). *Cheats at Work: An Anthropology of Workplace Crime*. London: George Allen & Unwin.

MAUSS, MARCEL (1985 [1938]). 'A Category of the Human Mind: The Notion of Person; the Notion of Self', in Michael Carrithers, Steven Collins, and Steven Lukes (eds.), *The Category of the Person*. Cambridge: Cambridge University Press: 1–25.

——(1990 [1925]). *The Gift: The Form and Reason for Exchange in Archaic Societies*, trans. W. D. Halls. London: Routledge.

MILLER, DANIEL (1986). 'Exchange and Alienation in the *Jajmani* System', *Journal of Anthropological Research*, 42: 535–56.

OUROUSSOFF, ALEXANDRA (1993). 'Illusions of Rationality: False Premises of the Liberal Tradition', *Man*, 28: 281–98.

PAINE, ROBERT (1969). 'In Search of Friendship: An Exploratory Analysis in "Middle Class Culture"', *Man*, 4: 505–24.

PARRY, JONATHAN (1986). '*The Gift*, the Indian Gift and the "Indian Gift"', *Man*, 21: 453–73.

PRUS, ROBERT C. (1989). *Pursuing Customers: An Ethnography of Marketing Activities*. Newbury Park, Calif.: Sage.

RUBEL, PAULA, and ROSMAN, ABRAHAM (1978). *Your Own Pigs You May Not Eat*. Canberra: Australian National University Press.

SACKS, KAREN (1984). 'Kinship and Class Consciousness: Family Values and Work Experience among Hospital Workers in an American Southern Town', in Hans Medick and David Warren Sabean (eds.), *Interest and Emotion: Essays in the Study of Family and Kinship*. Cambridge: Cambridge University Press: 279–99.

SAHLINS, MARSHALL (1974). *Stone Age Economics*. London: Tavistock.

SAID, EDWARD (1978). *Orientalism*. Harmondsworth: Penguin.

SCHNEIDER, DAVID (1980). *American Kinship: A Cultural Account*. (2nd edn.) Chicago: University of Chicago Press.

STRATHERN, MARILYN (1984). 'Marriage Exchanges: A Melanesian Comment', *Annual Review of Anthropology*, 13: 41–73.

——(1985a). 'John Locke's Servant and the *Hausboi* from Hagen: Thoughts on Domestic Labor', *Critical Philosophy*, 2: 21–48.

——(1985b). 'Kinship and Economy: Constitutive Orders of a Provisional Kind', *American Ethnologist*, 12: 191–209.

——(1988). *The Gender of the Gift: Problems with Women and Problems with Society in Melanesia*. Berkeley, Calif.: University of California Press.

THOMAS, NICHOLAS (1991). *Entangled Objects: Exchange, Material Culture and Colonialism in the Pacific*. Cambridge, Mass.: Harvard University Press.

TURNER, RALPH (1976). 'The Real Self: From Institution to Impulse', *American Journal of Sociology*, 81: 989–1016.

UEHARA, EDWINA (1990). 'Dual Exchange Theory, Social Networks and Informal Social Support', *American Journal of Sociology*, 96: 521–57.

WEBER, MAX (1946). 'Class, Status, Party', in Hans Gerth and C. Wright Mills (eds.), *From Max Weber*. New York: Oxford University Press: 180–95.

WEINER, ANNETTE (1977). *Women of Value, Men of Renown*. St Lucia: University of Queensland Press.

your blood too tense to circulate. You will laugh and feel horrible. You will smile and it will hurt and you will be happy for both. You will order take-out from that place on the corner that she always hated. You will eat too much and love it and be disgusted. By tonight, she will have left the state. By tomorrow, she will be at her parents' house. In two weeks, she will be Thailand's girlfriend.

She will haunt you. She will stalk you without mercy in the murky bog between sleep and wake. She will keep you hard and alone and you will hate her for it. She will be just around the corner and half a world away. She will live in your head as a despot and a minx. You will make love to her in your mind. Your days will be thick and gray with her ghost. Your fantasies will be hot and sweet and sticky at the end. You will blame her for things she has not done. You will contemplate a grand gesture. You will blame her for all the things you have not said. You will reach for her in the night. You will be too late.

You will find excuses to avoid speaking to her. She will not fight to accept them. You will find photos on her Facebook. You will find her smiling and drinking and happy without you and doesn't she look tan and happy and beautiful on that beautiful beach? You will find photos of the shirtless and happy Australian teacher that she's just friends with on that same beautiful beach. You will think that he's handsome.

You will go to a bar. You will go to another bar. You will yell and embarrass yourself. You will sulk and withdraw yourself. You will be hurt and unpredictable and aloof. You will be gaunt and tousled, with hungry eyes. You will be irresistible. Good for you.

When you go to the party, you will be grave and funny and comfortable around women you have no interest in. Your anger will be mistaken for charisma. Your indifference will be mistaken for confidence. You will inhale whiskey and exhale cigarette smoke. When the girl at the party asks for a light, she will be clever and bleak. Her features will be soft and her voice will be severe. You will want to lay with her on a bed of nails. The bed in your apartment will have to do.

The girl from the party is not sweet. She does not hesitate to kiss. She does not wait for your hands before hers explore your body. She does not notice your meekness and shock as her clothes crumple at the foot of your bed. She engulfs you in a black fire of skin and tattoos as

WELLMAN, BARRY, and WORTLEY, SCOT (1990). 'Different Strokes from Different Folks: Community Ties and Social Support', *American Journal of Sociology*, 96: 558–88.

WHITEHEAD, HARRIET (1986). 'The Varieties of Fertility Cultism in New Guinea: Part I', *American Ethnologist*, 13: 80–99.

WILLMOTT, PETER, and YOUNG, MICHAEL (1960). *Family and Class in a London Suburb*. London: Routledge & Kegan Paul.

YOUNG, MICHAEL, and WILLMOTT, PETER (1986 [1957]). *Family and Kinship in East London*. (Rev. edn.) London: Routledge & Kegan Paul.

4

Occidentalism as a Cottage Industry: Representing the Autochthonous 'Other' in British and Irish Rural Studies

Jane Nadel-Klein

A cartoon appeared a couple of years ago in my local newspaper, purporting to explain ethnic violence in Eastern Europe. In it, a Western-suited man (Gorbachev) stands helplessly by as men in loose peasant blouses and cummerbunds (the 'Zugs') massacre each other in the street. 'Why do we kill each other?' reads the legend below, 'Because it's our nature!' In this cartoon, bloodshed is explained in terms of instinct, or 'nature', and the violent men are obviously denizens of a Europe that does not fit into the cartoonist's conception of Western civilization. They are peasants, rural folk who have not grasped modernity's message of reason.

This cartoon does not merely primitivize peasants and rural people. It says they are pre-cultural animals who act on instinct, and that only the men in suits can save them. The cartoonist has embodied modern, Western identity in the figure of an authoritative, rational male who participates in an international system of knowledge and goods. He stands for progress.[1] Extrapolating from this image, we can say further that this figure is both urban and urbane, that he is not limited by merely 'local knowledge'. He is, in fact, the truly cosmopolitan man whose perspective encompasses the globe and its history, the representative of the modern state that subordinates petty local grievances to the transcendent ideal of citizenship (see Nairn 1977: 16). The peasants, on the other hand, are not merely rural and untutored. Their Hobbesian 'state of nature' makes them dangerous. They stand for parochialism and the opposition to progress.

In this case it is the Balkans that are said to be backward and out of touch with the rest of us. But Eastern Europe is by no means the only region of Europe to have provided a site for Western beliefs in the existence of primitive, backward, or autochthonous others subsisting in the margins of 'home' and threatening the achievements of Western civilization from within. Moving westward, we have Ireland.

Richard Lebow has explored the history of racist images of the Irish in *White Britain, Black Ireland*. In the late eighteenth century, a visitor to Ireland deplored Irish poverty, commenting that the Irish 'were beings who seem to form a different race from the rest of mankind' (quoted in Lebow 1976: 41). And Lebow tells us further that, in the 1850s, *Punch* magazine claimed that the Irish were ' "the missing link between the gorilla and the Negro" ' (1976: 40).

The newspaper cartoon bears a striking resemblance to some of the mid-nineteenth-century images in *Punch* that Lebow explores. The *Punch* cartoonists drew the Irishmen of their day as swarthy, stooping figures, semi-idiots, drunks, or even as monsters who threatened the health of the body politic. One such cartoon, published in 1846, depicts the dangers of the movement to repeal the Act of Union between Britain and Ireland. It bears the title 'The Irish Frankenstein', and features a huge, shillelagh-wielding creature clad in rags threatening a respectable, well-dressed Englishman (Lebow 1976: 46).

These commentaries on the Balkans and the Irish are examples of a prevalent theme in the depiction of modern life that draws upon the idea of cultural anachronism (Chakrabarty 1992), or the idea that living people and their ways of life can be out of date with 'the present'. The notion of anachronism is a powerful element in the cultural construction of what we call 'the West', one that looks to images of rural, marginal, or 'back-ward' society to create an internal other that validates a culturally deracinated, technologically driven 'progress' (our most important prod-uct) as the linchpin of Western identity. As Michael Herzfeld points out, this contributes to auto-essentializing claims that Western, or Western-'like', societies 'subordinate context to invention' and 'take control of their own destinies' while primitive or peasant societies merely succumb unthinkingly to the pressures of the moment (1987: 85).

This idea has historically been constructed within an evolutionist dis-course that has enabled the village and its associated referents (peasants, fisherfolk, the rural lower classes in general) to emerge as a peculiar set of symbols: an authenticating but ambiguous embodiment of the West's evolutionary roots. Representations of villages are not always entirely negative. Often they are full of romantic ambivalence: they bespeak a way of life both past and passing; they tell us what we think we have lost or point to what we think we have surpassed. However, even in their more benign form, they deny the 'coevalness' of villagers with modern civilization (Fabian 1983). They also appear frequently and in many forms. Consider, for example, this excerpt from an advertisement that appeared in a recent edition of the *New Yorker*. It invites one to 'Walk England' in a setting where time has presumably stood still:

English Adventures. Travel back in time on our luxury tours to the enchanted villages and spectacular mountains of Wordsworth's Lake District, including visits to the Roman Wall and Yorkshire Dales. (*New Yorker*, 28 Sept. 1992)

Rural people are assumed to be clinging to an outmoded way of life ('back in time') that may have an exotic, touristy charm ('enchanted'), but no more positive or active role to play in contemporary life than as a destination for 'luxury tours'. Constructed as anachronisms, villages and villagers—like the people of the Balkans, the Irish, and, as Herzfeld shows us, the Greeks—are thus denied full access to the hierarchical politics of inclusion in 'the West'. They are the indigenous and working-class rural people who coexist spatially, but neither temporally nor culturally, with bourgeois society.[2] The very idea of the West thus bifurcates: geographically—on the map—it is static and incorporates vast and diverse territory; conceptually—or, in Benedict Anderson's terms, imaginatively (1983)—the commitment to modernity excises working-class rural dwellers from the body politic. It is the second, more powerful aspect of this bifurcation that concerns us here, for it is predicated upon the notion that to be truly Western one must think, live, and act independently of local custom and kinship, free from the parochial constraints of any particular community. The fully Western person is a cosmopolitan person, and the global extension of Western culture is the logical outcome of modernity. To pursue a horticultural metaphor, an occidentalized construction of Western identity conflates rootedness with being root-bound. Every gardener knows that the root-bound plant can neither grow nor flower.

In this chapter, I continue the argument I began in 'Reweaving the Fringe: Localism, Tradition and Representation in British Ethnography' (1991), that the ways in which regions and communities are defined and portrayed as local, marginal, or traditional continue to constrain our understanding of the relationships between such places and what Arjun Appadurai calls 'the global ethnoscape' (1991). These portrayals circulate among cartoons, fiction, journalistic essays, and ethnographies that speak textually to one another. In the terms of this volume, they occidentalize by constructing an essentialized view of the 'real West' as governed by urban, bourgeois, cosmopolitan values, and by replicating orientalist criteria that essentialize non-Western societies as timeless, inflexible others (Said 1978). Local communities are seen not merely as socially encapsulated but as insular, their values tribal (manners beastly, customs quaint). While bourgeois society pursues the quest for efficiency and order, local communities are, at best, uncertain allies in the struggle for progress. Thus orientalist and occidentalist images interact dialectically to produce a particular construction of the West that situates both rural/ local and non-Western communities as crucial opposites to what it de- fines as modern, industrially technological, and middle-class. The one, however, remains peripheral to the other.

Class, community, and murder

As I began to think about occidentalism in the anthropology of 'the West' in general, and of Britain and Ireland in particular, I found that I felt a bit like Alice trying to reach the garden of wonderful, talking flowers. The more she walked in its direction, the further away it got. I decided to take Lewis Carroll's advice, therefore, and turn away from anthropology at first, in the hope that I would find myself walking back in at the gate. Turning, as I sometimes do in moments of confusion, from my profes- sion to my avocation, I began to consider some literary depictions of the rural other, more subtle—but perhaps more significant because more pervasive—than the cartoons of Balkan and Irish peasants. George Marcus and Michael Fischer point out, after all, that 'third-world literature' offers important information and insights to anthropologists (1986: 74). Why not, then, 'first-world literature'?

Josephine Tey suggested a way that I might sneak up on the exotic within. After all, as she wrote in her well-wrought mystery *The Singing Sands*, one does not have to travel all the way to the Orient to find the exotic, non-Western primitive. The Highlands and Islands of Scotland are at hand:

Arabia? Oh, yes, they had a whole shelf of books about the country. Almost as many people wrote books about Arabia as about the Hebrides. There was, too, if Mr. Tallisker might be permitted to say so, the same tendency to idealise the subject in its devotees. 'You think that, boiled down to plain fact, they are both just windy deserts.' Oh, no; not entirely. That was being a little—wholesale. Mr. Tallisker had much happiness and beauty from the Islands. But the tendency to idealise a primitive people was perhaps the same in each case. (Tey 1953: 139)

Some mystery novels display orientalism in its purest sense. Robin Winks, historian and mystery reviewer, points out the popularity of the

'sinister Oriental' in British detective fiction, exemplified by such characters as Sax Rohmer's Dr Fu Manchu and Ian Fleming's Odd Job (1977:
491–3). Yet, far more characteristically, mystery novels (at least British
mystery novels) make the exotic virtually part of the local landscape, as
seemingly natural and, therefore, unproblematic. I have in mind here the
classic British village murder mystery. P. D. James once said in a television broadcast that murder-mystery writers have a profound reliance on
the idea of social order. Even a cursory glance shows a plethora of mysteries embedded in rural settings that provide a routinized, highly ordered,
and stratified context for their dramas. This genre is an under-examined
form of 'indigenous media' (Ginsburg 1991), one that mythologizes the
relationship between bourgeois society and the 'village way of life' in an
age of uncertainty over the viability of both (cf. Strathern 1984). Despite
his obviously benighted and bigoted antagonism towards mysteries as a
genre, Edmund Wilson was on to something when he suggested that
people enjoy them because they reassure us that villains get caught (1944:
75). The issue is not only, or even primarily, 'Who Cares Who Killed
Roger Ackroyd?' (Wilson 1945), but the function of that ultimately
reassuring social universe into which the reader is transported.

In the normally harmonious world of the quiet (sleepy) little village,
middle-class normalcy—signified by a fastidious observance of formality,
indirect references to emotion, if any, and a suitable deference of labourers to gentry—prevails until the social fabric is rent by discovery of a
corpse; then, the image of the tight-knit community is threatened. The
local people, or villagers, are suddenly revealed as 'others' and often
appear to close ranks against inquiries by outsiders or even familiar, but
upper-class, investigators. Not until the mystery is resolved can people go
back to acting as if 'God's in his heaven, all's right with the world'. Social
integration prevails with the discovery or capture of the murderer, however, and in this, as in other aspects, the murder mystery bears a strong
resemblance to a number of structural-functionalist accounts of British
and Irish community life that were published between the 1930s and the
1960s (for a good review, see the discussion in Bell and Newby 1971).

Murder transforms the archetypal English village into an exotic den of
intrigue. Considerable social commentary of a quasi-ethnographic kind
may be found in these accounts. Many murder novels offer great detail
on village, regional, or occupational culture, dialect, custom, and class
relations.

With occasional exceptions, the social structure of British village murder mysteries is quite predictable. (That, after all, is one reason why we

read them.) The principal sleuth is usually a male from the upper or middle classes (Lord Peter Wimsey, Adam Dalgleish, Albert Campion, Roderick Alleyn, Richard Jury, and Melrose Plant), or a 'genteel' woman (Miss Marple, Miss Silver).[3] This status gives them a knowledge and power to take action which are unavailable to 'the lower orders'. The key characters, like the detectives, often have local connections to the hereditary, landowning élite; or they are upper middle-class individuals who have chosen rural homes in order to find a haven from urban pressures, to pursue, as Raymond Williams suggests, that elusive sense of returning to an ever-receding point in their pastoral ideal, to a time when England was a 'happier country' (R. Williams 1973: 10).

Local or village people are set apart in these accounts. On the whole, they are portrayed as lower class, poorly educated, resentful of and curious about outsiders, and publicly, at least, deferential to the upper classes. Since they are seldom key players in the plot, except, occasionally, as victims or inadvertent witnesses, we might wonder why they are there at all. I suggest that locals provide more than neutral background, or even local colour. They are employed to generate an atmosphere of unknown forces and to generate tension through the widening breach of social complementarity that invariably accompanies an unsolved homicide. A network of hidden signals and shared codes thwarts those who attempt to penetrate local knowledge. Suspicion of outsiders and fear of 'gentry' (police or amateur detectives) often inhibit locals from revealing key information about who went where, when, and why.

Of course, to use locals in this way does not require that they be given a distinct and identifiable location or culture. Sometimes all that is described is a generic village with local people present as servants, tradespeople, or observers from windows. For Agatha Christie's Miss Marple, indeed, all of human nature can be found in a village, and her famous deductions are predicated upon the parallels she is sure to find between suspects in a capital crime and the characters she has known in her village, St Mary Mead.[4]

The village genre of murder mysteries constructs a stratified social universe of inclusion and exclusion, a hierarchy that achieves a mythic quality, transcending the character and plot machinations of any individual author. I have selected a few examples from different works to illustrate how this form of ethnographic popular culture draws upon and reinforces stereotypes of backwardness, of locals as yokels.

While a village may contain both upper- and lower-class residents, the former are often referred to as 'county' or 'gentry', and it is clear that they do not count as 'local'. Their social networks and interests transcend the immediate community. They are connected to their peers all over the nation through their schools, military service, family ties (one of the Dorset Chittendons), and travel (usually Continental, though ex-colonials make frequent appearances). Lower-class people in murder mysteries, on the other hand, are truly local, in the sense of being preoccupied with purely village affairs, having a deep and detailed knowledge of the activities of a small, immediate network, and occupations (farming, fishing, mining, domestic service) that keep them within walking or cycling distance of their own cottages.

Mystery authors clearly equate being local with being lower class and demonstrate this by using speech patterns to type-cast the social strata of their characters.[5] Middle-class speech is not usually rendered as regionally special, often flowing rather indistinguishably from the author's own narrative style. Upper-class dialogue, on the other hand, is sometimes quite caricatured. An example is the staccato, elliptical style of retired military officers who drop consonants and first-person pronouns with equal ease, or the drawling silliness of an aristocratic twit. But however affected or eccentric, upper-class speech, like that of the middle class, is *not* treated as varying regionally. Colonel or Lord So-and-So speaks the same in Yorkshire as he does in Cornwall. The 'imagined community' (Anderson 1983) of the élites is a national, hegemonic one. This may even be brought out explicitly, as in the following extract from Josephine Tey's *The Singing Sands*, set in the southern Highlands of Scotland, where a 10-year-old boy uses local dialect as a gesture of independence:

Pat spoke from choice what his mother called 'clotted Perthshire,' his bosom friend at the village school being the shepherd's son, who hailed from Killin. He could, of course, when he had a mind, speak faultless English, but it was always a bad sign. When Pat was 'not speaking' to you, he was always not speaking in the best English. (1953: 24)[6]

The lower-class and parochial identity of villagers, on the other hand, is often marked by having them speak emphatically—not to say dramatically—in dialect. Consider the following, set in the Yorkshire dales:

'Strangled by a madman,' she repeated in a whisper. 'And right 'ere in our village. I don't know what the world's coming to, I don't. We're none of us safe any more, and that's a fact. Best keep yer doors locked and not go out after dark.'

'Rubbish!' Mrs. Anstey said. 'It was 'is wife as done it. Fer t'money, like. Stands to reason. Money's t'root of all evil, you mark my words. That's what my Albert used ter say.'

'Aye,' muttered Mrs. Sampson under her breath. 'That's because 'ee never made any, the lazy sod.' (Robinson 1988: 59)

Further, while members of the upper classes usually are individual characters (if often rather stereotyped), villagers frequently lack individuality. They are restricted to a few essential qualities, chiefly an avid curiosity and great excitement in the face of tragic events. Alternatively, they may appear exceptionally slow-witted. The following passage conveys the significance of Raymond Williams's comment about Dorothy Sayers's 'middle-class fantasies about the human nature of the traditional inhabitants' (R. Williams 1973: 249):

Harriet explained that there was a dead man lying on the shore and that the police ought to be informed.

'That do be terrible, surely,' said the woman. 'Will it be Joe Smith? He was out with his boat this morning and the rocks be very dangerous thereabouts. The Grinders, we call them.'

'No,' said Harriet; 'it isn't a fisherman—it looks like somebody from the town. And he isn't drowned. He's cut his throat.'

'Cut his throat?' said the woman, with relish. 'Well, now, what a terrible thing, to be sure.'

'I want to let the police know,' said Harriet, 'before the tide comes in and covers the body.'

'The police?' the woman considered this. 'Oh, yes,' she said, after mature thought. 'The police did ought to be told about it.' (Sayers 1932: 15)

Novels located in culturally 'remote' regions, such as Cornwall, East Anglia, or the Highlands of Scotland, may have considerable geographical detail, and attend to minor elements of folk culture. Within such settings, the primordial, tradition-bound character of rural regions becomes powerful, even overwhelming. Tey's detective in *The Singing Sands* sets out for 'the great, clean Highland country; way into the wide, unchanging, undemanding Highland world where people died only in their beds' (1953: 7). And later, 'In the "old" places anything was possible. Even beasts that talked' (1953: 28).

Community solidarity is sometimes emphasized by the implied or explicit claim that local people are hostile to outsiders: the aura of cultural foreignness that hangs ominously around 'the folk' is enhanced by the hint of physical danger. This is especially so in the case of fishing and mining communities. Their inhabitants not only live together, but share a hazardous occupation that marks them off as especially tough and insular. Alan Hunter suggests, for example, that the fisherfolk of his novel form a true secret society:

[Superintendent Gently] dropped in at the Beach Store to buy himself an ice-cream. On his way through the village he had encountered a group of fishermen. They were lounging under a wall and smoking their short clay pipes: they watched him in a heavy silence as he drew level with and passed them. Then one of them had spat—had the timing been coincidental? (Hunter 1959: 99)

And then:

[T]hey were more like a band of brothers, a religious order almost: they were the receptacle of secrets past common understanding. And to share them you must belong, to partake of the revelation; after which . . . wasn't it possible? . . . you could murder and get away with it! (1959: 102)

One common setting for cultural strangeness is the low-lying East Anglian coast, sometimes land, sometimes sea. The marshes and mudflats are treacherous, the inhabitants are rural and exotic. For example, Francis Beeding's *Death Walks in Eastrepps* (first published 1931) contains the following description of local people: 'The East Anglian mentality, the Inspector owned, was difficult. Folk were reticent, almost taciturn, indifferent to the stranger. They kept themselves to themselves, and were proud of it' (1980: 87). The fishermen, in particular, are more different than the rest:

He knew too well what the talk would be. These were fishermen, slow of speech and action, sturdy, with salt sense, but full of superstition. They would be talking again of Eric, the red-haired ghost of the Danish wanderer, shipwrecked on that shore a thousand years and more ago. (1980: 167)

Fishermen are similarly depicted in Alan Hunter's *Gently in the Sun*, set somewhere on the north-east coast of England: 'Bob Hawks . . . went queer years ago—which is saying something when it comes to fishermen. They aren't ordinary people like you and me' (1959: 56).

In the generally more complimentary image of fisherfolk as hard-working and shrewd given by author Henry Wade in *Mist on the Saltings*, another East Anglian offering, one still finds comments that essentialize their character and reiterate the idea that fisherfolk tend to be both furtive and untruthful:

The sea-board folk were intensely secretive about themselves and their doings, even in the most trivial matters, and if obliged to give information would always say whatever they thought most convenient, without any regard to its accuracy. (Wade 1985: 222)

Nothing these writers say through their narratives, by the way, is at all inconsistent with the kinds of comments about fisherfolk that I heard as

CONTENTS

the night goes sharp and wet. The night is teeth and nails and kisses. There are no regrets here. There are no girlfriends here. There are no Australians or mothers or friends from yoga here. Good for you.

In the morning you forget so very many things. You forget the party and the name of the girl lying next to you. You forget that you're alone when there's someone else in the room. You forget you were ever angry through the fog of your hangover. You stand and stir and stumble forth, and see the world in shifting, painful clarity. You wander the apartment in shambling steps, thirsting and hungry, your head splitting.

You put the teakettle on and linger in the hall while it brews. Something inside you stirs. You've broken something and the world didn't end. You've broken something and it felt good. The girl from the party wakes and stretches. When you pull back the sheets on her, you will forget to feel guilty. When her skin engulfs you, it feels like a soft goodbye. When the teakettle screeches, you have better things to do. Good for you.

an ethnographer doing field-work in eastern Scotland. From the beginning of the east-coast herring trade in the eighteenth century, when special new fishing villages were established along the coast, a stigma was attached to fisherfolk. They were often said by their landward neighbours to be 'a breed apart', or of another, inferior 'race', possibly descended from shipwrecked Phoenician or Viking mariners or perhaps from survivors cast off from the Spanish Armada (Nadel 1984, 1986).

Mining communities get similar treatment. In Reginald Hill's *Underworld*, a sophisticated novel as much about class conflict and modern industrial struggle as about murder, the community itself is none the less seen as violently, primordially other:

Silence fell in the room, a silence compounded of horror and excitement. It was the excitement that made Ellie [a policeman's wife, intellectual and middle class] feel more alien than anything else . . . The excitement was the buzz of speculation and anticipation which must have run around frontier towns when the word spread that a lynching was in the offing. Rough justice, sorting out your own messes, taking care of your own . . . all the old vigilante cliches ran through her mind. Burrthorpe was a frontier town, not in the geographic, political sense, but in terms of its monogenesis, its cultural separateness, its awareness of constant threat . . . Deep beneath the streets and houses lay the reason for their existence, the hope of their continuance. When finally the coal was exhausted or adjudged too expensive to be worth the hewing, Burrthorpe would literally be cut off from its roots and die. (1988: 199)

Fiction writers may at times be both good ethnographers and good informants. Their detectives must also be good field-workers, carefully negotiating social alliances to maximize the flow of information from different factions or groups within a small community. In Tey's *The Singing Sands*, the detective searches for clues on a Hebridean island whose population is divided between Roman Catholic and Presbyterian. He is warned of the animosity between the two factions and proceeds carefully. The following passage could easily come from an ethnographic chapter on field-work:

In the shop were several men from the fishing-boats in the harbour and a little round man in a black raincoat who could be nothing but a priest. This was a fortunate thing. Even the Presbyterian third, he felt, could hardly hold against him a fortuitous meeting in a public store. He edged in beside His Reverence and waited with him while the fishermen were being served. After that it was plain sailing. The priest 'picked him up' and he had five witnesses to it. Moreover, Father Heslop deftly included the proprietor . . . Grant deduced that the proprietor was not one of his flock. So he was very happily parcelled out among the islanders over the paraffiny buns and the margarine, and there would be no internecine war over the possession of his person. (1953: 83)

Deep down in the Gemeinschaft

Murder mysteries share some essentialized images of rural life with community studies. Just as these detective stories rely upon a subtext of the primitive, the not-truly-Western, within the cultural order, the social science tradition of community studies is animated by ideas of rural settlements as simpler than and somehow different from the rest of Western society.

This should come as no surprise. Recent critiques of representation in anthropology have suggested that the line between fiction and ethnography is not a clear one (Clifford 1986; Marcus and Cushman 1982). This may have a particular relevance for what Marilyn Strathern (1987) calls 'auto-ethnography', or Anthony Jackson's (1987) anthropologist working 'at home'. When the ethnographer is a native, both of the general host culture and of the ethnographic audience, it is more difficult to claim special objectivity or authority at the level of description.

Powerful localizing images circulate through the culture of which both ethnographer and novelist are a part. Richard Fardon points out that ethnographies are written within regional traditions that condition their structure and content (1990: 24–5). While his explicit concern is 'exotic' field-work and the influence of academic texts upon ethnographic investigation and writing, anthropologists working within their own societies are culturally embedded in a far more complex way. Their own literary and popular cultural traditions form both subject and object of their consciousness, making it difficult to mediate analytical boundaries between ethnography and autobiography.

A prevailing ethos among the denizens of the largely urbanized United Kingdom valorizes an idealized, archetypal vision of rural life as a precious remove from normal, middle-class pressures (Newby 1979). As Peter Laslett says, 'the English still seem to want to live in the structures of the pre-industrial world, prizing the thatched cottage and the half-timbered house as the proper place for the proper Englishmen to dwell in' (1984: 25). Patrick Wright refers to this imagined, nostalgic landscape as 'culturally resonant real-estate' (Wright 1985: 2). More wryly, Raymond Williams notes that '[t]he loved places are the "unspoiled" places, and no group agrees with this more readily than those who live in the "spoiled"' (R. Williams 1973: 253). The spoiled places, the sites of industry and urbanism, nevertheless provide the core of the capitalist, state-organized Western experience that undergirds the occidentalist vision. Social scientists, like other largely urban professionals, are by no means immune to the pastoral ideal.[7]

To an extent, British ethnographers writing about British society are necessarily engaging in an act of self-representation, which, as Nicholas Thomas puts it, 'never takes place in isolation and . . . is frequently oppositional or reactive' (1992: 213). Reflexivity 'at home' is refracted through an endless hall of mirrors.

Both British community studies and village murder mysteries require a structure and an authorial voice that can convince readers of the account's plausibility. Similarities between the two genres thus exist on several levels. Both rely heavily upon a wealth of realist detail, organized as evidence, to argue that their interpretations of events and human relationships are superior to other possible competing explanations. Both presume the existence of a relatively stable social order where custom normally precedes and supersedes conflict. (When the agents of the state appear, whether in the form of planning officials or police officers, they are seen as intrusive outsiders.) And both presume an essential cultural difference between rural communities and modern, industrial society, thus implicitly upholding the notion of the conceptual, exclusive, and progressive West.

Moving closer to anthropology than the murder mystery, but not quite there yet, are extended, semi-popular essays on village life that also imagine villages as semi-isolated habitats with certain characteristics that make them essentially different from the rest of British society. Ronald Blythe's *Akenfield* (1969) is a case in point. It is a set of human portraits drawn from an East Anglian agricultural village that finds itself increasingly tied to the modern world of commercial farming. The author is himself an East Anglian.

Blythe's brief 'Introduction' frames his view of village life. There he establishes the village's pre-Norman lineage, and follows this with Akenfield's appearance in the Domesday Book. Succeeding years bring enclosures, wars, and mechanization, but through it all, the villager abides by the rhythm and mandates of the soil:

Deep in the nature of such men and elemental to their entire being there is the internationalism of the planted earth which makes them, in common with the rice-harvesters of Vietnam or the wine-makers of Burgundy, people who are committed to certain basic ideas and actions which progress and politics can elaborate or confuse, but can never alter. (Blythe 1969: 15)

A number of elements in *Akenfield* make Blythe's choice of idiom a curious and self-contradictory one. First, not all residents are native villagers. Like Laslett in *The World We Have Lost* (1984), Blythe (1969: 16) recognizes that townspeople subscribe to what he calls 'the national village cult', the belief that life, to be properly experienced, must be lived in the country. Small wonder that Akenfield, like other rural areas, has seen the influx of urban newcomers in search of this village ideal. Meanwhile, the land cannot support everyone and many of the young people must leave. And finally, many of the voices that Blythe records recall hard and bitter times. Not all of them regret modern changes, nor does the village seem as timeless as his own Introduction suggests it should. Blythe's panegyric to a universal and 'elemental' peasant nature is thus almost immediately undercut by his own description of contemporary life in East Anglia. The apparently unintentional presence of this contradiction is itself eloquent testimony to the enduring power of such romanticized images.

Many nineteenth- and early twentieth-century writings on rural or village life in Britain recapitulate the connection of rural localism with primitivism, and anthropology lent its support. Much recent commentary on the history of anthropology has pointed to the imperialist legacy of the discipline, and to the emergence of cross-cultural, but non-relativist, comparison from the encounter between Europeans and the inhabitants of their various colonies or objects of 'discovery' (Asad 1973, 1991; Kuper 1988; McGrane 1989; Wolfe 1991). Evolutionary schemata were drawn to make the greatest possible contrast between the 'savage' and the 'civilized', similar in conceptual space to the contrast between oriental and occidental. This contrast was constructed not only in terms of culture and custom, but also in terms of evolutionary distance (Bowler 1989; Kuklick 1984; Kuper 1988). The civilized European was seen to represent the fulfilment of human potential to achieve order and regularity: in short, mature humanity; the primitive tribesman was seen as the survival of humanity's childhood. In his study of developmentalism in Victorian thought, for example, Peter Bowler notes that 'Victorian anthropologists assumed that contemporary "primitive" tribes were exact equivalents of the Europeans' stone-age ancestors' (1989: 11).

But one did not need to travel to Africa, the Antipodes, or back to the Stone Age to discover incompletely civilized people. What worked to justify colonial relationships abroad was also employed to explain class hierarchy at home. For example, Henrietta Kuklick points out that many Victorian anthropologists equated 'contemporary primitives, ancient

European peoples, and the people living in less-developed sections of modern societies—rural residents and the "dangerous classes" ' (1984: 63). She says further that they 'agreed that the rulers of tribal societies resembled British gentlemen in manners and attitudes, while the lower orders in Britain displayed primitive physical capacities of strength and endurance their social superiors lacked' (1984: 64).

Images of villagers as 'the lower orders' seem part of the dialogue about race, class, and society that emerged within the new social science disciplines, including anthropology, as they defined themselves in part through classifying and ranking all those who fell outside the narrow spectrum of bourgeois morality and behaviour. While the effort to employ crude physiological criteria to distinguish among social classes[8] was largely abandoned, another, subtler form of evolutionist hierarchy was maintained in a number of post-war, largely functionalist community studies of Great Britain and Ireland—the western-most 'Atlantic Fringe' of Europe, as Conrad Arensberg (1963) has put it—through the attempt to maintain a notion of social types and forms. This hierarchy, with its 'discrete category of complex societies', as Michael Herzfeld has pointed out (1987: 53), contributed to the conceptual exclusivity with which Europe itself was defined.

My point here is not to review the numerous critiques of these studies. A good reference for this is the volume edited by Tony Bradley and Philip Lowe (1984), *Locality and Rurality: Economy and Society in Rural Regions*. In many of these studies, rural communities and regions were theorized as endpoints on the rural–urban continuum, as well as endpoints on the map, by anthropologists and by others. Many of these implicitly, if not explicitly, suggested that rural social organization was somehow 'simpler' than, and prior to, that of towns and cities.

Such images of essential simplicity are generally drawn from a 'Fringe' defined in territorial terms, Celtic or otherwise (see Hechter 1974). Arensberg articulated this in 1937 in the first chapter of *The Irish Countryman*, where he stated that 'an unbroken ancient [Celtic] tradition' has been preserved in Ireland because it has been 'isolated' (1959: 17).[9] More recently, Robin Fox (1978) has represented the Tory Islanders as an even purer—and more isolated—vessel for ancient Irish tradition than the farmers of County Clare. The Scottish Highlanders enjoy a similar reputation. As Malcolm Chapman (1978) points out, Scottish Gaelic society, the Highlanders in particular, have been portrayed as European equivalents of noble savages.[10] Consider, for example, W. J. Gibson's comment: 'In no part of the British Isles are the survivals of an earlier and

simpler state of society more definite or more picturesque than in the
Outer Isles of Scotland' (1946: 147). Indeed, Robert Redfield includes the
Scottish Highlanders in his musings on the fate of folk societies. He
apparently sees no irony in citing Toynbee to the effect that the Highlanders, along with the Maoris and the Araucanians, are examples of folk
societies that have retained some 'moral independence' within the civilizations that have engulfed them (1953: 45).

There is clearly a considerable degree of subjectivity in how the margin
gets defined. East Anglia, after all, is less than 100 miles from London.
Edwin Ardener, who remarks on western Scotland as 'an area in which
canonical levels of "remoteness" are to be found' (1987: 40), says that
Europeans are ' "space specialists": we easily realize our conceptual spaces
as physical spaces' (1987: 40). The British tourist industry, as we have
seen from the 'Walk England' advertisement, clearly relies on such notions of distance. Our autochthonous others, our orientals who give the
occident its boundaries, live elsewhere. We can go and visit them, but we
must go home again.

The imagined countryside

It is time, then, to examine more closely what ideas have been embedded
in the concept of rurality. In many of the post-war British community
studies, descriptions of rural communities tended to see integrated, internally static social systems, with kinship, mutual aid, harmonious (if not
egalitarian) social relationships, and, sometimes, occupational solidarity
as key factors in elaborating the rural–urban continuum. Class is given
fairly short shrift. As in the murder mysteries, it is taken for granted that
country folk are of the working class or its rural equivalent, in the sense
that they do not possess land or productive capital. In general, they are
tenants or agricultural labourers. And social conflict is not emphasized.
Historical references to enclosures, dissenting religious or political resistance movements, or 'alternative' sources of income (poaching, smug-
gling), which may be called the dynamic, resistive face of 'village life and
labour' (Samuel 1975), are few. Contemporary class asymmetry (relationship with landlords, merchants, employers) appears as exogenous, not
part of rural life, but rather something imposed upon it.[11]

One example of the emphasis upon rural life as static is found in the
work of W. M. Williams, who studied communities in northern and in
south-western England ('Gosforth' in Cumberland and 'Ashworthy' in
the West Country) (W. M. Williams 1956, 1963; see also Frankenberg

1969). While criticizing 'the orthodox "Gemeinschaft" view of rural social structure' as simplistic in ignoring the impact of changes emanating
from the wider society, he none the less maintains the view that 'rural life
is characterized by conditions of "dynamic equilibrium"', which ensure
'continuity of social life' (W. M. Williams 1974: 67).

Ronald Frankenberg's volume *Communities in Britain* explicitly employs these ideas to typologize a range of settlements within British
society: 'I believe that as one moves from rural to urban, one sees the
results of a process of proletarianization in which local gives way to
cosmopolitan, and multiplex to undisguised class relationships' (1969:
156). While Frankenberg says that his continuum is meant to be morphological, not evolutionary, his criteria embody the opposition of 'simple' to
'complex'; his very statement that 'the local gives way to cosmopolitan'
makes it difficult to accept his claim. The notion of morphological neutrality becomes especially problematic when he cites J. A. Barnes (1954)
with reference to the difference between 'simple, primitive, *rural* or small
scale societies as against modern, civilized, *urban* or mass society' (1969:
243, emphasis added). It is true that Frankenberg recognizes that even
the most rural communities of Britain are influenced by and tied into
industrial civilization, and thus lie nearer to the urban than to the rural
end of the continuum; however, he then says that 'thus the Irish countryside, studied by Arensberg, approximates to Barnes's "primitive" model,
but the urban societies at the end [of the continuum and of the book] are
similar to his model of modern society' (1969: 244).

In the Introduction to Ruth Crichton's *Commuters' Village*, we see a
similar formulation emphasizing the power of multiplex relationships to
efface class divisions within the village context. In a homily on the generic
virtues of English village life, she says:

Few people who live and work in a village have any doubt that social integration
is worth fostering. . . . [V]illage life offers something of high value—a sense of
belonging to a face-to-face group. The small size of the community and the
relative stability both give a feeling of security—of having a place in the order of
things . . .

Unlike suburbia, with its segregation of status groups, the village gives its inhabitants an opportunity of knowing people within a wide social range. Rich and
poor, skilled and unskilled, village worker and commuter can see each other as
whole people—the grocer as parish councillor, the doctor as cricketer, the schoolmaster as sidesman in church, the chimney sweep as amateur actor. (1964: 9)[12]

The expectation that rural society, like 'primitive' society, will be characterized by an emphasis on kinship organization has conditioned much of the ethnographic writing on Britain. Alwyn Rees says of Llanfihangel, a parish in rural Wales, that '[t]he solidarity of the kindred is a constant source of surprise to the stranger' (1950: 79). He explains this, moreover, as a 'heritage from the tribal past' (1950: 81).

On the other hand, James Littlejohn's *Westrigg: The Sociology of a Cheviot Parish* is an instructive example precisely because kinship is not found to be a significant part of social life. In this account of a rural Border parish, published in 1963, Littlejohn explores historically the disappearance of kinship bonds and mutual aid. He describes the parish in demographic, occupational, and class terms. Westrigg has a small, dispersed population, its employment basis is primarily commercial farming and forestry, and the people there increasingly describe themselves as isolated. The younger generation is leaving for opportunities elsewhere.

Littlejohn compares Westrigg to rural Ireland and Wales:

> The Irish countryman explains his act of mutual aid 'as part of the traditional reciprocation of sentiment and duty which makes up his system of kinship.' Rees shows that assistance is part of the relationship of kinsfolk and neighbours. There are no kinship ties among the farmers of Westrigg. (1963: 28)

It seems, in fact, to be strikingly bereft of the expected components of communal solidarity. Market-place competition, class relations, and bureaucratic organization prevail. These factors cause Littlejohn to question whether Westrigg actually is 'rural' at all:

> [E]xcept for the fact that farms and forests are 'small firms' the description so far might apply in many features to any industrial population, and it may be asked at this point how far the parish is a 'rural community': the term normally implies some sort of unit with a social life of its own, an 'area of common life'. (1963: 37–8)

Littlejohn's problem is not simply that rural life is being transformed, but that the category itself constrains thought. It obscures the dynamics of an encompassing world–system that continually reconfigures the boundaries between core and periphery. It is an example of the way in which dichotomizing categories such as rural/urban, simple/complex, traditional/modern, and even periphery/core contribute to an essentialized, occidentalized, vision of Western society as having 'margins' that harbour pre–modern ways of life. The converse point is made by Theodore Bestor in his criticism of applying a village model to understanding social life in Tokyo's neighbourhoods. In his words, 'the village metaphor implies that one possible explanation for a highly urbanized society that maintains the integrity of community life . . . may be that the society is somehow not truly urban' (1989: 44–5).

Conclusion

As I understand the significance of exploring occidentalism in constructions of Western society (Carrier 1992), it is a way of using Edward Said's
insights about essentializing and homogenizing—and ultimately, distancing—the way we see other cultures to consider the assumptions we employ
in constructing our cultural home base, as it were. Representations of
Britain are imbued with the idea that here we have the home of modernity,
the site of the industrial revolution and of a rational, state-organized
social order securing property and peace: the essential, and quintessential,
West. I have suggested that writers in several genres have underpinned
this vision with its antithesis, the village, as the 'orient within'. In this
view, rural life is modernity's evolutionary precedent, surviving as an
anachronism that shows us how far we have progressed.

From cartoons and murder mysteries to functionalist community studies, we can see a tendency to present bourgeois society as the normal,
defining condition of Western civilization. Such a vision cannot admit the
social vitality of alternative ways of life, but must see them as backward,
deviant, or even pathological. Rural areas defined as marginal become
objects of social policy and effectively disenfranchised as wards of the
state. They have, however, been captured as an economic resource, as
part of the national mania for heritage (see Hewison 1987; Wright 1985),
and tranquilized as tourist destinations.

The rural–urban contrast[13] has thus become a social discourse with
consequences. The contrast is not a simple complementary opposition,
but a duality that is inherently hierarchical. It tends to reify the concept
of the social margin or periphery in terms of geography, class, and the
bourgeois bureaucratic value of social efficiency. In so doing, it lends
itself to employment in the administration of power, appearing most
strikingly perhaps in the context of policy arguments over economic and
political development (Broady 1973; Forsythe 1984; Gilder 1984; Nadel
1983; Parman 1990; Steel 1975). In this respect it is part of the struggle
over local self-determination that Herzfeld identifies as 'the disputed
ownership of history' (1991: p. xi). Finally, as I have suggested elsewhere,
the contrast continues to have implications for the professional practice of
anthropology as a discipline specializing in the exotic (Nadel-Klein 1991).

What counts as Western is as vital an issue now for Europe as at any
time in its history. The Englehart cartoon on the Balkans suggests that a
new Europe is at war with the old, and that the men in suits—embodiments
of a transcultural bourgeois rationality—must mediate and ultimately

erase local differences. Recent events in Europe indicate that this project is far from being completed, and perhaps will never be. Quite apart from events in Bosnia, the effort to achieve a common monetary system and market is facing serious difficulties.

An extensive public relations effort is being made to address this. Efforts to produce a pan-European identity can be read in the publications of the Commission of the European Communities, which are published in Danish, Dutch, English, French, German, Greek, Italian, Portuguese, and Spanish. According to a recent pamphlet called *A People's Europe*, 'European integration is . . . meant to benefit ordinary people.' A 'Eurobarometer opinion poll carried out in 1991' found that 'more than half the people in the 12 Member States of the European Community (53%) claim to feel a sense of European identity "sometimes" or "often" '. While this implies that some 47 per cent never do, in fact, feel such identity, the authors of the pamphlet go on to proclaim that '[t]hroughout the Community, people's sense of belonging *not merely* to their own country but to a wider Europe is steadily growing' (European Communities 1992: 1, emphasis added). 'Real' European identity thus is being proclaimed by Brussels as a cosmopolitan one. The language of EC publications reveals an insistence that the future lies in transcending locality.

Perhaps it is no accident that the peoples of Europe are now struggling with and resisting the idea of adopting a singular identity at a time when indigenous peoples elsewhere are discovering a source of power in doing exactly that. Australian Aboriginal people debate accepting 'Koori' as a pan-Aboriginal designation, Native Americans discover commonality, and the very category 'indigenous' has become a transnational, transcultural political identity.

Increasingly, it seems, cultural identities are losing—or changing—their spatial moorings. Recent debates on how space and place should be retheorized in anthropological thinking (Gupta and Ferguson 1992; Rodman 1992) suggest that we need to despatialize the way we identify not only the locations of specific cultures, but also core and periphery, centre and margin. Like the distinction between First and Third Worlds, the division between margin and centre rests upon privileging the conceptual West, where pre-modern 'others' linger at the edges, over the spatial, inclusive West, and can more usefully be seen as a construct based heavily upon class and power. It has been defined by a view of the world that takes the middle-class reality of advanced capitalism as normal and unremarkable, while the cultures of villages and other rural communities

ICARUS FALLS

Alex Shvartsman

MY WORLD IS A PAIR OF PHOTOGRAPHS. THEY STAND ATOP a nightstand at my bedside, encased in acrylic frames. A young woman in an orange jumpsuit smiles from one of the photos. She wears a nametag, but I can't make out what it says, not even when I squint. I'm pretty sure that she's me. The rest of the room is bland and nondescript, like hospital food. I try to shake off the fog inside my head, but it hangs there, thick and heavy as a murky autumn morning at the Boston harbor. I examine the cheap floral prints on the walls and the sparse, utilitarian furniture around my bed. I desperately scan the room for clues, anything to help me remember, but there isn't much to go on.

The other photo is of a middle-aged woman with braided hair and kind eyes. I concentrate on her face and will the fog in my mind to dissipate, but it doesn't obey. Relentlessly, irrevocably, I'm losing my memories, but I cling to the one that is most important. This is my daughter, Kate.

"Kate. Kate," I keep whispering until I drift off and lose myself in the fog.

are merely objects upon which to act, to gaze (see Urry 1990), or to house in glass cases.

Coda

As a piece of indirect evidence for my argument about the process of cultural marginalization, I should like to note that museums provide a good index of what we in the West find 'remarkable', as opposed to ordinary. In Scotland, one can find a number of small museums devoted to folk life displays (the Scottish Fisheries Museum in Anstruther, for example). However, I have never seen, either in Scotland or anywhere else, a museum where one could walk in and feel 'at home'—a museum of contemporary middle-class life.

Notes

1 Raymond Williams (1973: 37) notes that even those who have indicted capitalism have adopted the rhetoric of progress in conceptualizing its place in human history.
2 For an interesting parallel, see Susan Hegeman's discussion of beliefs that Appalachia housed an unchanged Elizabethan culture preserved by the descendants of the original Scottish and English settlers (Hegeman 1991: 82–3).
3 There are, of course, exceptions, such as Reginald Hill's Andrew Dalziell or Joyce Porter's Dover. These policemen are aggressively, even boorishly, defiant of gentility. They may be said to uphold the norm by inverting it.
4 See the brief discussion by Margaret Yorke on 'St. Mary Mead and Other Troubled Villages' for a mystery writer's point of view (Yorke 1977: 258–60).
5 Such writers as Margery Allingham, Agatha Christie, Michael Innes, Ngaio Marsh, Dorothy Sayers, and Josephine Tey are well known for doing this, but many other authors pursue the class theme as well.
6 An upper-class woman in Angus made the same point to me when apologizing for her offspring's use of 'braid Scots', emphasizing that the child could perfectly well use 'proper English' when she wanted to (Nadel-Klein 1991: 513).
7 As John Nalson tells us, in writing about 'The Quiet Revolution in Traditional Society', a 'small wave of professionals' (1982: 71), including Max Gluckman, either rented or bought farm property in the hills of north-east Staffordshire. They were, according to Nalson, seeking refuge from the pressure of life in Manchester, but ironically and inadvertently contributing to a rise in local property values and the demise of family farms in the region.
8 Considerable racial typologizing was done for Britain by men such as John Beddoe. While the main criteria seem to have been hair colour and head-form, speech, surname, and history of migrations were taken into account.

Drawings sometimes include 'native dress' (Beddoe 1885: 259). Scottish High-landers are described thus:

> Quick in temper and very emotional, seldom speaking without being influ-enced by one feeling or another; more quick than accurate in observation; clear thinkers, but wanting in deliberation; they have a fertile and vivid imagination; love the absolute in thought and principle; dislike expediency and doubt; sympathetic with the weak, patriotic and chivalrous. Disposed to a sentimental melancholy, yet hopeful and sanguine. Often witty and eloquent; lovers of the animal kingdom, sometimes excel in zoological science. (1885: 246)

9 See Hugh Brody's critique of *The Irish Countryman* as being an ahistorical and functionalist account of stability (1974).

10 New Age literature reproduces this construction of the Highlands, and the Celtic Fringe more generally, as a site of primitive tribalism. Whether that literature is articles on spirituality and the new manhood, or catalogues selling crystals and other objects of power (such as the *Pyramid Books and the New Age Collection*—'Together We Celebrate Life, Light, Love!' (Pyramid Books 1992)), 'Celtic' culture appears as a source of ritual inspiration and of spir-itual kinship with Native Americans. See e.g. such entries as: 'Consult the Celtic Oracle!' (a deck of cards), or 'Practical Celtic Magic'. Other 'remote' sources of mystical power presented in this catalogue include Viking/Norse, Ancient Egypt, Ancient Greece, Africa, India, China, Japan, Tibet, Salem, and the gypsies.

11 These criticisms are not meant to apply, I must mention, to the more recent body of literature on Great Britain and Ireland that was developed in the 1970s and 1980s, exemplified by the work of Anthony Cohen. Cohen himself (1982, 1985, 1987), Judith Ennew (1980), Susan Parman (1990), Reginald Byron (1986), and others are very explicitly historical and contextual in their approaches, exploring the social construction of identity through experience and symbol.

I must also note my omission of another important strand of British ethno-graphy, which is the focus on immigrants and their communities. It is my observation as an ethnographer in Scotland that villagers themselves do a fair bit of occidentalizing in construing their country to be one where 'foreigners' do not ever really fit in.

12 The village of Puttenham, located in the 'green belt' of Surrey about 30 miles south of London, gives a rather different picture of how various status groups see each other. I did a short piece of field-work in Puttenham in 1967, exploring the relationship between social class and participation in voluntary associations. At the time, its population of about 600 had a number of differ-ent groups, including former agricultural workers (many housed on the coun-cil estate), commuters (mainly stockbrokers, accountants, and other workers

in the City), and a group of 'gentry'. Wage workers and stockbrokers seldom met in the same clubs, teams, or societies. It was abundantly clear at that time that, despite Puttenham's status as a small village, members of these different groups did not see each other as 'whole' people, in Crichton's sense, but were limited in their mutual social knowledge by class (Hurwitz 1967).
13 This shares a semantic space with the paired oppositions of folk/urban, simple/complex, primitive/civilized, local/cosmopolitan.

References

ANDERSON, BENEDICT (1983). *Imagined Communities: Reflections on the Origin and Spread of Nationalism*. London: Verso.

APPADURAI, ARJUN (1991). 'Global Ethnoscapes: Notes and Queries for a Transnational Anthropology', in Richard Fox (ed.), *Recapturing Anthropology: Working in the Present*. Santa Fe, Calif.: School of American Research Press: 191–210.

ARDENER, EDWIN (1987). ' "Remote Areas": Some Theoretical Considerations', in Anthony Jackson (ed.), *Anthropology at Home*. ASA Monograph 25. London: Tavistock: 38–54.

ARENSBERG, CONRAD (1959 [1937]). *The Irish Countryman*. Gloucester, Mass.: Peter Smith.

——(1963). 'The Old World Peoples: The Place of European Cultures in World Ethnography', *Anthropological Quarterly*, 36/3: 75–99.

ASAD, TALAL (ed.) (1973). *Anthropology and the Colonial Encounter*. London: Ithaca Press.

——(1991). 'Afterword: From the History of Colonial Anthropology to the Anthropology of Western Hegemony', in George Stocking (ed.), *Colonial Situations: Essays on the Contextualization of Ethnographic Knowledge*. Madison, Wis.: University of Wisconsin Press: 314–24.

BARNES, J. A. (1954). 'Class and Committees in a Norwegian Island Parish', *Human Relations*, 7: 39–58.

BEDDOE, JOHN (1885). *The Races of Britain: A Contribution to the Anthropology of Europe*. Bristol: J. W. Arrowsmith.

BEEDING, FRANCIS (1980 [1931]). *Death Walks in Eastrepps*. New York: Dover.

BELL, COLIN, and NEWBY, HOWARD (1971). *Community Studies*. New York: Praeger.

BESTOR, THEODORE (1989). *Neighborhood Tokyo*. Stanford, Calif.: Stanford University Press.

BLYTHE, RONALD (1969). *Akenfield: Portrait of an English Village*. New York: Pantheon Books.

BOWLER, PETER (1989). *The Invention of Progress: The Victorians and the Past*. Oxford: Basil Blackwell.

BRADLEY, TONY, and LOWE, PHILIP (eds.) (1984). *Locality and Rurality: Economy and Society in Rural Regions*. Norwich: Geo Books.

BROADY, MAURICE (ed.) (1973). *Marginal Regions: Essays on Social Planning.* London: Bedford Square Press.

BRODY, HUGH (1974). *Inishkillane.* New York: Schocken Books.

BYRON, REGINALD (1986). *Sea Change: A Shetland Society, 1970–1979.* St John's: Institute of Social and Economic Research, Memorial University.

CARRIER, JAMES G. (1992). 'Occidentalism: The World Turned Upside-Down', *American Ethnologist*, 19: 195–212.

CHAKRABARTY, DIPESH (1992). 'The Death of History? Historical Consciousness and the Culture of Late Capitalism', *Public Culture*, 4/2: 47–66.

CHAPMAN, MALCOLM (1978). *The Gaelic Vision in Scottish Culture.* London: Croom Helm.

CLIFFORD, JAMES (1986). 'Introduction: Partial Truths', in J. Clifford and George Marcus (eds.), *Writing Culture: The Poetics and Politics of Culture.* Berkeley, Calif.: University of California Press: 1–26.

COHEN, ANTHONY P. (ed.) (1982). *Belonging: Identity and Social Organisation in British Rural Cultures.* Manchester: Manchester University Press.

——(1985). *The Symbolic Construction of Community.* Chichester: Ellis Horwood.

——(1987). *Walsay: Symbol, Segment and Boundary in a Shetland Island Community.* Manchester: Manchester University Press.

CRICHTON, RUTH (1964). *Commuters' Village.* London: David & Charles.

ENNEW, JUDITH (1980). *The Western Isles Today.* Cambridge: Cambridge University Press.

EUROPEAN COMMUNITIES (1992). *A People's Europe.* European File Series. Luxembourg: Office for Official Publications of the European Communities.

FABIAN, JOHANNES (1983). *Time and the Other: How Anthropology Makes its Object.* New York: Columbia University Press.

FARDON, RICHARD (ed.) (1990). *Localizing Strategies: Regional Traditions of Ethnographic Writing.* Edinburgh: Scottish Academic Press.

FORSYTHE, DIANA (1984). 'The Social Effects of Primary School Closure', in Tony Bradley and Philip Lowe (eds.), *Locality and Rurality: Economy and Society in Rural Regions.* Norwich: Geo Books: 209–24.

FOX, ROBIN (1978). *The Tory Islanders: A People of the Celtic Fringe.* New York: Cambridge University Press.

FRANKENBERG, RONALD (1969). *Communities in Britain: Social Life in Town and Country.* Harmondsworth: Penguin.

GIBSON, W. J. (1946). 'The Village in the Outer Isles of Scotland', *Sociological Review*, 38: 247–69.

GILDER, IAN (1984). 'State Planning and Local Needs', in Tony Bradley and Philip Lowe (eds.), *Locality and Rurality: Economy and Society in Rural Regions.* Norwich: Geo Books: 243–57.

GINSBURG, FAYE (1991). 'Indigenous Media: Faustian Contract or Global Village?' *Cultural Anthropology*, 6: 92–112.

GUPTA, AKHIL, and FERGUSON, JAMES (1992). 'Beyond "Culture": Space, Identity, and the Politics of Difference', *Cultural Anthropology*, 7: 6–23.

HECHTER, MICHAEL (1974). *Internal Colonialism: The Celtic Fringe in British National Development, 1536–1966.* London: Routledge & Kegan Paul.

HEGEMAN, SUSAN (1991). 'Shopping for Identities: "A Nation of Nations" and the Weak Ethnicity of Objects', *Public Culture*, 3: 71–92.

HERZFELD, MICHAEL (1987). *Anthropology through the Looking Glass: Critical Ethnography in the Margins of Europe.* Cambridge: Cambridge University Press.

——(1991). *A Place in History: Social and Monumental Time in a Cretan Town.* Princeton, NJ: Princeton University Press.

HEWISON, ROBERT (1987). *The Heritage Industry: Britain in a Climate of Decline.* London: Methuen.

HILL, REGINALD (1988). *Underworld.* New York: Warner Books.

HUNTER, ALAN (1959). *Gently in the Sun.* New York: Berkeley Medallion.

HURWITZ, JANE (Nadel-Klein) (1967). 'Puttenham, an English Country Village', senior thesis (Barnard College).

JACKSON, ANTHONY (ed.) (1987). *Anthropology at Home.* ASA Monograph 25. London: Tavistock.

KUKLICK, HENRIETTA (1984). 'Tribal Exemplars: Images of Political Authority in British Anthropology, 1885–1945', in George Stocking (ed.), *Functionalism Historicized: Essays on British Social Anthropology.* Madison, Wis.: University of Wisconsin Press: 59–82.

KUPER, ADAM (1988). *The Invention of Primitive Society.* London: Routledge.

LASLETT, PETER (1984). *The World We Have Lost: Further Explored.* New York: Charles Scribner's Sons.

LEBOW, RICHARD NED (1976). *White Britain and Black Ireland: The Influence of Stereotypes on Colonial Policy.* Philadelphia: Institute for the Study of Human Issues.

LITTLEJOHN, JAMES (1963). *Westrigg: The Sociology of a Cheviot Border Parish.* London: Routledge & Kegan Paul.

McGRANE, BERNARD (1989). *Beyond Anthropology: Society and the Other.* New York: Columbia University Press.

MARCUS, GEORGE E., and CUSHMAN, DICK (1982). 'Ethnographies as Text', *Annual Review of Anthropology*, 11: 25–69.

——and FISCHER, MICHAEL M. J. (1986). *Anthropology as Cultural Critique.* Chicago: University of Chicago Press.

NADEL, JANE (1983). 'Houston's Little Sisters: A Cross-Cultural Perspective on Offshore Oil', *Human Organization*, 42: 162–7.

——(1984). 'Stigma and Separation: Pariah Status and Community Persistence in a Scottish Fishing Village', *Ethnology*, 23: 101–15.

——(1986). 'Burning with the Fire of God: Calvinism and Community in a Scottish Fishing Village', *Ethnology*, 25: 49–60.

NADEL-KLEIN, JANE (1991). 'Reweaving the Fringe: Localism, Tradition and Representation in British Ethnography', *American Ethnologist*, 18: 500–17.

NAIRN, TOM (1977). *The Break-up of Britain: Crisis and Neo-nationalism.* London: New Left Books.

NALSON, JOHN S. (1982). 'Quiet Revolution in Traditional Society', in Ronald Frankenberg (ed.), *Custom and Conflict in British Society*. Manchester: Manchester University Press: 70–93.

NEWBY, HOWARD (1979). *Social Change in Rural England*. Madison, Wis.: University of Wisconsin Press.

PARMAN, SUSAN (1990). *Scottish Crofters: A Historical Ethnography of a Celtic Village*. Fort Worth: Holt, Rinehart & Winston.

PYRAMID BOOKS AND THE NEW AGE COLLECTION (1992). Untitled catalogue. Chelmsford, Mass.

REDFIELD, ROBERT (1953). *The Primitive World and its Transformations*. Ithaca, NY: Cornell University Press.

REES, ALWYN (1950). *Life in a Welsh Countryside*. Cardiff: University of Wales Press.

ROBINSON, PETER (1988). *A Dedicated Man*. New York: Avon Books.

RODMAN, MARGARET (1992). 'Empowering Place: Multilocality and Multivocality', *American Anthropologist*, 94: 640–56.

SAID, EDWARD (1978). *Orientalism*. New York: Vintage Books.

SAMUEL, RAPHAEL (ed.) (1975). *Village Life and Labour*. London: Routledge & Kegan Paul.

SAYERS, DOROTHY (1932). *Have his Carcase*. New York: Harper & Row.

STEEL, TOM (1975). *The Life and Death of St. Kilda*. London [?]: Fontana Collins.

STRATHERN, MARILYN (1984). 'The Social Meaning of Localism', in Tony Bradley and Philip Lowe (eds.), *Rurality and Society: Economy and Society in Rural Regions*. Norwich: Geo Books: 181–98.

——(1987). 'The Limits of Auto-anthropology', in Anthony Jackson (ed.), *Anthropology at Home*. ASA Monograph 25. London: Tavistock: 16–37.

TEY, JOSEPHINE (1953). *The Singing Sands*. New York: Macmillan.

THOMAS, NICHOLAS (1992). 'The Inversion of Tradition', *American Ethnologist*, 19: 213–32.

URRY, JAMES (1990). *The Tourist Gaze*. London: Sage.

WADE, HENRY (1985 [1933]). *Mist on the Saltings*. New York: Perennial Library; Harper & Row.

WILLIAMS, RAYMOND (1973). *The Country and the City*. New York: Oxford University Press.

WILLIAMS, W. M. (1956). *The Sociology of an English Village: Gosforth*. London: Routledge & Kegan Paul.

——(1963). *A West Country Village: Ashworthy*. London: Routledge & Kegan Paul.

——(1974). 'Dynamic Equilibrium in Ashworthy', in Colin Bell and Howard Newby (eds.), *The Sociology of Community*. London: Frank Cass & Co.: 64–8.

WILSON, EDMUND (1944). 'Why do People Read Detective Stories?' *New Yorker* (14 Oct.): 73–5.

——(1945). 'Who Cares Who Killed Roger Ackroyd? A Second Report on Detective Fiction', *New Yorker* (20 Jan.): 52–8.

WINKS, ROBIN (1977). 'Sinister Orientals: Everybody's Favorite Villains', in Dilys Winn (ed.), *Murder, Ink: The Mystery Reader's Companion*. New York: Workman Publishing: 491–3.

WOLFE, PATRICK (1991). 'On Being Woken up: The Dreamtime in Anthropology and in Australian Settler Culture', *Comparative Studies in Society and History*, 33: 197–224.

WRIGHT, PATRICK (1985). *On Living in an Old Country: The National Past in Contemporary Britain*. London: Verso.

YORKE, MARGARET (1977). 'St. Mary Mead and Other Troubled Villages', in Dilys Winn (ed.), *Murder, Ink: The Mystery Reader's Companion*. New York: Workman Publishing: 258–60.

5

Imaging the Other in Japanese Advertising Campaigns

Millie R. Creighton

Against a white misty background a white woman stands in a rounded doorway; her long blondish-white hair is drawn to one side thus half circling her head in curls. A white cloth is draped around her body from the waist down. Naked from the waist up, her arms lie across her breasts thus concealing the nipples, while still revealing the majority of breasts and skin. This was the focal image of an ad prominently displayed inside Tokyo commuter trains, on the walls of major transit stations, and on poster boards lining the streets of shopping districts throughout the summer of 1990. The advertisement was for a Japanese wedding hall 'marriage', whose English name was written in the *katakana* syllabary, commonly used in Japanese to designate words of foreign origin.[1] The visual imagery attempted to capture the viewer's attention and promote a special feeling. The informative content was minimal. The brief message, 'Dramatic Wedding: *Ai no Uedingu Suteeji*' ('Dramatic Wedding: Love's Wedding Stage'), appeared in a combination of English and Japanese. The ad was directed not at foreigners but at Japanese, since wedding services as a commercial industry are directed primarily at young Japanese about to marry, and their parents who are usually involved in arranging and financing weddings. This advertisement was not particularly *medatsu*, or 'eye-catching', since such advertising imagery featuring foreigners, or more precisely Caucasians, is prevalent in Japan.

The prevalent use of foreigners, particularly white foreigners, or *gaijin*, in Japanese advertising, the nature and functions of these depictions, can all provide insights to the representation and perpetuation of otherness in Japanese society. These issues are particularly important, given that for over a decade now Japan, which constructs identity around an assertion of homogeneity, has designated *kokusaika*, 'internationalization', as a primary national goal. Although a buzz word of the 1980s and 1990s, internationalization is a somewhat paradoxical goal for a nation that in certain periods of its history insulated itself from outside influences, and which asserts strong cognitive boundaries between those who belong to the category of 'we Japanese' and those who do not. Noting the contradictions involved, one journalist went so far as to claim that internationalization was in actuality 'an anti-Japanese activity' (LaBrack 1983). The Japanese government promotes internationalization in part because it recognizes that Japan has risen to the ranks of Western international powers, and as a result must take on responsibilities consistent with its new world prominence. Internationalization can also serve to placate pressures from Western governments to reduce trade barriers or further open Japanese society to outsiders. The prevalent representations of *gaijin* and other foreign imagery often create the impression that Japan is fully open to outsiders, when in reality barriers to either trade or full participation of foreigners in Japanese life remain strong. Advertisers have their own profit motive for parading representations of *gaijin*. They recognize (and attempt to reinforce) a popular interest in foreigners as outsiders, and are also able to capitalize on the use of foreigners to contrast with Japanese images of themselves.

In a semiotic analysis of American advertising images, Judith Williamson claims that ads 'are selling us something else beside consumer goods: in providing us with a structure in which we, and those goods, are interchangeable they are selling us ourselves' (Williamson 1978: 13). I also suggest that advertising images, in providing representations of 'not us', help to create and sell otherness. This construction and representation of the other is not separate from the construction of self-identity, since the creation of self-identity often involves locating or imagining a contrasting other to highlight the distinguishing characteristics believed to define the self. Japanese national identity has long been affirmed through the contrast between 'ware ware Nihonjin' (We Japanese) and 'yosomono' (outsiders). As Roy Andrew Miller (1977: 77) points out, '[a]ny facet of Japanese life or culture is thrown into sharp relief when it is brought into direct confrontation with a similar or parallel foreign phenomenon'. The prevalence of both foreign places and foreign faces in Japanese advertising functions to delimit Japanese identity by visual quotations of what Japan and Japanese are not.

There has been a long history in Western academic and popular thought regarding the construction of the Orient as other, but, as Jane Desmond (1991: 150) has pointed out, 'this process is a two-way exchange'. For quite some time, Japan has also been constructing an occidentalist other in the form of the white Westerner. This occidentalist construction is reflected in the actual usage of the word *gaijin*. The word, literally meaning 'outside person', is most frequently translated as 'foreigner', but is commonly used only in reference to whites, who are assumed to be Westerners. A relevant linguistic code distinction occurs between the Japanese words *gaijin* and *gaikokujin* (Manabe, Befu, and McConnell 1989: 40). Blacks and non-Japanese Asians are conceptualized differently and, in recognition of the fact that they come from foreign countries, may be referred to as *gaikokujin* (person from an outside country) but are seldom called *gaijin* since, as I said, this word suggests someone white. Certain groups, such as people of Korean descent who are legal residents of Japan, are none the less conceptualized as 'outside people' even if they are not from other countries. The designation *zainichi kankokujin* (Korean residents of Japan) is commonly used.[2]

The social construction of *gaijin* denies the individual uniqueness of Westerners, transforming all Caucasians into an essentialized category that reduces the complex variations among them. Just as Western orientalisms created self-occidentalisms through an implied contrast with a simplified West, Japanese renderings of *gaijin* are occidentalisms that stand opposed to Japanese orientalisms about themselves. Representations of the *gaijin* other create and highlight contrasting statements about the specialness of being Japanese. Among the essentialized self-orientalisms created are Japanese assertions of uniqueness and cultural homogeneity.

Representations of *gaijin* in Japanese advertisements frequently contrast with representations of Japanese. *Gaijin* are much more likely to be shown with free body posturing, or with hair and clothes in total disarray. *Gaijin* are often shown overtly breaking the conventional rules of Japanese society, or as individuals who struggle incompetently with the habits and customs of Japanese life. Nude representations of *gaijin*, particularly naked shots of the upper bodies of both men and women, are common in advertisements for products and services where naked depictions of Japanese would be considered inappropriate. It is true that naked images of Japanese, particularly Japanese women, do appear on late-night television broadcasts defined as erotic viewing, in *manga* ('comic books'), and in ads for products directly or indirectly defined as part of the sex trade. However, nude depictions of Japanese for everyday, mainstream products and businesses are not common, whereas nude depictions of *gaijin* for these are not unusual. Although this discussion focuses on the representations of *gaijin* in Japanese advertising, there are similarities with the ways *gaijin* are represented in other circumstances, such as in newspapers and Japanese-made television programmes. In these cases, as well, *gaijin* are used to

I hear Kate talking to the nurse in the corridor. "Damn reporters are still camped out in front of the building," she says. "I wish they'd leave us alone."

I know what a nurse is, and what reporters are. General concepts are easy. I can recite the periodic table of elements and list each year the Red Sox won the World Series in the twentieth century. Some of the time useless trivia is easy, too. But I have no idea why the reporters are out there. I don't remember my life.

Kate walks into the room and smiles at me. "Is today a good day?" she asks.

The fog lifts a little bit, enough for me to remember that this is our ritual. The doctor said there would be a lot of bad days, but occasionally there would be good days, too. I remember this, but not much else. I shake my head.

Kate frowns and sits down by the bed. She takes my hand into hers. I ask her about the nametag in the photograph.

"That's you, Mom, in front of the *Icarus,* on the day you left for your mission. It says 'Anne Freeman, Captain.'"

Kate reaches into the drawer and takes out a small attaché case, its brown leather stiffened with age and cracking in several spots. She rummages through it and takes out a round plastic disc the size of a coaster. She places it atop the nightstand and presses a small button on its side. A hologram of a ship moving through space springs to life. The ship looks like a drop of quicksilver.

"This is the *Icarus,*" Kate says. "You were part of the team that designed it, and then you piloted it to the stars."

The fog in my mind is thick as ever. I don't recall any of this, but I know the Icarus of Greek myth. "Why would anyone name their ship after a man who crashed?"

"It's because he flew near the sun. Watch."

In the hologram, the quicksilver ship is flying directly into the sun. When it gets close enough for the giant fiery orb to blot out the sky, it releases red shimmering wings. They blossom outward, growing many times larger than the ship itself.

elicit exoticism, while they are at the same time portrayed as breaking Japanese conventions or humorously inept at Japanese life.

Many questions arise regarding the contemporary depiction of foreigners, the non-Japanese other, in modern Japanese advertising. First, why are such *gaijin* ads so prevalent? Are images of foreigners used to fulfil any calculated functions? Do such ads reflect social attitudes and roles? What differences are revealed in attitudes towards different types of foreigners? These are some of the questions I will attempt to address. Although representations of blacks and non-Japanese Asians will be touched on, the focus of this discussion will be representations of whites, those conceptualized as 'true' *gaijin*, for it is renderings of whites as *gaijin* which most represent the occident in this context.

Symbolism, fantasy, and foreigners in advertisements

Rather than emphasizing information about products, Japanese advertisements have an essentially symbolic nature, which renders them particularly interesting anthropologically. Because of their symbolic focus, these advertisements provide a fruitful means of getting at the characterization of *gaijin* in Japanese society. Depictions of foreigners fit into Japanese advertising images of 'fantasy excursions'. These generally contain minimal informative content, but instead present pleasant imagery and possibilities for playful excursion into a fantasy world. Representations of foreigners become just another series of intriguing image quotations and in the process the occident is brought under control while foreigners are rendered not really real—at least as individual people.

It is important to recognize that advertisements have a problematic relationship to what people think in that they are messages sent rather than lessons learned or common thoughts expressed. The renderings of *gaijin* discussed here are representations created by Japanese advertisers, not the products of a reified Japanese culture. This analysis concentrates on the images of *gaijin* in ads, and reflections on those images provided by the image-makers; it does not assert that all Japanese respond to these advertisements as the image-makers expect. However, the images are intentional representations designed to make people buy, projected by people with a well-developed understanding of what is likely to prompt members of that culture toward purchasing. All the advertising agencies discussed here, some of which are now the world's largest, devote extensive research efforts to studying how Japanese consumers respond to their images. For this reason, it seems appropriate to suggest that advertisers' explanations of how *gaijin* imagery is perceived are derived from studies of Japanese consumers as the image-receivers. Japanese advertisements, like the advertising catalogues analysed by James Carrier (1990: 702), are 'collections of images that professional image-makers have found to appeal to people'.

Japanese advertising has been characterized as mood advertising. It does not try to explain very much about what is being sold, or position products as superior to their competitors. Instead, it attempts to communicate a special mood or elicit emotional feelings. Advertising that focuses on images rather than informational content is, of course, not unique to Japan. Such advertising occurs, for example, in North America particularly when competing products are essentially the same. However, mood advertising is much more abundant in Japan. Additionally, although some informative and even competitive advertisements appear, they do so much less frequently than in North America. Although there are commercial and economic reasons for mood or image advertising, two explanations, stemming from Japanese cultural predispositions, also help account for it. Advertising is a means of competition, and competition is directly in conflict with espoused Japanese social values. Everyone and everything is supposed to strive continually for a harmonious, co-operative existence. I do not mean to suggest that competition is lacking in Japan; extreme competition does exist, just as conflict exists despite the espoused value given to harmony. However, competition tends to be channelled and open expressions of competition tend to be treated negatively. Advertisers are therefore left in an enigmatic position; they must compete without appearing to be overtly competitive. In particular, comparative advertisements, stressing the virtues of one product over another, tend to be received as overtly competitive and therefore inappropriate.

Another problem is posed by cultural expectations for humility—or, at least, outward expressions of humility. In a society where social etiquette expects that guests are offered painstakingly prepared foods with set self-effacing expressions such as, 'this might not suit your palate, but please eat it anyway' ('okuchi ni awanai ka mo shiremasen ga meshiagatte kudasai'), advertisements that extol the virtues of items being sold, or that even provide extensive information about them, violate expectations for formalized humility. Expectations of humbleness extend to the relationship between sellers and buyers. One advertising chief expressed the view that ads should not appear to make authoritative statements about products, but instead appear to acquiesce to the discerning intelligence of buyers. As he explains:

We never do any competition ads, those claiming that this product is better than that one. We never do them, absolutely never. It's partly because Japanese values frown on that sort of open display of competitiveness. But it's more than that really. The message we want to give customers is that they are the ones in control, they are the ones with discerning good taste and intelligent sensibilities. We're not telling them what to do.

In addition, consumer scepticism about informative ads renders mood advertising economically a more rational way of encouraging people to buy. This possibility first occurred to me on an earlier research stay in Japan, while I was talking to a group of eight Japanese housewives gathered at my Tokyo landlady's home for friendly conversation and a mid-morning snack of rice crackers and green tea. When I asked them whether they would be induced to buy a product whose merits were described in an ad, they all agreed that this would not be a good basis upon which to purchase something. As one woman expressed it, '[i]t is only natural for the sellers to present their own products in a good or favourable light. But how can you believe from their own words that it is really the best product?' With such scepticism regarding the supposedly objective data provided by comparative advertisements and 'informmercials', ads that instead evoke a pleasant mood or create interesting associations achieve greater success.

Fantasy vignettes and startling or impressive visual parades, seemingly divorced from any logical association with the product being sold, are characteristics of the Japanese commercial advertising industry. At the heart of Japanese mood advertising is what has been designated as the 'no meaning ad'. This concept has become such a prominent focus of Japanese advertising that the entire phrase was adopted from English, and is often written in the *katakana* syllabary as 'nō miiningu ado'. The 'no meaning ad' was frequently brought up by people I interviewed in the advertising industry as a partial explanation for the prevalence of foreigners and foreign scenes in Japanese commercials. For example, a creative director from the Osaka branch of Dentsu,[3] Japan's—and the world's—largest advertising agency, states:

To explain the abundance of foreigners in Japanese ads, well . . . American commercials, for example, are very 'realistic'. Japanese commercials and ads are not really trying to be realistic like Western ones; instead they are more image-provoking. Since the goal is just to create a nice or different feeling it does not seem strange to have so many foreigners. It is all part of the advertisements' goal to build a dream world [*yume no sekai*]. The products aren't so different, or at least they don't seem so different to Japanese consumers. So in order to capture the market you need to create a different image, a better fantasy feeling.

The sentiment that foreigners are aptly used to further this goal of creating fantasy moods is reiterated by a section head of the Osaka Yomiuri Advertising Company (Osaka Yomiuri Kōkokusha), who says:

My idea is that Japanese ads are not so realistic. Unlike typical ads in America, they are not there to give information or to depict everyday life. Instead ads create a mood. Something is wanted to help create that mood, or a fantasy feeling. Pictures of foreigners and foreign places help create this.

She went on to state that images of foreigners in advertisements also detracted from the feeling that 'it is just us trying to sell things to us'.

Looking at it from the perspective of someone who makes ads, there is also an attempt to get around certain feelings of Japanese people. . . . One reason for using *gaijin* is that it helps to reduce the sense of its being 'commercial business'. There is in one sense sort of a contempt for commercial advertising that involves the feeling that companies are trying to make 'us' buy products. That is why mood advertising is so important. If there are only Japanese in the ads, it just feels like 'us' trying to make 'us' buy things. Using *gaijin* reduces this feeling somewhat.

Her words provided further support for the idea that using foreigners in advertisements helps minimize the overtly competitive nature of advertising, while also contributing to Japanese occidentalisms by reinforcing a clear distinction between the Japanese as 'us' and *gaijin* as other.

Gaijin *as bearers of innovation and style*

Throughout Japanese cultural history foreigners have been accorded a dual nature. They are considered both as the bearers of highly valued innovation and style, and as moral threat. Emiko Ohnuki-Tierney argues that because foreigners are equated with the outside they are structurally equivalent to deities from whom both blessings and destruction flow. She writes, 'there has been a tendency to equate foreigners with deities, therefore often assigning to foreigners dual—both beneficial and destructive— natures and power' (Ohnuki-Tierney 1987: 145). For centuries Japan looked to China for this role, adopting many Chinese cultural institutions and aspects of material culture. However, from the Meiji Era (1868– 1912) on, the role of strangers/outsiders shifted to white Westerners, transforming the Chinese along with other Asians into marginals who were neither insiders nor outsiders (Ohnuki-Tierney 1987: 147).

Historical, political, and economic processes enveloping Japan prompted this shift by which white Westerners became the primary other in relationship to whom the Japanese dialectically define self. The Japanese began introducing Western material goods and ideas in the mid-sixteenth century. Then, feeling threatened by this outside influence, the governing political leaders imposed a policy of seclusion which closed Japan to the outside world for two and a half centuries, until Western powers forced Japan's reopening. The Meiji Era, the first after Japan's reopening to the outside world, was characterized by intense curiosity about the West combined with a strong consciousness of Western power, technological expertise, and economic dominance. Thus, from the beginning of Japan's modern history the white Western world became the model to emulate; it represented a standard by which to gauge Japan's progress and modernization. As a result of these processes the modern Japanese occidentalism of the *gaijin* is directed at white Westerners, not just any alien groups. The impact of these economic, political, and historical processes is recognized by many within the modern advertising industry, as reflected in these comments from a creative director at Dentsu regarding the imagery of white Westerners.

Another reason for the abundance of *gaijin* is that for a long part of Japanese history, from Meiji at least, we have always been looking at Western countries as progressive ones. These were places that Japan had to catch up with. From this there developed sort of a complex—'it's a white world'.

In addition to being a referent for progress, whites came to be considered a standard of beauty, particularly with the shift from kimono for everyday wear to *yōfuku* or 'Western-style clothing'. Several informants declared that Japanese people tended to accept the idea that Western-style clothing, because it originated abroad, would naturally be better suited to Western body types. Therefore it was in keeping with popular expectations for fashion and beauty products to portray foreigners in these ads. A male Japanese scholar who is now researching Japanese concepts of self and other referred to white women as standards of beauty to explain the prevalence of foreign imagery in advertisements.

European and American are the main *gaijin* used; Asians are not represented very much. Both men and women appear, but women are much more beautiful than men, who are not so important. From long ago there has been an image of European women as glamorous and beautiful.

Another male Japanese researcher expressed similar sentiments with an unsolicited amount of detail:

Particularly looking at European women from way back there has long been the idea that they are more stylish. This doesn't apply so much to men. It's very closely tied to the whole idea of fashion and that's what lots of ads are for, women's fashions. There are certain traits associated with European women such as differences in body type from Japanese women. A nicer hip shape for example, the hip is fuller and lifts up, not small or tucked in. European women have longer legs and a larger torso compared to Japanese women. So because of these things, whites are considered more stylish. Whether it is true or just an illusion I don't know, but this is the Japanese belief.

Although there was general agreement that *gaijin* have long been considered bearers of style and beauty, there may be gender bias in these two researchers' insistence that this only applies to foreign women. For example, in contrast to the two males quoted above, a female researcher concurs that white Westerners are accepted as more attractive models for Western clothing, but does not believe the emphasis is all on white women. She states: 'Fashion is a big part of the reason there are so many foreigners. For example, in men's wear. Japanese don't suit foreign goods and styles as much. We don't think those Japanese men look good in Western clothing.'

If white Westerners have become a standard since Meiji, the popular culture of post-war Japan served to reinforce this. As expressed by the president of one consulting firm, 'Post-war Japanese history is the history of Americanization.' The American occupation of Japan brought American popular and consumer culture to Japan. This persisted after the occupation ended because of continuing international economic and political dominance of the United States. The early post-war period in Japan brought with it a craze for movies—predominantly American-made movies—creating the feeling that foreign portrayals in such media were 'natural'. Television was established as a regular household furnishing during the 1950s, which coincided with the American occupation. Shows were either dubbed or side-titled American productions, or copies of such models. Again, this reinforced the feeling that it was only *atarimae*, or 'natural', to see representations of whites on the screen.

The Tokyo Olympics held in the 1960s marked a new age for Japan, representing the emergence from extreme post-war poverty into a more focal international role. The Tokyo Olympics thus had a significant impact on Japanese society, and they further perpetuated the acceptance of foreign images on the screen. The Tokyo Olympics also brought large numbers of foreign visitors to Japan. A *ramen* shop erected across from Yoyogi Park, home of the 1964 Tokyo Olympics, which still remains, reveals the extent of exoticism surrounding occidentals at that time. The lit awning of the noodle shop advertises in Japanese, 'gaijinsan mo, tabe ni kuru', '*Gaijin* come to eat here too'. The phrase was meant to attract Japanese, not foreigners, given the widespread assumption at that time that most foreigners could not read Japanese.

While pointing out one aspect to the dual nature of *gaijin*, their role as bearers of innovation, style, and value, these examples also reveal the occidentalism of the Japanese, an occidentalism that arose in response to specific historical, political, and economic processes. As Western—and in the case of twentieth-century Japan, more specifically American—influence dominated the international scene, American material and popular culture began to permeate Japanese society. *Gaijin* became not all or any foreigners, but an essentialized projection of white Westerners. Japanese occidentalism exoticized *gaijin*, enhancing the appeal of advertisements that imaged or even referred to these strange but attractive alien beings. In ways parallel to Western orientalism, Japanese occidentalism also involved a sexual projection of the other, particularly the allure of the occidental woman. However, as a response to the increasing impact of Western culture on Japan, Japanese occidentalism involved more than attraction to and exoticization of the Western other. The creation of *gaijin* as a social construction of Japanese occidentalism also mirrored a need to assert control over the moral threat of an intruding outside world.

Gaijin *as moral threat*

In explaining the prevalence of *gaijin* ads in Japan, marketing analyst George Fields (1983: 117) claims that foreigners are aliens who represent the 'E.T.s of Japanese advertising'. Such ads confront the fear of the foreign invader, transforming foreigners into 'tamed' beings who are kept in place by Japanese brands. Thus, 'the "ugly" unknowns are [rendered] extremely loveable, like household pets' (Fields 1983: 118). This interpretation relates to the second aspect of the dual role of *gaijin* in Japan—that of moral threat. According to Japanese occidentalisms, Western culture embodies egoism and individualism, attributes which contravene essential Japanese values. Even the sexuality allowed to *gaijin* can be seen as a projection of individual self-indulgence and sensuality. The cultural denial of egoism and individualism in Japan makes the West attractive precisely because of these traits, yet also marks the West as a primary threat to 'Japaneseness'. Core attributes of this self-orientalism include discipline, order, meekness, responsibility, and submission to group goals (Moeran 1984: 253, 259). Advertisers use these associations with the West to evade Japanese cultural values, thus allowing portrayals and statements that might not otherwise be acceptable. At some point, however, the use of *gaijin* imagery also involves taming the foreigner as moral threat, and a corresponding assertion of the superior value of Japaneseness.

In other words, *gaijin* images are used not only to provide a fantasy mood or simply because this has become the established custom, but because foreigners can be used to break social conventions more readily than Japanese. Where, in order to 'really say it', Peter, Paul, and Mary, American folk singers popular in the 1960s and 1970s, had to 'lay it between the lines', the Japanese advertiser may have to resort to using foreigners. *Gaijin* can do, say, and depict what a Japanese might wish to, but social values militate against. For example, in a society with extensive concepts of classificatory status (Lebra 1976) involving expectations for appropriate forms of dress depending on gender, age, and social rank, red has traditionally been considered an appropriate colour for little girls but too bright and conspicuous for adult women. Although a Japanese model in a bright red outfit might still spark disapproval, *gaijin* women are frequently presented in red dresses with flair and defiance.

Gaijin are a pragmatic tool consciously utilized by the advertising industry to portray images of romance, in evasion of a long-standing cultural expectation of public restraint in such matters. According to a creative director for Dentsu:

There are a lot of love scenes in ads—like kissing. In Japan for a long time there is an idea that kissing, even holding hands, is something that people shouldn't do in public. But having *gaijin* kiss is one way to portray romance, and it's o.k., because, after all, they are *gaijin*.

In a similar vein, many companies find it safer to portray nudity using foreigners, particularly when criticism might negatively affect a brand image. Commenting on the common usage of naked or near-naked *gaijin* women in advertisements, the librarian of Osaka Dentsu's advertising library says, 'ads can't use Japanese women for such nude scenes because it is too realistic, so *gaijin* are used'. There are many references to the bare-breasted women depicted in orientalism—perhaps modern Japanese advertising reflects the reverse trend, and indeed occasionally seems to be the orient's revenge. The retailing chain Parco featured a full frontal view of a Caucasian woman standing naked in one of their theme ads. Unlike the wedding advertisement described earlier, there was no attempt to cover or mask her nudity in any way. Images of naked Japanese women may be viewed, as I said, on late-night 'adult' television programmes in Japan where there is an intended and often pornographic purpose. However, one does not see an open, nude presentation of Japanese women to advertise 'respectable' brand-name products or a major department store. Such an advertisement would be as controversial in Japan as a fully naked women advertising a mainstream family department store would be in the West. Although I have mentioned naked depictions of *gaijin* women, the male *gaijin* body is similarly used to image sensuality. One example is the Zephyr lotion commercial highlighting the heavily muscled and sweat-glistening torso of a white male viewed from below the navel to the neck (Abe and Yamakawa 1990: 166).

Foreigners often provide a safer mechanism for expressing selfish sentiments in a culture which has long frowned on *wagamama*, or self-centred concerns. Related to this is the prevalent use of the English word 'my' in advertising and product names rather than the Japanese equivalents *watakushi no*, *watashi no*, or *boku no*. Ads and product labels commonly refer to 'my jeans', 'my car', 'my home', 'my peanut butter', and even—as I recently saw in a small town in Shikoku—'my toilet paper'. Kalman Applbaum contends that the proliferation of the English 'my' reflects increased exposure to Western values that are 'in marked contrast with the earlier generation's critical attitude towards individualism' (Applbaum 1992: 24). Although increasing exposure to Western individualism is related to the prevalent use of 'my', I would disagree with Applbaum's analysis somewhat, suggesting instead that what is most important is the code-switching from Japanese into English to make such individualistic assertions. Using the English possessive 'my' creates the feeling that this self-centred assertion is less 'really real' than use of the equivalent Japanese *watashi no* would. By switching to the English 'my', egoism and individualism persist as occidentalist projections, while the Japanese core of conformity, collectivism, and self-abnegation remains unblemished. In September 1990, the autumn theme poster for My City, a large retailing complex (and itself another example of the prevalent retailing use of the English 'my') in the central Shinjuku district of Tokyo, did use the Japanese word *watashi*. However, in this rare case the assertion of self-desire was seemingly made by the female *gaijin* depicted. This woman, with long reddish-blond wavy hair, was shown wearing a brown sweater, plaid pants, and a rust-tones shawl, to kick off My City's autumn campaign. The accompanying ad captions read, in a combination of *kanji*, *hiragana*, and roman letters:

aki iro.	shizen iro.	watashi iro.
[autumn colours.	natural colours.	my colours.]

Affectionate Colors
My City

An advertising campaign for the fast-food chain Lotteria featured a foreign woman to promote the introduction of their new *Kaisaa Sando* (Kaiser Sandwich). One Japanese customer noted that it was more important for fast-food outlets such as this, which she believed to be a Japanese version of the Wendy's or McDonald's type of hamburger shops imported from the States, to feature *gaijin* in order to create a foreign image than it is for what she called the 'real' Western fast-food chains. In actuality Lotteria is a Korean-based company, and given the problematic positioning of 'Koreanness', to be discussed below, it was perhaps even more essential for Lotteria to make such associations.[4] In Lotteria's Kaiser Sandwich promotion, the fuzzy image of a Caucasian woman was shown carrying a large bouquet, accompanied by a statement normally too *wagamama* (self-centred) for Japanese tastes. The *gaijin* woman exclaims in the ad, '*Suki na mono shika, tabetakunai,*' 'I don't want to eat anything that I don't like.' A Japanese person may frequently desire to express such sentiments, but Japanese values define such an assertion as overtly egoistic, ungrateful, and immature. To show how negative such a statement might be if made by a Japanese, I draw on Dorinne Kondo's account of a Japanese ethics retreat in which she participated and learned the expected cultural attitude toward food. She writes:

Even our food held a lesson for us. . . . Cleaning our plates, even if we didn't like what was served, would prevent selfishness and lead to a grateful, gentle heart. Giving in to likes and dislikes, on the other hand, was the beginning of selfish, egocentric behavior. (Kondo 1990: 91–2)

Advertisements and commercials featuring foreigners are commonly divided into two categories, 'talents' and 'anonymous' depictions. The adopted, and transformed, English word 'tarento' (talent) really indicates that the *gaijin* involved is famous. As in the use of *gaijin* imagery generally, 'talents' are frequently used to break with Japanese conventions, including linguistic ones. In the 1980s a kimono-clad, calligraphy-brush-wielding Woody Allen was featured in Seibu Department Store's 'Delicious Life' (*oishii seikatsu*) campaign (see Nishioka 1989: 131). 'Delicious Life' combines two words not normally put together in Japanese to break with conventional language use, providing an interesting, catchy idea

"Nano filaments," Kate says. "They capture the heat; enough energy to power an interstellar jump. Your team at MIT designed this, right around the time I was born."

We watch in silence as the ethereal wings turn from red to bright orange and begin to disintegrate while the drop of quicksilver is being pulled toward the sun. Then a perfect circle of pitch black opens directly in the path of the drop. It blocks off a small part of the fiery inferno below, like a miniature eclipse. The ship falls through and disappears, the circle collapsing in on itself behind it.

"This is the recording of the *Icarus's* maiden voyage. There isn't a man, woman, or child on Earth who doesn't know what you have accomplished."

There is at least one woman who doesn't. But the pride in Kate's voice makes me keep the observation to myself.

⸻⬦⬦⸻

Today is one of the good days. The fog isn't quite so dense. As I wait for Kate, I reach for the drawer and take out the attaché case.

This is my Keepsake Box. It's full of memories. Mementos accumulated throughout the course of my life. Kate says it's important that I go over the objects in the Keepsake Box daily. This is supposed to keep me anchored a little longer.

I touch the surface of a pink-and-pearl stone, its edges smoothed out by a millennia of currents. It's from the beach on Arcturus VI. My hand shakes as it caresses a handful of exotic-looking pebbles scattered throughout the attaché case. One for every planet I visited.

There are other treasures inside as well. An impression of a tiny foot taken on the day Kate was born. My Valedictorian medal from college. A yellowed flyer from my high school play. A Mickey Mouse watch my parents gave me when I turned eight.

The fog obscures the original memories of these objects from my mind. All I remember is Kate telling me about each of them, in turn, every day.

There are other things in the case, trinkets and souvenirs I don't recognize at all. The memories of them are so close, like tops of skyscrapers, disappearing into the fog.

which captured the public imagination, while the ads played on the additional incongruity of the clumsy *gaijin* engaged in traditional Japanese pursuits. In the 1990s humorous, and somewhat ridiculing, portrayals of Arnold Schwarzenegger swinging kettles or pounding dough while buried in flour for *ramen* commercials became a common sight.

Although prominent foreigners were used in Japanese advertisements from much earlier on, the 1970 advertising campaign for Mandom (a line of men's toiletries) featuring Charles Bronson is most frequently credited with establishing this 'talents' trend which still persists in Japanese commercials. While in Osaka in 1990, I had the golden opportunity to interview the creative director who developed the Mandom campaign. I believe that, as in the other cases discussed here, it was not only more 'exotic' and 'exciting' to have a foreigner for this promotion, but 'safer'. Bronson's image, a clear depiction of sensuality and indulgent individualism, was used to invert the established protocol for Japanese cosmetics and toiletries advertising.

The Bronson commercials were an attempt to change the way men's toiletries were presented while utilizing associations of the West with progress, to promote a more modern, Western image for the then fifth-place company in men's toiletries. According to the ad's creator:

Until then, when making men's cosmetics we always portrayed a soft, gentle look and always used Japanese men. . . . When creating the [new] name for the product 'Mandom' the desire was to combine the idea of 'kingdom' or 'freedom' with the word MAN, creating the idea of a 'man's world'. Until then the idea of cosmetics for men was to create a 'sweet smell'.

To go with the new image, a new bottle was designed to convey a sense of strength. This was achieved by making a huge cap, larger than the bottle. According to the creative director, '[t]he cap and bottle made a big impression. It conveyed a sense of strength rather than "sweetness".' To go along with this imagery, the ad makers decided to present a 'kitanai Amerika no otoko'—'a dirty American male'—in Mandom commercials, and featured Charles Bronson, looking all sweaty in grimy clothing. The catch-phrase used as a slogan for this promotional campaign was 'otoko no taishū' or 'a man's body odour'. Until that time, according to the creative director, the word *taishū* was considered a negative phrase with a rather bad connotation, having all the appeal of the analogous English 'body odour' or 'BO'. The idea of the advertising campaign was 'to take this negative thing and turn it into a plus'. In this instance, the use of Bronson as 'the dirty American male' with a 'man's BO' successfully accomplished these goals. Utilizing a foreigner made it easier to be this daring. Had the campaign backfired it would have been easier to revert to more conventional portrayals utilizing Japanese men than if a Japanese man had been used to break with the existing conventional expectations.

Taming the other

Despite the fact that *gaijin* are utilized in advertisements to circumvent certain Japanese cultural values, representations of *gaijin* end up reaffirming Japanese merit and centrality. In analysing why the Japanese study English, Applbaum (1992: 18) suggests that this is a symbolic way Japanese 'express recognition for the pervasiveness of Western culture' while at the same time gaining control over the tongue that had so much impact on their lives and country. In a similar way, prevalent representations of *gaijin* admit to Western dominance and influence, while the West of the occidentalized *gaijin* is brought under control. In recent advertisements, there has even been a shift whereby *gaijin*, once the revered standard of what Japan longed to become, are now used to highlight the economic dominance of Japan.

A Japanese article on advertising trends points out that 'desire requires something unreachable' ('akogare ni wa kyori ga hitsuyō') and Japanese are beginning to feel they have not only reached the standards of Westerners, but have surpassed them. A resulting conspicuous trend involves commercials making fun of foreigners (Asahi 1990). If for decades advertisements reflected a '*gaijin* complex' that 'it's a white world', with Japan's reclaimed assurance in its own cultural identity, *gaijin* faces are now used to suggest that maybe it is, or should be, a Japanese world after all. Humour in recent commercials is provided by beautiful and elegantly attired *gaijin* women trying to tell jokes in Japanese but stumbling inadequately with the language. A commercial for the Osaka Keihin shopping mall features a *gaijin* repeating the phrase, 'I can't keep up with the Japanese' (Asahi 1990).

Another example revealing the use of *gaijin* to assert the centrality and merit of Japaneseness is an advertising poster distributed by the National Rice Council. In order fully to understand the impact of this ad, it is important to realize that rice is both a metaphor and metonym for the collective Japanese self. It is not just any rice, but only the highly polished, short-grain Japanese rice (in contrast to other long-grain forms of Asian rice or rice grown in Western countries) that serves as a dominant symbol of Japanese identity. As a metaphor of identity, Japanese rice suggests purity, reaffirms a Japanese myth of cultural homogeneity, and asserts a 'natural' link between the Japanese and their land (Ohnuki-Tierney 1993). In this advertisement it is no longer the Japanese trying to 'catch up' with the West, but instead a *gaijin* businessman in Japan perplexedly trying to figure out why the Japanese are the front runners. As the *gaijin* businessman sits, holding a bowl of rice in his hands, he says thoughtfully to himself, 'I wonder what makes Japanese business so successful. It must be the rice they eat' (Ashkenazi 1993: 168). This example is particularly noteworthy given the international pressure, especially from the United States, on Japan to open its rice markets to imports, and Japan's intense resistance to this. In this case, internationalization involves invoking a *gaijin* presence that reaffirms the value and centrality of Japaneseness through Japanese rice, a core cultural symbol, and thus inverts international pressures to open Japan's rice markets while acknowledging the new international prominence of Japanese businesses.

By broadening this discussion to include 'living advertisements' as renderings of *gaijin*, I would like to use an example I have discussed in a previous work (Creighton 1991: 696–9) to show how occidentals are tamed and rendered ignorant foreigners, thus bringing the occident under control. In 1987 I and two other Caucasian women were hired by a prominent Tokyo department store to be 'living advertisements' by working as guides and translators for the store's annual exhibit of Japanese craft traditions. Throughout the exhibit we were dressed in traditional Japanese garb, including *yukata* (summer kimono), *obi* (the wide belt which holds a kimono in place), and *geta* (wooden sandals).

Due to the great interest directed at *gaijin* they have news value in Japan, and so the department store received a great deal of media coverage of our participation in the event. Media releases frequently reiterated stereotypes defining *gaijin* as other. For example, one newspaper headline exclaimed, 'Blue-Eyed Guides for an Exhibit of Japanese Tradition' ('Nihon no dentōten ni aoime no annainin') (*Nikkei Ryūtsū Shinbun* 1987). 'Blue-eyed' serves as a conventional marker for the otherness of *gaijin*. The headline underscored the contradiction involved in having *gaijin* explain traditional Japanese crafts to the Japanese.

Our employment was utilized by the Japanese media to tantalize its public with the blurring of boundaries between the Japanese self and the occidental other. *Gaijin* are supposed definitively to represent other, but the Japanese language is definitively a marker of Japaneseness (e.g. Miller 1977, 1982; Chamberlain 1971). A great deal of attention was directed at the fact that all three of us spoke Japanese. Kimonos are also a marker of

Japanese identity. *Gaijin* wearing kimonos are funny, even endearing, as long as they do not look quite right. We were dressed every morning by a professional kimono instructor who made sure we looked correct in the traditional costume. A great deal of media attention was also directed to the fact that all three of us were married to Japanese men, and hence had legal and family ties in Japan making us *gaijin* but not completely outsiders. That I was the *okaasan* (mother) of a son who is a Japanese national was also emphasized. *Okaasan* represent inside belongingness by symbolizing the family line (*ie*), a person's home-town community (*furusato*), and Japan as a nation. Others have mothers, but *okaasan* are supposed to be Japanese.

During one particular day, a television crew followed us around taping our activities for a feature report on our participation in the exhibit. Since a special *furusato* (home-town) noodle restaurant had been set up for the exhibit, the television crew wanted to interview us eating at the restaurant. Before the interview commenced, one of the women, who seldom ate Japanese noodles, leaned over to ask the other two of us, 'How do you eat these things anyway?' Neither our explanations nor the interview planned for the feature ever appeared on television. Instead, the presentation played with the blurred distinction between Japanese and other. Our family ties were presented, our knowledge of Japanese traditions and the Japanese language were emphasized (and exaggerated), we were presented as occidentals who seemed more competent at being Japanese than Japanese. However, before the all-important distinction between Japanese self and *gaijin* other could break down there was a climactic release in the form of a female English-speaking voice (accompanied by subtitles for the Japanese audience) asking, 'How do you eat these things anyway?' A summarizing comment appeared on the screen proclaiming, 'So even these so-called experts on Japan do not comprehend the proper way of eating Japanese noodles.' The potential threat of the foreign invader was vanquished by this finale in which *gaijin* were revealed as ignorant, incompetent foreigners after all, and the distinction between Japanese and other was reaffirmed.

All of the advertising discussed in this section shows *gaijin* used symbolically to bring the potentially threatening occident under control, rendering them cute, cuddly, and incompetent, hence unthreatening. But more than this, they serve to reaffirm Japanese centrality and the value of being Japanese. Since these advertisements focused on the threatening aspect of *gaijin*, it is important to restate the dual nature of the *gaijin*. Advertisements that tame the *gaijin* as a moral threat and advertisements that depict *gaijin* as attractive, positive forces can be mutually reinforcing. The cultural distancing involved in controlling the threatening aspects of *gaijin* and the outside world they represent makes it easier to solicit widespread acceptance of Western things defined as positive. Thus, advertisements can simultaneously promote Western goods by presenting *gaijin* as the bearers of style and innovation, while reaffirming Japanese value and centrality.

Orientalizing a homogeneous self

This discussion has focused on renderings of *gaijin*, white Westerners, because they most represent the occident in Japan. Directing some attention at other categories of foreigners will reveal how Japanese interest in foreigners helps reinforce orientalisms about themselves, particularly an assertion of homogeneity. The contrasting ways in which non-white foreigners, whom Japanese classify differently from whites, are rendered also reaffirm the suggestion that the Japanese occidentalism of the *gaijin* is distinctly Western, and not just alien.

Perhaps the most problematic depictions of foreigners in recent Japanese advertising involve representations of blacks.[5] Caricatured black images appear as comic, low-class, or foolish figures. Whereas there are large numbers of white people who appear either as 'talents' or as unknown individuals, depictions of blacks are few relative to whites, and these black individuals must be famous to be featured. Typically they tend to be well-known athletes, dancers, or musicians.

The stereotyping of blacks is long established in Japan. For example, Japan was rocked by a *Dakko-chan* doll craze beginning in 1960. Dakko-chan was a caricatured black figure with big eyes and huge red lips, which came attached to a pole. When prompted by pushing on the pole bottom, Dakko-chan would scurry up the pole. When it became Japan's top-selling toy in its first year, the maker Takara adopted it as the company logo. The Japanese continue to buy 100,000 Dakko-chan dolls a year (Jones 1988).

In the mid-1980s, *Chibikuro Sanbo* (Little Black Sambo) dolls became a huge fad in Japan, more than a decade after the North American debate about whether the book *Little Black Sambo* should be removed from school libraries because of its stereotyped representations. The wide-eyed character dolls were depicted as silly, clumsy, foolish, and uneducated. For example, the caption on one Sambo product read, 'When I'm hungry there's no stoppin' me. I'll be up in a palm pickin' coconuts before you can count to three. An I can count way past three, too!' (Shapiro 1988). The manufacturers defended the products, saying the figures were 'humorous' and 'friendly' and that, therefore, Japanese children who enjoyed them would 'not grow up to be racists'. A similar controversy arose over a line of mannequins featured at Sogo Department Store. Again, the caricatured large forms, with crossed eyes, large lips, and jazz poses, caused accusations of discrimination and poor taste. Debates also raged over the trademark character for the Japanese drink Calpis (*Carupisu*), which for years had been the same black person with large lips, dressed in hillbilly clothes with a straw hat, consuming the white drink, accompanied by the phrase 'hatsu koi no aji' ('The taste of first love').

An employee of Japan's largest ad agency claimed there was no racist intention behind any of these controversial advertising representations. He admitted that the images reveal Japan's inexperience with racial diversity and lack of true internationalization, stating,

there is a long way to go before most people have experience with whites even. Right now they are still just '*misemono*', a curiosity, something to be seen. Japanese have had even less experience with blacks; are even less likely to understand them. I think there is no desire to be discriminatory. It is just not understood that such problems arise.

These controversies over the representation of blacks in commercial products and advertisements occurred around the time of Nakasone's now famous *faux pas* about American minorities. In 1986, when he was Prime Minister, Nakasone remarked on the higher Japanese IQ relative to Americans. When criticized for this statement, Nakasone made matters worse by explaining that he had been referring to the negative impact of blacks and other American minorities in pulling down the general IQ level.

Despite the loud protests of racism and discrimination directed at Japan by foreigners, particularly North Americans, because of these issues, the white Western world shares the blame for helping to create the unfortunate stereotyping of blacks in Japan in the first place. Japan was introduced to the comic use of black representations when it was first reopened to the outside world by Commodore Perry in 1853. Perry's crew produced a minstrel show for their Japanese hosts, featuring white crew members with blackened faces (Thorton 1986: 95). When Japanese first began coming to the United States they likewise witnessed the lower position of blacks in American society, as a diplomatic envoy in 1860 encountered the separation of whites and blacks, and the presence of slavery. Many Japanese have derived their only understanding of blacks through translations of literature written by whites, or through images from popular foreign films. In the 1980s a collection of racially oriented jokes denigrating blacks was written by a white man well known in Japan as the host of a television English show. Published in Japan under the title *It's Only a Joke* (Spector 1984), the book was distributed as an educational guide to the study of English. Like Nakasone's comments, which more than anything else suggested that America's problems stemmed from its heterogeneity, negative representations of blacks tend to reinforce a belief in the value of the presumed homogeneity of Japan.

There are very few depictions of non-Japanese Asians, who, according to one advertising specialist, are not considered 'true *gaijin*'. As I noted, they are not considered insiders in Japanese cuture, nor are they sufficiently distant to provide an appropriate contrasting other. Their marginal status makes them problematic and contributes to a Japanese tendency to look down on other Asians. Non-Japanese Asians do appear in advertisements for designated ethnic products, such as speciality Chinese foods, or for cleaning products that suggest stereotyped labour roles.

Presentations of foreign scenery illustrate this diminished interest in other Asian areas. Japanese advertisements respond to the public interest created by particular events, notably the Olympics. For two years preceding the 1992 Olympics held in Spain, Japan was enmeshed in a Spain boom. Museums and department stores hosted exhibitions of Spanish artists; Barcelona emerged as a popular new vacation destination. A similar boom was noted for the Calgary Olympics, during which time commercials featured scenes of Calgary and panoramic imagery of the Canadian Rockies. The situation was notably different for the 1988 Olympics, held in Seoul. The few commercials invoking Olympic symbolism in that year tended to ignore the host country. One commercial showed the legs of a runner as he raced around a track, thus highlighting the Olympics as an event but removing it from any association with its location in Korea in that particular year.

The problematic nature of Korea in relation to Japan is further seen in the case of Koreans living in Japan. The president of a marketing trends consulting firm categorized foreigners into three groups, white foreigners (*gaijin*), non-white foreigners (blacks, Asians, etc.), and non-foreign foreigners. This third, marginal group is comprised largely of descendants of people brought to Japan as labourers from other Asian countries, particularly Korea, in the pre-World War II period. Although these people were born in Japan, have lived their entire lives in Japan, and speak

Japanese as a first language, they do not have Japanese citizenship and are instead legally designated as 'foreigners'. Their case provides another example of how orientalisms and occidentalisms are used to draw lines within a society, rather than just between societies. Resident Koreans are not included in Japanese self-orientalisms. Denying the inclusion of resident Koreans and other groups within Japan, such as Ainu and *burakumin* (descendants of an occupational caste), allows the projection of an orientalist self-construction of Japan as a homogeneous society.

The representations of racial diversity discussed here are seldom true images of internationalization, serving instead to further the internalization of a homogeneous self-construct in one other significant way. While white Westerners are treated as representatives of an essentialized occident, with frequent disregard for the diverse cultural and historic differences among Western societies, at the same time representations of the racial diversity of foreigners more generally serve as a means of projecting heterogeneity outside. This coincides with John Russell's (1991*b*: 13) assertion that 'In some ways the black other occupies the same symbolic space and function as *burakumin* and Koreans, two categories of other with which blacks are often equated.' Projecting heterogeneity onto the outside world reaffirms the uniqueness and specialness of Japan by contributing to an orientalist self-assertion of homogeneity that denies the diversity within Japanese society.

Conclusions

To a large extent representations particularly of whites, but also of blacks and other Asians, have reinforced their otherness, thus serving to reaffirm the homogeneous unity and uniqueness upon which Japanese identity is largely based. The imaging of white foreigners in Japanese advertisements reflects the dichotomized role of *gaijin* in Japan. They tend to be either objects of glorified attention or conversely a standard of negative traits. In either case they are often stripped of individual identity and their own personalities; encountered and experienced as representative *gaijin* (see Creighton 1991) rather than real individuals. Makers and analysts of Japanese advertisements readily admit that, for the most part, Japanese remain ignorant of the people within the *gaijin* packaging. Much of Japanese advertising is a performance of visual imagery, and appropriately these foreigners are simply *misemono*, 'spectacles' or 'things to look at'.

This attitude was frequently attributed to a sort of ignorance arising among a people who have had few possibilities of interaction with other cultural groups, socialized to perceive themselves as Japanese, as basically the same. Images of foreigners are fantasy depictions, attention-getters, flights of fancy, which help construct Japanese identity by portraying what Japanese are not, and thus perpetuate a discourse of otherness. Although abundant, these representations tend not to bring any deeper understanding of the outside world. Their very abundance often gives the false impression that Japan is largely open to the outside world and to foreigners.

However, trends within Japan, reflected in Japanese advertising, suggest that many Japanese—although they may not use these labels—are questioning Japan's occidentalisms and self-orientalisms. Within both the general public and the advertising world, many people have listened and responded to foreigners' criticisms of their treatment as essentialized *gaijin*. This has prompted a realization of the need for a more sophisticated understanding of foreigners and for greater care with such issues and representations.

Throughout the 1980s, and now into the 1990s, the Japanese government has peddled internationalization as a national goal. A great deal of criticism has been directed at the possibilities for the true attainment of such a goal. As already noted, one author referred to internationalization as a contradictory goal, claiming that it was basically an 'un-Japanese activity' (LaBrack 1983). Others have condemned such goals as empty words, given the repeated assertions of Japanese uniqueness (Dale 1986). Thus far, internationalization has been emphasized in a very literal sense— an attempt to link nation to nation. However, in a society in which the interconnectedness of people in face-to-face networks of interpersonal relationships is paramount, for the internationalization of Japan to be realized it will, I suspect, require more of a grass-roots basis. For example, the tremendous increase of 'international' marriages greatly affects how Japanese, related in personal networks, understand, accept, and interact with foreigners. The increased numbers of foreigners visiting or living in Japan, and the increasing numbers of Japanese travelling or studying abroad, also have a slow but real impact on Japanese perceptions and interactions with others.

One marketing consultant expressed the view: 'The internationalization of Japanese society will start from inside, and will come.' I believe there is a great deal to this sentiment. There have been big changes in Japan in the past few decades. Where once most people saw only *images* of foreigners, and never a foreigner in person, this is less and less the case.

Although some older Japanese still relate to foreigners as *misemono*, many Japanese young people have grown up to accept their presence as natural. For these younger Japanese such foreigners are less likely to elicit attention as *gaijin*, since they have always been just 'people in the neighbourhood'.

In the 1980s Japan was intent upon learning more about foreign places and foreign peoples. In the 1990s, I believe there will be a greater openness and acceptance of foreign persons. There are clearly many Japanese who have become aware of foreigners as real people, not just as *gaijin*, and many Japanese are more aware of some of the problems of representation discussed here. The 1990s may be a decade of marked change in attitudes towards foreigners, as young Japanese who have grown up seeing them as ordinary people come of age. There are also intentional promptings to encourage Japanese of all ages to reflect on their own degree of acceptance of others, trends which are beginning to be reflected in modern advertising. One example is the question of the decade put to the Japanese public in 1990 in the autumn advertising campaign for a major urban retailing concern, Isetan Department Store. The ad shows a black woman, a white girl, and an Asian man, suggested to be non-Japanese by his somewhat darker skin colour and style of clothing. The theme phrase reflects the common use of punning in Japanese advertising. The phrase has a certain ambiguity because in Japanese the ideographs used to write it can be read two different ways, resulting in two slightly different meanings. These are:

> nannin made aiseru ka
> [Up to how many people are you able to love?]

or:

> nanbito made aiseru ka
> [Up to what kind of people are you able to love?]

In the internationalized reality of the 1990s, this remains an important question not just for the Japanese, but for all of us.

Acknowledgements

The research on Japanese advertising presented here was conducted under a Japanese government grant, issued under the Nakasone fund, to support research related to internationalization. Earlier versions of this chapter were presented at the annual meetings of the American Anthropological Association held in Chicago in Nov. 1991, and the Japan Studies Association of Canada held in Ottawa

I wonder if there should be a wedding ring, or some other memento of Kate's father, but I can't find one. Instead I pick up a small round mirror, a gift from my best friend in first grade. A gaunt, wrinkled face stares back at me from the mirror, unbrushed wisps of thin white hair curling above the shoulders. It's not the face of the young adventurer from the photo, not the face I care to remember.

I put away the mirror and wait for Kate to arrive. I must tell her that this is a good day.

I wake up with a jolt, my head filled with memories. It is an overwhelming sensation, like the desert that was once an ocean suddenly being refilled with water. It takes me time to adjust. My mind is sharp and clear, and there is no fog. I feel almost happy, until I let myself sort through the memories.

There is the sound of Champagne being popped at the MIT Theoretical Physics Department on the day we make the breakthrough that would lead to interstellar flight. We run out of bubbly and move the celebration to a nearby bar. Too many tequila shots later, I leave with Bruce, a construction worker.

The silence on the other end of the line lasts for too long. "You should get an abortion," Bruce finally says. "I'll pay for half."

When Kate is born I expect Bruce to show up, or at least to call. He never does. A year later, I learn that Bruce died in a car accident. I don't go to the funeral.

Kate is getting older and she is asking about her father. I tell her that Bruce was a marine biologist who drowned while saving the life of a colleague. On her fifth birthday I give her a vintage attaché case I bought at a garage sale. I tell her it was her father's Keepsake Box.

"What's a keepsake box?" asks Kate.

"It's a place for you to store the things that are really special, memories that you want to cherish forever." I open the case. Inside there are a handful of colorful pebbles collected during a college vacation. "These are your dad's memories," I tell her. I invent a story to go with each pebble, tales of her father's exciting adventures from around the world.

The overwhelming joy of learning that I've been selected to pilot in Oct. 1992. Members of Dentsu branches in both Tokyo and Osaka, and members of the Tokyo offices of the *Mainichi* newspaper, offered invaluable help with this research. I am especially grateful to Jacob Kovalio for comments on earlier versions of this chapter. An earlier version (Creighton 1994) appeared in Jacob Kovalio (ed.), *Japan in Focus* (Toronto: Captus Press).

Notes

1 Foreign words and phrases are commonly adopted into the Japanese language but the writing system reserves a special syllabary, *katakana*, for these words to mark them as words of foreign origin, in contrast to words of Japanese origin which are written in *kanji* (ideographs) and the *hiragana* syllabary. Switching from one writing form to the other allows the incorporation of foreign words into the language while symbolically reaffirming the distinction between Japanese and other.

2 The different referents for types of foreigners show that they are not all categorized together. Whites, no matter what their country of origin, are called *gaijin*, a word which could in theory be used for non-white foreigners but usually is not. In addition to the referent *gaikokujin*, blacks are most commonly called *kokujin*, while other Asians are either called 'Asians' (*ajiajin*), or referred to as people of a specific country (i.e. 'Chinese'—*chūgokujin*). Difference is not strictly dichotomized but forms an array of classificatory otherness, such that the various groups are situated more closely or distantly *vis-à-vis* each other within the cognitive space of this array. I return to this point later in this chapter.

3 The word 'Dentsu' appears in this chapter without a macron, in keeping with the company's own romanized version of its name.

4 I am grateful to Robert J. Smith for pointing out this possibility to me.

5 Although a brief description of representations of blacks is presented here, this is currently the subject of much more extensive research. For example, John G. Russell (1991*a*) has researched Japanese renderings of blacks, and his research has been published in Japanese in a book entitled *Nihonjin no kokujinkan: mondai wa 'Chibikuro Sanbo' dake de wa nai* (The Japanese View of Blacks: A Problem Bigger than just 'Little Black Sambo').

References

ABE TOSHIYUKI and YAMAKAWA HIROJI (eds.) (1990). *The CM kanpanii: jidai o bijinesu suru imeeji komyunikeeshon*. Tokyo: Daiyamondosha.

APPLBAUM, KALMAN (1992). ' "I Feel Coke": Why the Japanese Study English', *Asian Thought and Society*, 17: 18–30.

ASAHI SHINBUN (Yukan) (1990). 'Datsu "akogare" "imeeji": Dajyare renpatsu no bijo ya nansensu Nihongo gakkō', *Asahi Shinbun* (2 June): 14.

ASHKENAZI, MICHAEL (1993). *Matsuri: Festivals of a Japanese Town.* Honolulu: University of Hawaii Press.

CARRIER, JAMES G. (1990). 'The Symbolism of Possession in Commodity Advertising', *Man*, 25: 693–706.

CHAMBERLAIN, BASIL HALL (1971 [1905]). *Japanese Things: Being Notes on Subjects Connected with Japan.* Tokyo: Charles E. Tuttle Co.

CREIGHTON, MILLIE R. (1991). 'Maintaining Cultural Boundaries in Retailing: How Japanese Department Stores Domesticate "Things Foreign"', *Modern Asian Studies*, 25: 675–709.

——(1994). 'Images of Foreigners in Japanese Advertising', in Jacob Kovalio (ed.), *Japan in Focus.* Toronto: Captus Press: 225–40.

DALE, PETER N. (1986). *The Myth of Japanese Uniqueness.* New York: St Martin's Press.

DESMOND, JANE (1991). 'Benin Art Revisited: Photographs and Museum Collections', *Visual Anthropology*, 4: 147–60.

FIELDS, GEORGE (1983). *From Bonsai to Lévi's.* New York: New American Library.

JONES, TERRIL (1988). 'Racial Gaffe Rekindles Criticism from Overseas: Black Mannequins, Toys Seen as Sign of Same Attitudes as Watanabe's Remark', *Japan Times* (2 Aug.): 3.

KONDO, DORINNE K. (1990). *Crafting Selves: Power, Gender, and Discourses of Identity in a Japanese Workplace.* Chicago: University of Chicago Press.

LABRACK, BRUCE (1983). 'Internationalization—an Anti-Japanese Activity: Fine as Catchword, but Those Returning to Japan Find that the Old Ways are the Only Ways', *Japan Times* (7 Aug.): 12.

LEBRA, TAKIE SUGIYAMA (1976). *Japanese Patterns of Behavior.* Honolulu: University of Hawaii Press.

MANABE, KAZUFUMI, BEFU, HARUMI, and McCONNELL, DAVID (1989). *An Empirical Investigation of Nihonjinron: The Degree of Exposure of Japanese to Nihonjinron Propositions and the Functions these Propositions Serve.* Nishinomiya: Kwansei Gakuin University.

MILLER, ROY ANDREW (1977). *The Japanese Language in Contemporary Japan: Some Sociolinguistic Observations.* Washington, DC: American Institute for Public Policy Research.

——(1982). *Japan's Modern Myth: The Language and beyond.* New York: Weatherhill.

MOERAN, BRIAN (1984). 'Individual, Group and *Seishin*: Japan's Internal Cultural Debate', *Man*, 19: 252–66.

Nikkei Ryūtsū Shinbun (1987). 'Nihon no dentōten ni aoime no annainin', *Nikkei Ryūtsū Shinbun* (11 May): 4.

NISHIOKA FUMIHIKO (1989). *Jishin o mochitai anata no imeeji seisan no geijutsu.* Tokyo: JICC Shuppankyoku.

OHNUKI-TIERNEY, EMIKO (1987). *The Monkey as Mirror: Symbolic Transformations in Japanese History and Ritual.* Princeton, NJ: Princeton University Press.

Ohnuki-Tierney, Emiko (1993). *Rice as Self: Japanese Identities through Time.* Princeton, NJ: Princeton University Press.

Russell, John G. (1991a). *Nihonjin no kokujinkan: mondai wa 'Chibikuro Sanbo' dake de wa nai.* Tokyo: Shinhyoron.

——(1991b). 'Race and Reflexivity: The Black Other in Contemporary Japanese Mass Culture', *Cultural Anthropology*, 6: 3–25.

Shapiro, Margaret (1988). 'Old Black Stereotypes Find New Lives in Japan: Marketers Defend Sambo Toys, Black Mannequins, Insist Racism Was Not Intended', *Washington Post* (22 July): A18.

Spector, Dave (1984). *It's Only a Joke.* Tokyo: ARK.

Thorton, Michael Charles (1986). 'Collective Representations and Japanese Views of African-Descent Populations', *International Journal of Sociology and Social Policy*, 6: 90–101.

Williamson, Judith (1978). *Decoding Advertisements: Ideology and Meaning in Advertising.* London: Boyars.

6

Duelling Currencies in East New Britain: The Construction of Shell Money as National Cultural Property

Deborah B. Gewertz and Frederick K. Errington

It has become increasingly common for indigenous and minority groups throughout the world to promote and defend their own representations of identity by invoking images and other embodiments of tradition, history, and ethnicity.[1] In this chapter we examine such a politicization of culture in Papua New Guinea, one which centred on a recent phase in a history of contrast between native and introduced currencies.[2] As part of an ongoing struggle to determine the representation of self and other, both indigenous people and their colonizers had long invoked contrasting sets of orientalisms and occidentalisms about shell money and (for want of a better term) money. In the case we will examine, locally generated orientalisms and occidentalisms had also become part of the efforts by members of a particular group to define and validate themselves in the contemporary world of Papua New Guinea: they sought to portray a set of their activities centring on shell money as cultural property and, moreover, as a matter of special national concern—as constitutive of national identity. Our discussion, thus, will explore a range of different historical factors at work in the emergence of politically significant essentialisms—in this case those focusing on currency. In so doing, we will stress the importance of these essentialisms as they contributed to the self-representations which were asserted as comprising national identity.

The effort to establish national identity through the creation of national cultural property has, of course, been reported elsewhere (see Morphy 1983; McBryde 1985; Dominguez 1986; Handler 1985, 1988). Here we seek to elucidate the process by which certain activities, objects, and events became eligible for promotion to national cultural property, and hence as definitive of national identity. We do so by examining an instance in which the central and contrasting essentialisms—the powerfully, dramatically, simplified contrasts—on which national identity so often rested were generated and invoked. Exploring this process is especially important to an understanding of post-colonial politics in such places as Papua New Guinea. Nationalism, necessitating both the creation of unity and the maintenance of a relatively coherent cultural distinctiveness within the world at large, was likely to be especially difficult to achieve in a context like Papua New Guinea where there was enormous cultural pluralism and little collective history.

In short, we examine here one strategy for establishing national identity. Specifically, we analyse an attempt by members of a specific group, one which had become relatively powerful during the colonial and post-colonial periods, to promote, through invoking historically salient essentialisms concerning currency, certain of their cultural practices as representative of the nation as a whole. These cultural practices, as we shall see, had much to recommend them in providing one possible basis of a Papua New Guinea nation, a polity both unified and distinctive. However, that they were needed at all to consolidate Papua New Guinea's diversity virtually ensured that they would be strongly contested.

Setting the scene

Near the end of our 1991 field-work in the East New Britain province of Papua New Guinea, a collection of post-colonial characters converged to engage in a drama which struck us at the time as typical of this general process by which essentialisms were employed to construct identity. Indeed, it contained what has become a relatively standardized cast and plot and presented events as having enhanced—dramatic—significance. Yet, particularly on reflection, this drama seemed more than merely typical. It was especially instructive both in its form and its content (cf. Silverman 1977). As a confrontation between locals and those foreigners wishing to exploit them, it was an assertion of the political autonomy prototypic of a post-colonial, nationalist will (cf. Kapferer 1988, 1989). It also starred, in this assertion, a set of local cultural practices remarkably well suited for promotion to national cultural property. Clearly, not just any set of cultural practices would do: not just any set could convince a critical audience to suspend its disbelief (and distrust) and entertain the idea that the portrayal represented more than matters of local concern.

The case we observed focused on the media of value and transaction themselves. It focused on what became presented, by means of essentializing contrasts, as the relationship between indigenous and Western currencies—between shell money and money. In thinking about the drama, we came to realize the extent to which these currencies were (to paraphrase both Malinowski 1954: 44–7 and Lévi-Strauss 1962: 89) good to use as well as good to think. Shell money and money were thoroughly embedded in the daily lives of most the East New Britains we knew. Moreover, for them, the relationship between shell money and money encapsulated and embodied in a remarkably salient way the colonial and post-colonial encounter, and hence encapsulated and embodied the twinned orientalisms and occidentalisms that were the response to that encounter. In addition, the two currencies conveyed that encounter in a way that could be readily recognized by Papua New Guineans generally. As we shall see, the representational value in East New Britain of shell money—in its contrast to money—might (to paraphrase Bourdieu 1977: 167) have come without saying, but it had long ceased to go without saying.[3]

The drama

The characters[4]

The Foreign Missionary (Father Joseph Crane, an American priest stationed in the Duke of York Islands, interested in increasing church revenues through the sale of native artefacts).

The Artefact Dealer (Herr Franz Muller, owner of an artefact gallery in Munich specializing in Papua New Guinea *Kunst*).

The Member of the Indigenous Élite (Dr Isaac Tolanger, director of a Papua New Guinea research institute empowered to grant or deny export permits).

The Expatriate Adviser (Dr Martin Brown, an American anthropologist and expert on indigenous arts and crafts).

The Tolai Elder (Mr Paulis Toling, businessman and politician of a Tolai village).

The Community Government Officer (Mr Patrick Sulia of the Sepik, who was stationed in the Duke of York Islands).

The Field-Workers (Drs Frederick Errington and Deborah Gewertz, periodically resident on Karavar Island in the Duke of York group).

The Tolai Youth (a sardonic assortment).

The plot

Before the curtain goes up, Community Government Officer Sulia informs the audience that there has recently been trouble concerning the export of a *tubuan* figure, a mask used in the male ritual of the neighbouring and closely related Tolai and Duke of York peoples. Father Crane tried to send one to Muller in Germany, but was stopped when Sulia discovered that the elders giving Crane local permission to export were none other than his catechists.

Scene 1: the Berlin Museum

Franz Muller studies traditional arts and crafts of New Britain, which was part of the German colony of New Guinea prior to the assumption of Australian control after World War I. He collects photographs and descriptions of 'traditional' masks and ritual figures—many, such as those once made for the cannibalistic *iniet* organization, no longer in use—and of coils of shell money—decorated with, by now, archaic designs. He sends these to Father Crane, who contracts with New Britain villagers to reproduce them. The villagers are happy to earn money, and are also moderately interested to learn about their forgotten heritage.

Scene 2: Port Moresby, Papua New Guinea

Muller has sent Brown photographs, allegedly covering the entire contents of the two large shipping containers of artefacts and shell money he and Crane wish to export. Suspicious of both Muller and Crane and unfamiliar with the cultural area from which the artefacts come, Brown is reluctant to approve their export until he consults with Tolanger, a Tolai. Tolanger is particularly alarmed at the proposed export of the shell money which is of central importance in the *tubuan* organization and in many other social interactions. He flies to Rabaul, the capital of East New Britain and the centre of the Tolai homeland, to intercept and examine the shipment.

Scene 3: Rabaul

Tolanger, in the company of Paulis Toling and Tolai youth, meet Crane by his two containers at the Rabaul international wharf. (Muller by this time is no longer in Papua New Guinea.) Crane removes some innocuous artefacts from the front of the first container and evasively claims that all the rest are just like these. Tolanger, smelling a rat (if not a *tubuan* mask), insists that all the contents be revealed. He, Toling, and the Tolai youth watch with angry amusement—chewing betel nut and smoking in the shade of a nearby tree—while Crane, perspiring freely, begins to unpack the containers in the noonday tropical sun. Soon a *tubuan* mask is revealed—not included in the list of contents submitted for export—as well as a number of coils of shell money. Tolanger initially blocks export permission for the entire shipment.

Scene 4: Port Moresby

Tolanger describes his encounter with Crane to the field-workers, who are paying him a courtesy call. He explains the need for a policy on national cultural property which would protect Papua New Guinea as a whole against cultural loss. In addition, the policy would protect objects associated with secret organizations—even those objects explicitly made for sale and export—from being displayed to the public, any public. He would have this policy cover objects of significance to contemporary secret organizations, such as that of the *tubuan*, as well as objects significant to those organizations which had not existed for decades. Rather than viewing Muller and Crane as perhaps stimulating crafts production and reviving culture, he sees them as encouraging natives to debase their tradition and as stealing their heritage. Of most concern to Tolanger, significantly, is their attempt to export shell money. Under no circumstances, he explains, should this be permitted since shell money is 'vital to the culture and to the country'. Perplexed by the intricacies of the cultural politics of representation—the dispute about preservation and self-determination—the field-workers leave to begin thinking about this chapter.

Initial thoughts

As we have already suggested, whenever we thought of these East New Britain events they took the form of a drama because the characters—their conversations and concerns—had become relatively standardized not only throughout Papua New Guinea, but elsewhere in the 'Third' and 'Fourth' Worlds. Moreover, the events had enhanced significance, were particularly compelling, to the actors and audience alike. Indeed, variations of this drama have been enacted in recent years among, for example, the Maori, Australian Aborigines, and Native Americans. In these cases, as in the East New Britain drama we have described, an overriding concern has been focused on the ownership and display of objects—generally sacred objects—expressing (and inventing) particular cultural traditions.[5]

What struck us as remarkable, though, about the East New Britain drama was that it focused not primarily on sacred objects but on shell money. Certainly contentions over Hopi Kachina dolls and Aboriginal sacred sites had prepared us to understand why Tolanger and other Tolai might object to the export and profane viewing of sacred objects such as the *tubuan*. The controversy over shell money, however, concerned an object that by its very nature was thoroughly—quintessentially—public.

Shell money, called *tabu* (or *tambu*) by the Tolai and *divara* (or *diwara*) by the Duke of York Islanders, consisted of small cowrie shells (*Nassa camelus*) strung onto strips of rattan and counted either individually or measured on the body in standard lengths, particularly what European commentators call the 'fathom'. Continuously spliced, these strips could be arranged in large, wrapped (and sometimes decorated) coils, containing hundreds of fathoms. (In regard to their shell money, the neighbouring Tolai and Duke of York Islanders were identical.[6])

Although there was some (mostly early) debate challenging the status of shell money as money (Malinowski 1921; Roheim 1923; Einzig 1949; Douglas 1967), most of those who have worked in East New Britain have agreed that it did have the status of money. T. S. Epstein, for instance, described it as

true money. It acted as a generally accepted medium of exchange: food was bought and sold for money; it provided a measure of value; forces of supply and demand determined the tambu price for most articles sold. Moreover, it was a liquid asset as well as a store of value: large coils represented the accumulated wealth of the Tolai [and Duke of York Islanders]. (T. S. Epstein 1968: 26)

We must also add that shell money was the single standard by which not only everything but everyone was distinguished. The differences in the amount of shell money that an individual owned and used in public ceremonies distinguished those persons of importance from those of mere respectability and the latter from those of no consequence. Shell money was fundamental to the prestige system and to the ordering of social life (see, among others, Errington 1974*a*; Bradley 1982; Neumann 1992: 183–90).

Finally, it should be noted that in the modern era shells were purchased with money (now the Papua New Guinea Kina) often from tradestore owners who acquired them from as far afield as Malaita in the Solomon Islands. Indeed, the shell money that Crane and Muller wished to export in the form of coils might never have been in circulation (it would, though, have been entirely acceptable for circulation). It might, for instance, have been purchased by Crane from outside Papua New Guinea and strung by his parishioners. Yet, in our discussion with Tolanger, neither the shell money's actual provenance nor its economic history seemed especially relevant to him. He was far more concerned with its cultural than with its fiscal significance. Thus, consistent with what we interpret as his concerns, a national newspaper ran a picture of Tolanger, Toling, and two unidentified Tolai standing beside some fifteen coils of shell money. The caption read: 'Cultural Shipment Confiscated' (*Post-Courier* 1991: 3).

Given that shell money in various forms—from unstrung shells to long lengths—could be bought and sold for money and was itself a public medium of exchange, our initial response was 'why all the fuss?' As we shall see, although the effort to export shell money as artefact was new, the antecedents of the fuss were of long standing. Because shell money had been both means and marker of intercultural negotiation, it had acquired a particularly salient representational value. Shell money embodied the condensed orientalist and occidentalist essentialisms that comprised for local people a particular version of colonial history; its continued use in everyday life imbued common and pervasive transactions with emblematic significance. Tolanger's indignation, in other words, was well justified, but for reasons that took us considerable time to unravel.

In unravelling these reasons, moreover, we began to speculate that, by virtue of their political potentialities, these events precipitated by Crane and Muller were remarkably serendipitous. For members of a group as well educated and prosperous as the Tolai were relative to other Papua New Guineans (contacted earlier by Europeans than many others in the country, Tolai were 'given a headstart in educational and economic development' (Bray 1985*b*: 191)), these events were an opportunity to promote local self-identity and so to augment national influence and prominence.[7]

Duelling currencies

Unlike a great many indigenous currencies in Papua New Guinea, the shell money used by the Tolai and Duke of York Islanders retained, as we have indicated, the full range of uses that it had at the time of contact. It remained of great significance as a means of paying for goods and services and as a means of establishing and maintaining social relationships. All of the many modern field-workers among the Tolai and the Duke of York Islanders have recognized the continuing centrality of shell money in social life (e.g. Bradley 1982; A. L. Epstein 1963, 1969, 1979; T. S. Epstein 1968; Errington 1974*b*; Neumann 1992; Salisbury 1966, 1970*b*; Simet 1992).

However, we suggest that what has been written so far as to the centrality of shell money does not fully account for the alarm that the prospect of its export as artefact created. To explain this alarm, we need the *Icarus,* and the subsequent realization that this is only the second happiest day of my life. I worry about leaving Kate behind, but it's only for a few months. How can I resist the opportunity to visit the stars? Who could say no to sharing immortality with Gagarin and Armstrong?

The feeling of frustration when I first learn they intend to use cryogenics. "How can you expect me to sleep through this moment?" They lecture me about the challenges of engineering a ship small and light enough to make the jump. "It's only a few weeks. People spend months, years at the International Space Station." They tell me I'll wake up briefly on the other side, only to make the necessary adjustments for the return jump. At least I will get to see Arcturus.

Photo-ops in front of the *Icarus.* A whirlwind of interviews and events. Fame is… hectic. The night before liftoff, saying goodbye to Kate, hugging and holding her tight. She wants me to bring her a pebble from Arcturus, like the ones she thinks she has from her dad. I explain that I won't be landing on a planet this time around; maybe on the next trip. She shrugs and places one of my publicity photos into the Keepsake Box instead. Aboard the *Icarus,* I climb into the cryogenic chamber. The lid closes, and I feel the prick of a needle.

When I wake up, everything feels wrong. My body, the room I'm in, the concerned looks on the faces of doctors I don't recognize.

"You've been asleep for forty years," one of them tells me. I don't believe him. For me, it's only been moments. "Something has gone awry. The *Icarus* made a successful jump, but the cryopod failed to wake you up. I'm so sorry." I look at my hands. They're small and wrinkled.

I catch up on forty years worth of history from my hospital bed. Someone else was the first to set foot on an alien planet. Someone else brought back mementos of another world to share proudly with their daughter or son. I slept and I aged, until they had bothered to find and retrieve the *Icarus* at the request of the Smithsonian. They were stunned to discover that I was still alive.

I hug the stranger that is my daughter. She grew up an orphan, sustained only by the memories of a father she soon learned to be fake, and real memories of a mother foolish enough to leave her behind. Somehow, she still manages to love me.

to understand not only its centrality but also its status as cultural property. (After all, the United States dollar was central to American life, yet Americans were pleased when foreign investors sought to acquire dollars. To be sure, there were restrictions on the export in large quantities of dollars, but dollars were not usually regarded as cultural property.) Thus, we need to understand not only how shell money operated for Tolai and Duke of York Islanders, but what it signified *vis-à-vis* its proposed export to Germany.

To elucidate the alarm—and the drama—we must recognize that much of the interaction between colonized and colonizer coalesced around the orientalized and occidentalized similarities and differences between shell money and money. Such perceived similarities and differences, not only between currencies but between those who used them, had long been part of the politics of representation that both reflected and shaped Tolai and Duke of York histories. Although much, including much about the relationship among currencies, will probably never be known (such as how European currency was indigenously evaluated when introduced in the late nineteenth century), there are some provocative data in the colonial record which may serve to illustrate the general process.

Consider, for example, the following early account: in 1888, Reverend Danks, one of the first Methodist missionaries to work in the region, represented his (potential) flock, which then consisted primarily of Duke of York Islanders and Tolai, as largely the product of their shell money and their use of it. He believed that because they valued shell money they were 'frugal and industrious' and that 'their commercial transactions extend to places they have never visited'. On the other hand, he also believed that shell money fostered undesirable traits: 'A people whose greatest love is reserved for money, and whose highest aim is to get money, is an exceedingly hard-hearted and an intensely selfish people' (Danks 1888: 316). An interesting point, and one we shall return to, is that Danks's perception of these local people as both industrious and avaricious reflected the contradictory perceptions, the ambiguous moral value, of money in *Western* ideology. Evidently, in his view (but, as we will show, not in theirs), their actions were both social and anti-social because their money was like our money, ambiguously 'devilish acid or . . . instrument and guarantor of liberty' (Bloch and Parry 1989: 30).

The colonial record also suggests that, at least initially, shell money prevailed over money as the more desirable currency.[8] This preference was noted in the German Administration's Annual Report for 1900–1:

It was often very difficult for the European firms to obtain the shell required to purchase copra etc. In this respect they were completely dependent on the natives, and at times the exchange rate for shell money was forced up absurdly high . . . In view of these facts, the Government, by an Ordinance of 18 October, 1900, prohibited trading in *diwara* . . . From the same date the use of any kind of shell money in commercial transactions was forbidden. (trans. Sack and Clark 1979: 220)

Apparently, then, from early in their (and Papua New Guinea's) contact history, Tolai and Duke of York Islanders were perceived as adept in controlling Europeans so as to drive hard bargains that yielded them good returns in shell money. In this encounter, shell money remained so strongly the currency of preference for indigenes that its use had to be limited by colonial law.

Indeed, it would appear that during the colonial period shell money had an oppositional role to money, perhaps serving to sustain local identity through resistance to external forces. Certainly during the periods of Errington's 1968 and 1972 research and our 1991 joint research, Duke of York Islanders frequently described shell money in terms of an essentialized contrast to money: shell money was extolled as 'heavy' (*mawat*)—as substantial and significant—as capable of generating the activities on which both male and female reputations were built and social order rested; money was denigrated as 'light' (*biaku*)—as flimsy and inconsequential— as incapable of creating or sustaining personal worth or enduring social relationships (see Errington 1974*b*). Additionally, we were frequently told by our Duke of York assistants that they would have preferred us to pay them in shell money, if only we had enough to give them. They said that shell money stayed on the island or region to generate further exchanges, while money merely flitted away in the purchase of easily broken, imported goods. Locals actively sought opportunities to convert money into shell money; men often wished us to photograph them next to their rolls of shell money.[9]

This evidence suggests that the historical preference for shell money was not a preference for one morally ambiguous medium over another, as Danks might have thought. Rather, it was a preference for a medium that, through its acquisition, accumulation, and distribution, established personal reputation and social good, as well as cultural identity and worth.

Yet the ongoing 'structure of conjuncture' (see Sahlins 1981, 1985) in which these negotiations concerning cultural identity and worth took place also transformed the system in which Duke of York Islanders and

Tolai were negotiating. Subsequent to the 1900 ordinance prohibiting transactions between Europeans and indigenes in shell money, local peoples, in such contexts as labour and land values, world copra prices, taxes, and the cost of trade goods, have been strongly affected by international capital and its fluctuations.[10] Although most Duke of York Islanders and Tolai continued to value shell money highly, they have certainly become interested in acquiring money. Without doubt, they became fascinated with it: as shell money was the basis of an indigenous leader's power, money appeared the basis of colonial power.

Their fascination with money, hence, went well beyond a need to pay taxes or to purchase trade goods. (In fact, in parts of East New Britain, it has recently become possible to pay taxes with shell money.[11]) Sporadically since the 1930s, many Duke of York Islanders and some Tolai have organized themselves under the traditional leadership of 'big men' into 'cargo' movements. They wished not simply to acquire money for European goods; they wished also to engage Europeans as comparable in power—as social equals. For example, one of their cargo activities during the 1930s, called the 'dog' movement, was designed to determine why Europeans repudiated them as if they were dogs (see Worsley 1968: 48; Errington 1974*a*). Locals eventually decided that they were treated with such little respect, as so powerless and insignificant, because they did not know how to participate in European business practices: they did not know, for instance, how to build a factory, to order goods, to acquire money. Their post-war 'Kaun' movement (from the word 'account'—as in bank account) was a collective effort to raise large sums of money in order to duplicate such European business practices as ordering from overseas.[12] It was an effort designed to duplicate these practices so as to affirm local identity—to represent themselves—as equivalent in worth to Europeans. Indeed, other Tolai who joined the Mataungan Association— a micronationalist movement which emerged in 1969 and was dedicated to immediate self-government—believed themselves already equivalent in worth to Europeans.[13] To be a Mataungan, one analyst of the movement said, was 'to stand on one's own two legs in front of Europeans and to decide for oneself whether to say "Yes" and then, whether to add "Sir" ' (Grosart 1982: 142).

Such instances of local resistance, differentiation, and qualified emulation did not, of course, make the Tolai and Duke of York Islanders unusual in Papua New Guinea. However, we think that the colonial experiences of these shell-money users was importantly distinctive. In this part of East New Britain, some of the risks of historical action (Sahlins 1985: 143–56) were reduced in that both shell-money users and Europeans shared, and perceived with *relative* accuracy that they shared, *somewhat* comparable organizing principles: both relied upon a universal currency. This, we suspect, contributed to a situation in which crucial aspects of colonial hegemony could be countered rather effectively and over a long period: simply put, much of the discourse between colonizers and colonized was conducted in terms that, for shell-money users, both validated their concepts and enabled them to negotiate their autonomy with considerable skill.

From the very first, each found the other able and willing to transact— to do 'business'. Furthermore, the initial sense of mutual similarity did not dissolve into one of *great* difference as was so often the case in contact situations.[14] And, as far as we know, the Duke of York Islanders and Tolai did not come to regard themselves as diminished by virtue of the differences they did recognize between themselves and the Europeans, did not apparently experience their ritual complexes and attendant valu- ables as 'rubbish' in contrast to those of Europeans. (For a contrasting case see Burridge 1969; see also Macfarlane 1985.) For instance, the leaders of their cargo movements were 'big men' whose power continued to be based—as it had been before the Europeans arrived—on the use of shell money in ritual and marriage transactions. Shell money and money, in other words, remained sufficiently similar that the latter did not invali- date the former.

Although shell money and money were comparable in many important ways, there were also subtle but significant differences. As we shall see, these eventually became the basis of an essentializing local critique of money that would provide cultural animation for Tolanger's alarm. This critique stemmed from their perception (shared with Europeans—as in- dicated above) that money itself had an ambiguous moral value. In this respect, they regarded shell money to be superior to money.

From the Western perspective, the ambiguous moral value of money may well have been rooted, as Maurice Bloch and Jonathan Parry sug- gested, in the disjunction in capitalist societies between short-term and long-term interests, between matters of everyday strategizing (often in pursuit of individualistic, self-indulgent pleasures) and matters of social reproduction (Bloch and Parry 1989: 23–30). In Western capitalist societies, therefore, it was likely to be a matter of concern and contention whether those activities which were focused on the accumulation of money subtracted from or augmented the social whole. (Thus, the ambivalence in the fascination with which Americans watch Donald Trump.) Yet, such a distinction between short-term personal and long-term public interests did not arise with shell money. Duke of York Islanders and Tolai viewed sociality as generated by the use of shell money, especially—at least until recently—through the shell-money exchanges and other transactions of big men. The shell-money expenditures of big men were the politics both of self-aggrandizement and of social reproduction. Of course big men could act asocially as, for example, with the practice of sorcery. However, the possession of shell money seemed to be regarded as inherently socializing. As Richard Salisbury said for the Tolai, a big man 'creates a name, not for himself alone, but in terms of which other people can organize themselves' (Salisbury 1970*a*: 30; see also Bradley 1982; Neumann 1992: 183–203.)

Europeans might readily have agreed with these East New Britains that 'money maketh the man', but Europeans probably would have dissented from the idea that 'the monied man maketh society'. As one might expect, this difference generated misunderstanding and conflict. To judge from their cargo activities, including the 'dog' movement, Duke of York Islanders and Tolai (like many other Papua New Guineans) were troubled that their transactions in money had not established enduring relations with Europeans. Unlike their transactions in shell money which generated local sociality, transactions with Europeans frequently led nowhere (see Parry 1989 for a comparable point). The difference in the capacity of shell money and money to establish relationships that not only were enduring but effected social reproduction was, we think, interpreted by many Duke of York Islanders and Tolai as indicating its superiority: shell money was 'heavy' because it entailed transactors in pervasive and ramifying ways, as money apparently did not (see Counts and Counts 1970 for supporting comparative evidence). In this regard the cargo activities we have discussed among the Duke of York Islanders and the Tolai could be seen as efforts to bring money up to the standards of shell money to effect social reproduction.

Thus, shell money had not only retained its value as a medium of exchange in Duke of York and Tolai social life, but had remained the exemplar of what a medium of exchange should be like. As such, we think, it came to stand in cultural opposition to Western money, the two sorts of money being essentialized orientalist and occidentalist renderings of what were, obviously, more complex and ambiguous social relations (see e.g. Carrier, this volume).

Essentialisms in the generation of shell money as cultural property

While most Europeans were no doubt unaware of the criteria against which their currency was being judged, they certainly understood that local people wished to alter their social arrangements with Europeans. Cargo movements in the East New Britain area and elsewhere in Papua New Guinea were chronic sources of European concern: at best, they were seen as distracting local people from what Europeans regarded as productive labour; at worst, they were seen as politically subversive. Indeed, many Europeans feared industrial action, if not insurrection. To be sure, some Europeans admitted that local people were justified in viewing economic and social differentials as unfair. But even the more sensitive of these Europeans were likely to regard these differentials as unavoidable, at least for the time being. Thus, in 1941 the *Rabaul Times* explained the robbery of a Chinese carpenter, relatively well paid by non-European standards, by three of his Papua New Guinean plantation co-workers in the following manner:

[T]he three felt considerably annoyed [by the disparity in pay] . . . for was one not a senior lorry driver, another a 'boss' boy, while another was an old hand copra cutter? To them it was a very unjust world, even as millions of low paid workers have felt in every country before them. They adopted the primitive method of remedying this injustice—of effecting an equal distribution of wealth. (*Rabaul Times* 1941*b*)

Eventually, in a gradual move from their own 'primitive method' of control through outright oppression, Europeans were to pursue more sophisticated ways to remedy their anxieties about the possible consequences of colonial injustices. Consider, for example, a set of European-published pamphlets about money and its uses. In these pamphlets money, and, by direct extension, European life and the colonial presence, were represented as proper and inevitable. These pamphlets are especially interesting for they illustrate a process by which increasingly explicit meanings—in this case those embodied in money and in shell money—came to have additional representational value. These pamphlets, which contributed to the on-going transformation of that which came without saying into that which could no longer go without saying, proceeded through a set of European-generated essentialisms distinguishing between 'us' and 'them'. Shell money came for Europeans to embody an orientalism that took on meaning in contrast to an occidentalized Western currency. Ironically echoing, and perhaps drawing on, these European essentialisms, local people came to represent shell money as more than a medium of exchange. It became cultural property and a fit subject for the alarm that was central to our initial drama.

The pamphlets

During the late 1960s, the Reserve Bank of Australia, in association with banks operating in Papua New Guinea, issued a series of clearly written, though disingenuous, pamphlets entitled *Your Money, Prices, Banks and Banking, Keeping a Cheque Account*, and *What is Wealth?* These pamphlets were designed 'for use by secondary school children and others who want to learn something about money and saving' (*Your Money* n.d.: p. i). They were widely available throughout the country at banks, libraries, and schools. Not surprisingly, these pamphlets failed to deal at all directly with colonialism and its effects. Presenting the desire for wealth as 'natural because we all like to make progress and have a better standard of living' (*What is Wealth?* n.d.: 8), they answered the question of why some people fulfil this natural desire more completely than others by referring to hard and efficient work:

Some people do not understand how richer persons get good homes, motor cars, refrigerators, radios and furniture while other people who also work hard, still have to live in small huts.

The people who own these things have got them . . . by saving, by working and earning money, by growing crops for sale, by raising livestock, by trading or by obtaining them from relatives. Most of them have worked hard but also efficiently. People train as Teachers and Government officials. Others train as Doctors, Lawyers or Engineers, and so on. They earn more money in this way because of their training. Other people train as organisers of businesses and factories so that they can also earn more money.

In every country of the world, there have always been some people who are more wealthy than other people. (*What is Wealth?* n.d.: 9–10)

Nowhere in these pamphlets was there any mention of race, class, or relative position in colonial society—factors which determined access to training. For instance, those with sufficient training to read the pamphlets must have been aware that even they had to transact their banking needs at a desk apart from those used by Europeans.[15]

Local readers of the pamphlets, moreover, were told nothing about the importance of ownership in the productive process, and about the potential profits ownership conferred. Instead, one pamphlet answered the question of 'Why cannot we be given Motor Cars, etc.?' (*What is Wealth?* n.d.: 10) by portraying high prices as reasonable, indeed, as fair. Factory owners, it seemed, must charge high prices because 'it costs a lot of money to make a motor car and the people who buy cars must pay a big enough price for each one so that the people who own factories can get back all the money they have spent' (*What is Wealth?* n.d.: 11).

In both implicit and explicit opposition to the European self-representations of their money-based economic system as rational, reasonable, fair, natural, and leading to progress was the native system. Those who did not recognize the inherent superiority of Western socioeconomic relations were backward, misguided, and patronized as foolish. The many thousands of Papua New Guineans who noticed that it was the Europeans who owned most of the motor cars were pleasantly told, in effect, that their questions concerning colonial patterns of distribution were based on ignorance of how an economic system must operate.

Throughout the pamphlets, moreover, indigenous systems were portrayed as curtailing progress—as materially unproductive—because they channelled wealth into the ownership of pigs and the staging of feasts rather than into savings or investment (*What is Wealth?* n.d.: 10). Thus, of the nine 'main ways of increasing wealth in the Territory' with which *What is Wealth?* concluded, the first was: 'Saving by people so that savings can be put to some purpose which is productive' (*What is Wealth?* n.d.: 20).

Native economic systems were, as well, presented as cumbersome and inefficient in the modern world:

Can you imagine the difficulty in exchanging, at a shop or a store, a pig for a radio set or a guitar? Even if you could bring the pig to the shop or store which had the radio set or guitar for sale, the shop-keeper might not want the pig. However, he would always accept money. Besides, the pig might not be worth the same as the radio set or guitar, so how would you settle the difference in value? (*Your Money* n.d.: 2)

These pamphlets comprised only a small portion of a late-colonial discourse, and we do not know how many people read them. Yet they illustrated and contributed to a process of increasing self-consciousness about critical differences between 'us' and 'them' and about the power of representations. The pamphlets and the kind of discourse they embodied seem unlikely to have convinced a Tolai and Duke of York Island audience for two reasons: on the one hand, as implied in our discussion of the increasingly recognized incomparabilities between shell money and money, many locals would have found the pamphlets' premises both implausible and amoral. On the other hand, the very training advocated in the pamphlets was to have the unexpected consequence of producing an indigenous élite highly suspicious of the particular essentializing contrasts meant to inspire them. Moreover, such an élite would become relatively strong in East New Britain, which had a higher proportion of students (mostly Tolai) in secondary schools between 1972 and 1982 than any other province in the country (Bray 1985*a*: 17).

Most Tolai and Duke of York Islanders would have rejected the European self-representations presented in the pamphlets as implausible largely because they would not believe that colonial patterns of distribution were just.[16] As we have already suggested, local people had long understood that factory ownership was important and that owning a factory (or its fruits) was not simply a product of efficient work.[17] Furthermore, they did not think that prices—certainly high with respect to their limited earning capacities—were reasonable and fair. As Hank Nelson pointed out, '[f]or much of the time labour [in Papua New Guinea] was so cheap and so ineffective at pushing for higher pay that there was little incentive to reduce the size of the labour force' (1982: 80).

Equally, we surmise that many villagers would have objected to the European evaluation of their investments in social relations as non-productive. While accepting that 'we all want money . . . for the things that money can buy' (*Your Money* n.d.: 5), villagers would have depicted themselves as valuing the social uses to which money and the things it can buy could be put—lest they seemed selfish, socially naïve, and irresponsible. To illustrate this latter point: during our visit to the Duke of York Islands in 1991, people were pleased when we noticed that our gifts—whether watch, pocket knife, flashlight, or shorts—changed hands multiple times, often before our eyes, and that even soft drinks, purchased by us or by others, were passed on several times before they were finished.

Conversely, we were asked by villagers on numerous occasions to tell stories that essentialized the contrast between 'them' and 'us': tales of the homeless (about whom they had heard on radio and in newspapers), tales about impoverished isolation and social dislocation.[18] These stories, parables really, were all to convey the ambiguous moral value of money—its aspect as 'devilish acid'—mentioned earlier. They confirmed for these villagers the asocial individuality and social inequality of European society; they confirmed the truth of one of their own essentialisms about the West which might be formulated as 'no money—no food—you die!'[19] Simply put, our village informants would not have accepted as likely or desirable the European orientalisms and occidentalisms in the pamphlets, in part because these representations contradicted their own essentialisms.

The indigenous élite would also have rejected the European representations of self and other. This élite had emerged in part because, with Independence in 1975, many positions formerly held by Europeans had been localized. Members of this élite, who had begun to 'earn more money . . . because of their training' (*What is Wealth?* n.d.: 9), knew very well the practical and moral difficulties of efforts to sequester income from the social claims of kinsmen and others. (For discussion of the degree to which members of the Papua New Guinea élite remained socially entailed, see Gewertz and Errington 1991: 101–25.) Moreover, despite the implicit promise of the pamphlets (and of late colonialism) that training could lead to socio-economic equality—that backward tribalists, who brought pigs to exchange for radios, could readily become respected bureaucrats and bankers in the eyes of Europeans—members of this élite knew the process was more complex. In particular, their training or work had often taken them abroad into the racially divided West where the discrimination they encountered, their formal qualifications notwithstanding, made them very sensitive to demeaning characterizations.

The denouement

Tolanger, not only a member of the national élite but a shell-money-using Tolai, was unusually well suited to reject the kind of essentialized representations the pamphlets portrayed. He was also able, we suggest, to reformulate them. His people would have readily recognized the dissonance of bringing a pig to exchange for a radio. Their own currency could be represented as having retained its full range of uses and as having long been the standard against which European currency was evaluated: shell money, in this depiction, while a 'true money', was not a 'devilish acid'—the root of all evil. Both economically viable and morally superior, it could be regarded as encapsulating the virtues of a particular local tradition. Moreover, we surmise, if properly promoted as representation, shell money could denote the post-colonial nation as a whole: shell money could be elevated to the more powerful status of national cultural property because it could represent a successful emergence from the inequities of colonial history.

We can now speculate more fully concerning the bases of Tolanger's alarm: if shell money were to retain its special salience in East New Britain—much less be feasible as national cultural property, as a matter of national interest—it had to be *defined* as inalienable. It had to be defined, perhaps paradoxically, as beyond price. It certainly could not be allowed

I feel my mind crumbling piece by piece, like a sandcastle at high tide. The doctors said that the prolonged stay in the cryogenic pod had damaged my brain. My memories would disappear in a matter of weeks. The universe, which tried so hard and failed to kill my body, would have its revenge by erasing my consciousness instead.

Soon, too soon, it gets really bad and I forget more things than I remember. That's when Kate starts lying to me. She describes the planets I never got to explore, weaves details of a lifetime of joy and wonder, a lifetime I never lived. She makes up a new planet, new story for every pebble in the attaché case.

●—●◦●—●

I sit in the armchair by the bed, the attaché case open in my lap, when Kate walks in.

"Today is a very good day," I tell her by way of hello.

She steals a nervous glance at the pebbles, but my expression betrays nothing.

Everyone remembers that Icarus crashed, but they neglect the fact that he first flew, that he reached greater heights than any man had before him. They forget that Daedalus also flew, and his wings worked, and he landed safely. I may not have set foot on another world, may not have lived the wonderful life my daughter had invented for me, but I was still the first person to reach the stars, and that has to be enough.

"Sit next to me. I remember some things about your father."

My baby Kate, who is now Kate Terbanov, with a husband and children of her own, pulls up a chair. I present her with the only gift I have to offer—a memory of her father. Who gives a damn whether this memory is real or fabricated? I spin pleasant fictions about Bruce, things she can't check or verify, lies about his character and personality, and our romance, that are as appealing to the adult Kate as the adventures of an imaginary super-dad were to a child.

I can already feel the fog creeping back in, slowly reclaiming my mind. For all I know, this may be the last good day I have left. Kate and I make the best of it, building memories out of pebbles and attaché cases and hope.

to appear as an ordinary commodity *subject* to European currency. To have permitted Crane and Muller to transform shell money from currency into artefact, would, we suggest, have negated shell money's status as money, its capacity to act as a medium of value. It would have been intolerable for Crane and Muller to be allowed to submit shell money to their measure. Moreover, to let them define shell money as an exportable tourist object would be to relinquish its special power to represent—to embody—cultural heritage.

Thus, we think it likely that from Tolanger's perspective the purchase of shell money was not simply a matter of its convertibility—the value of one currency relative to another—but of its appropriation. Crane and Muller were perhaps adding insult to injury because they were buying large amounts of shell money in order not to use it. They were, in effect, re-engaging Tolanger, and others in East New Britain, in the colonial battle which the Tolai and Duke of York Islanders thought they had already won. Once again, the basis and matrix of indigenous social entailments were threatened with dissolution by an alien, 'devilish acid'.

(It is interesting, in this regard, to speculate about the possible cachet on the German market of the artefacts Crane and Muller wished to obtain. There was little doubt that their experience with artefacts had been sufficient to teach them about the international value of the locally authentic and significant. In fact, the less willing local people were to part with objects, the more valuable they were likely to be in Germany. That an alarm was raised at the proposed export of these 'artefacts' must have confirmed to Crane and Muller that they had chosen potentially profitable items.)

Appropriately—given the threat to social entailment the proposed export of shell money created—Tolanger, by raising the alarm, asserted a unity among what had in actuality become a fairly diverse group of Tolai. He was not only invoking orientalist and occidentalist essentialisms to counter and supplant those of Europeans, but was, we suggest, also using them to obscure what had become substantial class differences among shell-money users (for class formation in the Pacific generally, see Hooper *et al.* 1987). Although, as we have seen, dense networks of social relations constituted sociality among both Tolai and Duke of York Islanders, Tolanger was surely quite aware that some among them had become considerably wealthier than others—both in shell money and in money— and that their interests and possibilities had begun to diverge.[20]

The reasons it was important for members of the élite to maintain links within their own cultural groups were various and can only be enumerated

here: they included the importance of maintaining a local power base in electoral politics, of retaining a place of refuge if life away became too precarious, and of ensuring personal identity in a multicultural nation. From the point of view of villagers, themselves increasingly differentiated economically and educationally, connections with the élite were also important. They provided sources of donated income, access to jobs, points at which power and influence could be exercised and ties to the broader world known increasingly through the media.

By raising his alarm, it seems to us, Tolanger was not only keeping his home fences in good order, he was also validating a vision of local life as focused on shell-money use. At a time when class distinctions were becoming increasingly evident in Papua New Guinea (as the 'devilish acid' did its work), Tolanger was providing substantiation to the idea that a moral community of concerned shell-money users still existed: that he, Toling (the Tolai elder), and the Tolai youth were united in a way that obscured the extent to which their interests and possibilities had become disparate. (One Tolai member of the East New Britain Provincial Government had a rather cynical vision of how shell money helped maintain this moral community. He said that shell money is 'the opiate of the people—it keeps villagers thinking that they are equal to those with more money.')

The social life of meta-things

We have documented one attempt by a local culture to promote and defend its own representations of identity. For Tolai and Duke of York Islanders during the colonial period, this process involved the relationship between what we have termed 'duelling currencies'. Unlike most indigenous currencies in Papua New Guinea, shell money proved both durable and of important representational value: each characteristic contributed to the other. Indeed, European currency appeared to have been given a 'run for its money' and to have 'met its match'. Furthermore, more recently shell money had gained additional value: as a still-vital indigenous currency—again, one of the few monetary survivors of the colonial wars—it could, we suggest, come to represent the successful survival and continued vigour of a local tradition in the context of Papua New Guinea as a whole.

Thus, the drama Tolanger helped stage was directed at least as much to a contemporary Papua New Guinea audience as to the likes of Crane and Muller. It was a drama for several reasons. Because it focused on a

political circumstance commonly encountered with emergent national-isms, it employed a somewhat standardized cast and utilized a familiar 'rhetoric of motives' (Burke 1969). It had an audience or, more accurately, audiences. And it sought to present events as portentous. The themes of Tolanger's drama, focusing on freedom from foreign influence and deter-mination, were, of course, of wide pertinence to those in many former colonies. However, because his audience was largely composed of Papua New Guineans, these themes were meant to have, we speculate, more local referents, ones articulating the country's particular nationalist concerns.

As a state, Papua New Guinea was characterized by extensive cultural pluralism, and national culture was still largely composed of the heritage of particular groups. For example, National Day celebrations at the Na-tional High Schools involved performances by students of the 'signature events' of their particular cultural groups. National politics involved con-testation about which cultural groups would become most representative of the state, or, at the very least, which cultural groups were sufficiently strong and cohesive to be major national players. Political survival often depended on the successful manipulation of contrasting representations: politicians might have to justify why, for example, the next Prime Minis-ter should be an 'Islander' rather than a 'Highlander' or a 'Sepik'; why an international investor should locate a timber project, or resort, or process-ing plant among the Tolai rather than among the Chimbu or the Chambri. Hence, for example, the National Parliament building, constructed dur-ing the tenure of Prime Minister Michael Somare, a man from the Sepik region, had the overall design of a somewhat generalized Sepik men's house. Moreover, when we were in East New Britain in 1991 there was considerable national concern that there were too many Tolai in govern-ment, particularly because the Prime Minister then was a Tolai.

Tolanger's drama, focused as it was on shell money, was likely to engage both local and national audiences. As described, it encapsulated for the shell-money users a long colonial history of successful resistance. The drama rehearsed that history and defined the Tolai (and, by extension, Duke of York Islanders) as part of the current community of shell-money users. As well, through evoking contrasting orientalisms and occidentalisms and through presenting the essentialisms of locals as displacing those of Europeans, the drama powerfully validated a local life, to the extent that this life focused on shell money as a medium of exchange and value.

But the drama would also elicit mixed, or even unfavourable, reviews. While the national audience would be attentive, the nature of national

politics means that no claims for the priority of any cultural group would go uncontested.[21] Some of the local audience might also pan the drama. For instance, one of the minority representatives to the East New Britain Parliament complained to us about the shield, the symbol of provincial authority. It pictured items important only to the Tolai and Duke of York Islanders: the *tubuan* figure, a large roll of *tambu*, and the two birds representing the moieties.

Yet, at the very least, Tolanger was asserting—through his alarm and the national publicity it received—that the Tolai and Duke of York Islanders, unlike most other Papua New Guinea groups, had an indigenous universal currency that was still powerful. They were shown, in this respect, to be strong and cohesive and, as well, pre-adapted to modernity (though not in the way that T. S. Epstein (1968) described Tolai as primitive capitalists). In other words, more than any other group in Papua New Guinea, they were presented as both traditional and modern.

In this regard, the drama was addressing a more general nationalist dilemma: how to maintain both a distinctive cultural heritage and a rootedness that was not anachronistic but enabled functioning in the contemporary world. The East New Britain solution to this dilemma was inspired. Shell money, as it emerged from the contrasting local and European orientalisms and occidentalisms, had come to represent, to embody, and to enable the essentializing of both traditional and modern values. As we have outlined here, Tolanger's alarm—his response to Crane and Muller's proposed appropriation of shell money—concerned not only the valorization of the medium of value itself, but its valorization as a matter of national significance.[22]

Conclusion

As Robert Foster makes clear in a recent review article on national cultures, 'comparisons of nationalist ideologies . . . disclose radical differences in their ontological grounding, and thus the operation of radically different nationalisms' (Foster 1991: 254). Given cultural diversity and the widespread assumption—the ontological grounding—that cultural groups were always in relations of potential competition, the feasible strategies for pursuing nationalism in Papua New Guinea were limited.

One strategy we have outlined elsewhere. Interestingly, it also took the form of a drama, but a comic drama, about the arrival in East New Britain of the first Methodist missionary and his pacification of the savage cannibals he found there. In this drama, cultural roots were presented as truncated and the significance of deep cultural distinctiveness thereby denied. In other words, by diminishing some of the grounds of complementary opposition, various groups were portrayed as relatively comparable (Errington and Gewertz 1994).

Another strategy, the topic of the present chapter, consisted of efforts to promote the cultural characteristics of particular local groups as the national model. It also, as we have suggested, took the form of a drama, but one perhaps potentially more tragic than comic. In this drama, deep cultural distinctiveness was asserted rather than denied and the field of competition was thereby enhanced rather than diminished. Whereas the first strategy pursued unity through suppressing the competition, the second, and probably ontologically more appealing to Papua New Guineans, pursued unity through suppressing the competitors, at least those who failed to achieve pre-eminence.

It seems to us that for both strategies, the play was the thing. The object of both performances was to catch actors and audience up in the action so that they could forget their habitual 'articulation of separated items on a field of presentation' (Casey 1991: 21). In other words, the object was to reconfigure existing lines of cleavage, fragmentation, and distinction, whether based on culture or class. Thus, actors and audience would be remade, however temporarily, as citizens. Yet, it is not clear to us how effective these dramas ultimately could be. We doubt that many prospective citizens would have suspended for long what were, after all, in Papua New Guinea, myriad and compelling disbeliefs.[23]

Acknowledgements

We are grateful to the granting agencies that supported our field trip to the Duke of York Islands for four months in 1991. Errington received a grant-in-aid from the American Council of Learned Societies and a Faculty Research Fellowship from Mount Holyoke College. Gewertz received a Faculty Research Grant from Amherst College. These grants also enabled us to engage in two months of historical research in Papua New Guinea and Australia. We thank our Papua New Guinea colleagues at the National Archives and University of Papua New Guinea for their assistance. To Joe Nom of the University's New Guinea Collection and to Tom Barker, Marta Rohatynskyj, and Karolus Walagat of the East New Britain Provincial Government, we send a special thanks. In Australia, we worked primarily at the Mitchell Library in Sydney and at National Archives in Canberra. Librarians at both of these facilities were very helpful. In addition, we thank our friends and colleagues at the Research School of Pacific Studies—particularly Jim Fox and Michael Young—for facilitating our stay in Canberra by appointing us

Visiting Fellows. Errington had, prior to 1991, made two trips to the Duke of York Islands. In 1968, in collaboration with Shelly Errington, he spent a year on Karavar Island under a grant from the National Institute of Mental Health; in 1972 he spent four months on Karavar, sponsored by a Crary Summer Fellowship from Amherst College. He expresses gratitude to each of these institutions. We also wish to acknowledge the friends and colleagues who commented on early drafts of this chapter: Dorothy and David Counts, Jan Dizard, Robert Foster, Nancy McDowell, Donald Pitkin have made friendly, if sometimes critical, suggestions. Carolyn Errington, whose editorial skills have long been invaluable to us, deserves and is sent much more than thanks. Finally, we note that the order in which our names appear is arbitrary, for we wrote this article jointly.

Notes

1 The literature concerning attempts on the part of minority groups to promote and defend their own representations of identity has proliferated in recent years. For provocative presentations see Gwaltney (1981), Whisnant (1983), Clifford (1988: 277–346), Handler (1988), Nadel-Klein (1991*b*), and many of the essays in Hobsbawm and Ranger (1983). For recent analyses focusing on the Pacific in particular, see Babadzan (1988), Keesing (1989), Linnekin and Poyer (1990), LiPuma and Meltzoff (1990), and White (1991).

2 Despite the occasional anachronism, we use 'Papua New Guinea' in this chapter to refer to the geographical entity which only in 1975 became an independent nation of that name. Prior to that time, Europeans referred to it—or parts of it—in various ways.

3 We recognize that the value of money is always significantly a matter of representation—one of perception. See, in this regard, Virginia Dominguez's interesting study of how dollars came to be regarded in Israel as more 'real' than shekels (Dominguez 1990: 16–44).

4 All names except ours have been changed and identities, as far as feasible, obscured.

5 On the Maori, see, among others, Hanson (1989) and Wilford (1990). On Australian Aboriginals, see Morphy (1983), Myers (1988, 1991), and Nadel-Klein (1991*a*). On Native Americans see Clifford (1988: 215–51) and Raymond (1989, 1990). For works of more general interest see Fischer (1989), Karp and Levine (1991), and Terrell (1991). See also Hillerman's (1989) fictional account of the controversy surrounding the Smithsonian's claims to Native American bones in the name of 'science'.

6 This is not to say that the Tolai and Duke of York Islanders were the same people: their languages, as well as other aspects of their culture, were distinct though closely related. In our effort to understand the drama with its focus on shell money, we concentrate on certain important similarities between Tolai and Duke of York Islanders, including a largely common colonial history.

7 Indeed, in 1982, East New Britain had a higher percentage (31%) of students enrolled in grades seven to ten (approximately ages 13 to 16) than any other province in the country (Bray 1985*a*: 17). But Tolai fared even better educationally than others within East New Britain. For example, in 1983 81% of elementary-age Tolai children were enrolled in community primary school, compared to 63% on the Duke of York Islands, 59% in the two Baining census divisions, and 36% in the three Pomio census divisions (data extrapolated from Bray 1985*b*: 189).

8 Writing at the turn of the century, and basing his analysis on German colonial sources, Oskar Schneider confirmed this point. It was because shell money was more valuable than European currency to local people that the German administration both remunerated and fined them in shell money. Schneider wrote:

> All work is compensated with diwarra; the administration, thus, pays those who have been sent away to work one strand monthly, along with food once a day.
>   It is not only due to the buying power of the diwarra, but also its value [literally, belovedness], that it is taken as atonement for everything, even the worst crimes . . .
>   The administration also makes use of the value of diwarra. In 1896–97 the government pulled in 923 strands in fines from the natives, and, in addition, on various punitive expeditions, the islanders would only be granted pardon for their misdeeds after a payment of strands of diwarra. (Schneider 1905: 31–2, trans. Margaret Gates)

   See the history of New Ireland–European contact by Paula Rubel and Abraham Rosman (n.d.) for additional confirmation of the preference for shell money.

9 Strings of shell money were rarely purchased directly with money; unstrung shells sometimes were, at rates which varied considerably over time for the volume acquired. The most usual way to acquire shell money was through selling locally grown foodstuffs or consumable trade goods (such as biscuits and tobacco) (see, for confirmation, Neumann 1992: 166–71).

10 For an informative discussion of the sequential responses by the nearby Tangans to capital penetration, see Foster (1988: 22–70).

11 Some Duke of York Islanders had begun to pay Community Government taxes with strings of shell money: 2.5 fathoms per nuclear family was considered an amount equivalent to the annual tax of K5.00 (approximately $US 5.50). These fathoms were later converted into money when individuals purchased them for use, primarily in mortuary and marriage ceremonies. As we watched the Duke of York Islands Community Government President collect the taxes on Karavar Island, we saw several individuals buy the strings of shells their co-villagers had contributed. The President said that Tolai, as well, often bought Duke of York shell money in this manner but he was adamant that 'none would leave the province'.

12 As Counts (1971), McDowell (1988), and Kaplan (1989) have made clear, to use the more familiar term of 'cargo cult' would be inappropriately ethnocentric. 'Cults' existed only from the outside looking in. See more generally Lindstrom (1993).

13 Although the Kaun and the Mataungan Association were contemporaneous and committed to achieving social equality with Europeans, members of each had very different views concerning the desirability and feasibility of self-government. See Errington (1974*a*) for a more complete comparison.

14 e.g. the early encounter Marshall Sahlins (1981, 1985) describes, in which the Hawaiians regarded Captain Cook as the god Lono. (For a critique of Sahlins's account of Cook as Lono see Obeyesekere 1992.)

15 In this regard, the *Rabaul Times* reported in 1957 that

> The Commonwealth Bank will invite native village councilors and native clients to attend the opening of the new 'Native Accounts' premises at the Rabaul branch . . . The bank has had native accounts for many years but has only recently opened extensions to the buildings specially designed for native clients. (*Rabaul Times* 1957)

The number of active native clients in the Rabaul area had grown considerably during the late 1950s; by 1957, they numbered nearly 20,000. Presumably white depositors had begun to find banking side by side with so many native investors discomfiting.

16 Of course, Europeans were also exposed to, and in some cases also rejected, comparable, essentialistic messages intended to convince them that their own system of economic differentiation was equitable. Thus, in a series of moralistic advertisements for the Commonwealth Bank of Australia which appeared over a twenty-year period in the *Rabaul Times*, Europeans in Papua New Guinea—also subject to the vicissitudes of a coconut economy—were enjoined to be thrifty and save regularly in order to achieve economic autonomy and self-sufficiency. They were told, for instance,

> The petty borrower loses prestige and friends. He is trading on the thrift of others whilst practicing none himself. He is selling his pride on the instalment plan—a pound at a time. The man of self-respect, the man who values the good will of others, takes care that he is never in the position of being 'short of a pound'. (*Rabaul Times* 1941*a*)

17 Indeed, Errington's arrival on Karavar in 1968 was welcomed largely because it was hoped he could help build a factory or, barring that, provide access to the fruits of factories by teaching them the secret numbers necessary to receive large amounts of goods with little or no payment.

18 One Papua New Guinea journalist recently reported her shock at discovering homelessness in her own country. She wrote:

> There is no reason why Papua New Guineans should live in poverty. We have an abundance of agricultural land available where people can grow

their own food and hunt or fish from their own traditional hunting and fishing grounds . . . [As she and a colleague drove into the Baruni rubbish dump outside of Port Moresby, all they] could see near the huge mound of rubbish that was just thrown out by a garbage truck were women and children all bending down and retrieving whatever was edible from the refuse. I could not believe my eyes that this was happening in our own country. (Seneka 1991: 12)

Her response, however, can be regarded as somewhat stereotypic as this condition, and shocked responses to it, had existed in Port Moresby for at least a decade.

19 This apt phrase was coined by Nicholas Thomas (1992: 76) to capture Pacific Island perceptions of Western societies.

20 Interestingly, we often heard wealthy Tolai described by marginal peoples in East New Britain as like Europeans. Thus, they might provide you with food but would not eat with you. One man, in fact, told us that 'the Tolai think of themselves as a master race'. Similar perceptions of Tolai condescension have been reported by Andrew Lattas, among the Kaliai of West New Britain (personal communication), and Jane Fajans, among the Baining of East New Britain (personal communication). Tolai were, certainly, aware of possible ethnic discontent among these marginal peoples: Tolai Provincial Government officials had, for example, employed two Western anthropologists to study their ethnic minorities.

21 Jo Mangi (1989) makes a similar point and suggests that it might be necessary to refer to prehistory in order to establish a unitary identity for Papua New Guineans.

22 We have heard much of late about British objections to the substitution of a common European currency for the pound; we have heard, as well, worries about the intentions of the various republics formed from the old Soviet Union to use different currencies. Much commentary concerning these objections and worries involved a limited definition of value: it focused on fiscal encumbrances—on the difficulty, for instance, of measuring one currency against another—rather than on representational importance. But it is no accident that the coins and bills issued by most nation-states generally depicted either historically significant figures or contemporary occupants of historically significant positions—Abraham Lincoln, or the Queen. Tolanger's drama about the valorization of the medium of value had, in this respect, a world-wide cast. (On a different sort of representation and currency, see Hart 1986.)

23 The achievement of nationalism in Papua New Guinea may, in actuality, lie ultimately with the predominance of consumer capitalism, however lamentable that may be for other reasons (see Foster n.d.). In other words, for nationalism to work, Papua New Guinea may need less of the dramatic and more of the everyday.

References

BABADZAN, ALAIN (1988). 'Kastom and Nation Building in the South Pacific', in Remo Guidieri, Francesco Pellizzi, and Stanley J. Tambiah (eds.), *Ethnicities and Nations*. Austin, Tex.: University of Texas Press: 199–228.

BLOCH, MAURICE, and PARRY, JONATHAN (1989). 'Introduction: Money and the Morality of Exchange', in J. Parry and M. Bloch (eds.), *Money and the Morality of Exchange*. Cambridge: Cambridge University Press: 1–32.

BOURDIEU, PIERRE (1977). *Outline of a Theory of Practice*, trans. Richard Nice. Cambridge: Cambridge University Press.

BRADLEY, CHRISTINE (1982). 'Tolai Women and Development', Ph.D. thesis (London).

BRAY, MARK (1985*a*). 'An Overview of Issues', in M. Bray and Peter Smith (eds.), *Education and Social Stratification in Papua New Guinea*. Melbourne: Longman Cheshire: 1–30.

——(1985*b*). 'Social Stratification and Disparities in Access to Education in East New Britain', in M. Bray and Peter Smith (eds.), *Education and Social Stratification in Papua New Guinea*. Melbourne: Longman Cheshire: 182–93.

BURKE, KENNETH (1969). *A Rhetoric of Motives*. Berkeley, Calif.: University of California Press.

BURRIDGE, KENELM (1969). *New Heaven, New Earth*. New York: Schocken Books.

CASEY, EDWARD (1991). 'Between the Soft Space of Memory and the Hard Rock of Place: Remembering Forgetting', unpublished MS.

CLIFFORD, JAMES (1988). 'Identity in Mashpee', in J. Clifford, *The Predicament of Culture*. Cambridge, Mass.: Harvard University Press: 277–346.

COUNTS, DAVID, and COUNTS, DOROTHY (1970). 'The Vula of Kaliai: A Primitive Currency with Commercial Use', *Oceania*, 41: 90–105.

COUNTS, DOROTHY (1971). 'Cargo or Council', *Oceania*, 41: 288–97.

DANKS, BENJAMIN (1888). 'On the Shell Money of New Britain', *Journal of the Royal Anthropological Institute of Great Britain and Ireland*, 17: 305–17.

DOMINGUEZ, VIRGINIA (1986). 'The Marketing of Heritage', *American Ethnologist*, 13: 546–55.

——(1990). 'Representing Value and the Value of Representation: A Different Look at Money', *Cultural Anthropology*, 5: 16–44.

DOUGLAS, MARY (1967). 'Primitive Rationing', in Raymond Firth (ed.), *Themes in Economic Anthropology*. London: Tavistock: 119–47.

EINZIG, PAUL (1949). *Primitive Money in its Ethnological, Historical and Economic Aspects*. London: Eyre & Spottiswoode.

EPSTEIN, A. L. (1963). 'Tambu: A Primitive Shell Money', *Discovery*, 24: 28–32.

——(1969). *Matupit*. Berkeley, Calif.: University of California Press.

——(1979). 'Tambu: The Shell Money of the Tolai', in R. H. Hook (ed.), *Fantasy and Symbol*. New York: Academic Press: 149–205.

THE LIGHTKEEPER MISSES HIS WIFE IN 1996

Laurinda Lind

Every time, it's tragic for him to hear
how his wife died three years past, so they
should quit telling him and let him rest,
thinking she's a room away, yet hidden.

Back in the aughts, he was born in a lighthouse
and slept in a top drawer lest the St. Lawrence
wash in across the floor. Their island rock
was only big enough for them. They wove a garden

from peat bogs floating past, blasted loose from shore
when marsh gas exploded. The cat caught crawdads
in the shallows. Steamers leaked watermelons
that bobbed in the channel till the father rowed

back out for them. Winters, the boy, the future
keeper, frequently drowned due to inconsistent ice
and, with each revival, he must have seen her,
arcing toward him, a beam visible

even from earliest years—else,
why look for her now while the lens
is dim as dust, and why should she shine
to him still, when the light is nearly lost?

EPSTEIN, T. S. (1968). *Capitalism, Primitive and Modern*. Canberra: Australian National University Press.

ERRINGTON, FREDERICK K. (1974*a*). 'Indigenous Ideas of Order, Time and Transition in a New Guinea Cargo Movement', *American Ethnologist*, 1: 255–67.

——(1974*b*). *Karavar*. Ithaca, NY: Cornell University Press.

——and GEWERTZ, DEBORAH B. (1994). 'From Darkness to Light in the George Brown Jubilee: The Invention of Non-tradition and the Inscription of a National History in East New Britain', *American Ethnologist*, 21: 104–22.

FISCHER, MICHAEL (1989). 'Museums and Festivals: Notes on the Poetics and Politics of Representation Conference', *Cultural Anthropology*, 4: 204–21.

FOSTER, ROBERT (1988). 'Social Reproduction and Value in a New Ireland Society', Ph.D. thesis (Chicago).

——(1991). 'Making National Cultures in the Global Ecumene', *Annual Reviews in Anthropology*, 20: 235–60.

——(n.d.). 'Studying National Culture in Papua New Guinea', unpublished MS.

GEWERTZ, DEBORAH B., and ERRINGTON, FREDERICK K. (1991). *Twisted Histories, Altered Contexts: Representing the Chambri in a World System*. Cambridge: Cambridge University Press.

GROSART, IAN (1982). 'Nationalism and Micronationalism: The Tolai Case', in Roland J. May (ed.), *Micronationalist Movements in Papua New Guinea*. Canberra: Australian National University Press: 139–75.

GWALTNEY, JOHN (1981). *Drylongso*. New York: Vintage.

HANDLER, RICHARD (1985). 'On Having a Culture', in George Stocking (ed.), *Objects and Others: Essays on Museums and Material Culture*. Madison, Wis.: University of Wisconsin Press: 192–217.

——(1988). *Nationalism and the Politics of Culture in Quebec*. Madison, Wis.: University of Wisconsin Press.

HANSON, ALLAN (1989). 'The Making of the Maori', *American Anthropologist*, 91: 890–902.

HART, KEITH (1986). 'Heads or Tails? Two Sides of the Coin', *Man*, 21: 637–56.

HILLERMAN, TONY (1989). *Talking God*. New York: Harper & Row.

HOBSBAWM, ERIC, and RANGER, TERENCE (eds.) (1983). *The Invention of Tradition*. Cambridge: Cambridge University Press.

HOOPER, ANTONY, *et al.*, (eds.) (1987). *Class and Culture in the South Pacific*. Auckland: Center for Pacific Studies and Institute of Pacific Studies.

KAPFERER, BRUCE (1988). *Legends of People, Myths of State*. Washington, DC: Smithsonian Institution Press.

——(1989). 'Nationalist Ideology and a Comparative Ideology', *Ethnos*, 54: 161–99.

KAPLAN, MARTHA (1989). 'Meaning, Agency and Colonial History', *American Ethnologist*, 17: 3–22.

KARP, IVAN, and LEVINE, STEVEN (1991). *Exhibiting Cultures*. Washington, DC: Smithsonian.

KEESING, ROGER (1989). 'Creating the Past: Custom and Identity in the Pacific', *Contemporary Pacific*, 1: 19–42.

LÉVI-STRAUSS, CLAUDE (1962). *Totemism*. Boston: Beacon Press.

LINDSTROM, LAMONT (1993). *Cargo Cult: Strange Stories of Desire from Melanesia and beyond*. Honolulu: University of Hawaii Press.

LINNEKIN, JOCEYLN, and POYER, LIN (eds.) (1990). *Cultural Identity and Ethnicity in the Pacific*. Honolulu: University of Hawaii Press.

LIPUMA, EDWARD, and MELTZOFF, SARA (1990). 'Ceremonies of Independence and Public Culture in the Solomon Islands', *Public Culture*, 3: 77–92.

MACFARLANE, ALAN (1985). 'The Root of All Evil', in David Parkin (ed.), *The Anthropology of Evil*. Oxford: Basil Blackwell: 57–76.

MALINOWSKI, BRONISLAW (1921). 'The Primitive Economics of the Trobriand Islands', *Economic Journal*, 31: 1–16.

——(1954). 'Magic, Science and Religion', in B. Malinowski, *Magic, Science and Religion*. Garden City, NY: Doubleday-Anchor: 17–92.

MANGI, JO (1989). 'The Role of Archaeology in Nation Building', in R. Layton (ed.), *Conflict in the Archaeology of Living Traditions*. London: Unwin Hyman: 217–27.

MCBRYDE, ISABEL (ed.) (1985). *Who Owns the Past?* Oxford: Oxford University Press.

MCDOWELL, NANCY (1988). 'A Note on Cargo Cults and the Cultural Construction of Change', *Pacific Studies*, 11: 121–34.

MORPHY, HOWARD (1983). ' "Now You Understand": An Analysis of the Way Yolngu Have Used Sacred Knowledge to Retain their Autonomy', in Nicholas Peterson and Marcia Langton (eds.), *Aborigines, Land and Land Rights*. Canberra: Institute of Aboriginal Studies: 110–33.

MYERS, FRED (1988). 'Locating Ethnographic Practice: Romance, Reality and Politics in the Outback', *American Ethnologist*, 15: 609–24.

——(1991). 'Representing Culture: The Production of Discourse(s) for Aboriginal Acrylic Paintings', *Cultural Anthropology*, 6: 26–62.

NADEL-KLEIN, JANE (1991a). 'Picturing Aborigines: A Review Essay on After Two Hundred Years', *Cultural Anthropology*, 6: 414–23.

——(1991b). 'Reweaving the Fringe: Localism, Tradition and Representation in British Ethnography', *American Ethnologist*, 18: 500–17.

NELSON, HANK (1982). *Taim Bilong Masta*. Sydney: Australian Broadcasting Commission.

NEUMANN, KLAUS (1992). *Not the Way It Really Was: Constructing the Tolai Past*. Honolulu: University of Hawaii Press.

OBEYESEKERE, GANANTH (1992). *The Apotheosis of Captain Cook*. Princeton, NJ: Princeton University Press.

PARRY, JONATHAN (1989). 'On the Moral Perils of Exchange', in J. Parry and

Maurice Bloch (eds.), *Money and the Morality of Exchange*. Cambridge: Cambridge University Press: 64–93.

Post-Courier (1991). 'Cultural Shipment Confiscated', *Post-Courier* (17 Oct.): 3.

Rabaul Times (1941*a*). 'Advertisement for the Commonwealth Savings Bank', *Rabaul Times* (28 Mar.): page unknown.

——(1941*b*). 'Where the Cultures Meet', *Rabaul Times* (8 Aug.): page unknown.

——(1957). 'Native Clients Attend Bank Opening', *Rabaul Times* (29 Mar.): page unknown.

RAYMOND, CHRIS (1989). 'Some Scholars Upset by Stanford's Decision to Return American Indian Remains for Re-burial by Tribe', *Chronicle of Higher Education* (5 July): A5–7.

——(1990). 'Dispute between Scholar, Tribe Leaders over Book on Hopi Ritual Raises Concerns about Censorship of Studies of American Indians', *Chronicle of Higher Education* (17 Oct.): A6, 8–9.

ROHEIM, GEZA (1923). 'Heiliges Geld in Melanesien', *Internationale Zeitschrift für Psychoanalyse*, 9: 384–401.

RUBEL, PAULA, and ROSMAN, ABRAHAM (n.d.). 'Aliens on our Shores: A History of New Ireland–European Contact', unpublished MS.

SACK, PETER, and CLARK, DYMPHNA (eds.) (1979). *German New Guinea: The Annual Reports*. Canberra: Australian National University Press.

SAHLINS, MARSHALL (1981). *Historical Metaphors and Mythical Realities*. Ann Arbor, Mich.: University of Michigan Press.

——(1985). *Islands of History*. Chicago: University of Chicago Press.

SALISBURY, RICHARD (1966). 'Politics and Shell Money Finance in New Britain', in Marc Swartz, Victor Turner, and Arthur Tuden (eds.), *Political Anthropology*. Chicago: Aldine: 114–28.

——(1970*a*). 'Dukduks, Dualism and Descent Groups: The Place of Parkinson in Ethnological Theory'. Paper presented at the Bismarcks Conference, Santa Cruz, Calif.

——(1970*b*). *Vunamami*. Berkeley, Calif.: University of California Press.

SCHNEIDER, OSKAR (1905). *Muschelgeld-Studien*. Dresden: Ernst Engelmann's Nachfg.

SENEKA, KONIO (1991). 'The Cost of Urban Drift', *Times of Papua New Guinea* (4 July): 12.

SILVERMAN, MARTIN (1977). 'Making Sense: A Study of a Banaban Meeting', in Janet Dolgin, David S. Kemnitzer, and David M. Schneider (eds.), *Symbolic Anthropology*. New York: Columbia University Press: 451–79.

SIMET, JACOB (1992). 'Tabu', Ph.D. thesis (Australian National University).

TERRELL, JOHN (1991). 'Disneyland and the Future of Museum Anthropology', *American Anthropologist*, 93: 149–52.

THOMAS, NICHOLAS (1992). 'Substantivization and Anthropological Discourse: The Transformation of Practices into Institutions in Neotraditional Pacific Societies', in James G. Carrier (ed.), *History and Tradition in Melanesian Anthropology*. Berkeley, Calif.: University of California Press: 64–85.

What is Wealth? (n.d.). Reserve Bank of Australia.

WHISNANT, DAVID (1983). *All that is Native and Fine*. Chapel Hill, NC: University of North Carolina Press.

WHITE, GEOFFREY (1991). *Identity through History*. Cambridge: Cambridge University Press.

WILFORD, JOHN (1990). 'Anthropology Seen as Father of Maori Lore', *New York Times*, 20 Feb.: C1, 12.

WORSLEY, PETER (1968). *The Trumpet Shall Sound: A Study of 'Cargo' Cults in Melanesia*, 2nd edn. New York: Schocken.

Your Money (n.d.). Reserve Bank of Australia.

The Colonial, the Imperial, and the Creation of the 'European' in Southern Africa

Robert Thornton

South Africa's history has long been characterized as the struggle between an imperial power, England, and indigenous people who have sought to maintain their independence or autonomy. The interests of the imperial power, according to the standard view, were mainly to control the territory of southern Africa and to control access to natural and human resources within it. Far from being a merely historical interpretation, this view was tantamount to policy from the time that Cecil John Rhodes took his seat in the Cape Parliament in 1881 (Rotberg 1988: 128) soon after the crushing defeat at Majuba of the first British attempt to annex the Transvaal. It continued to be the policy of successive British governments and of imperialists within southern Africa up to the instigation of the Anglo-Boer War, which led to the eventual unification of what is today South Africa under British control, and to eventual independence of the Union of South Africa under a white government.

Historians and anthropologists have been aware of the many nuances and ambiguities in actual relations of power within and between European and African actors in this complex political arena (Gluckman 1940; Marks 1986), but, for the most part, the relationship has been treated as a categorical one between 'whites' or 'Europeans' on the one hand, and on the other 'blacks' or 'Africans' (e.g. Crapanzano 1985; Freund 1984: 55, 104; Hunter 1936; Macmillan 1963; Muller 1981; Omer-Cooper 1987; Wilson and Thompson 1971, and many others). The interests of the indigenous black African peoples have been understood as efforts to co-operate with, but at the same time to resist, this co-optation (e.g. Comaroff 1985; Marks 1986).

These standard histories (liberal, radical, and revisionist alike) focus on the gradual expansion of British territorial claims, the extension of capitalism and racism, and finally the spread of state bureaucratic control over the lives of all southern Africans. This began in 1798 when the British took over the small Cape Colony (in order to keep it from the French, not for its intrinsic interest to the British Crown or its Empire) and led finally to the violent capture of two independent creole[1] states of the Afrikaners or Boers—the South African Republic (known as the Transvaal) and the Orange Free State. The two Boer republics were amalgamated with the territories of Transkei (formerly Kaffraria) and Griqualand, and with the colonies of the Cape and Natal, and the whole was ruled directly from Britain until 1910. The subsequent Union of South Africa, created in 1910, metamorphosed into the Republic of South Africa in 1961. The Republic left the Commonwealth soon thereafter and was a pariah state until the beginning of the 1990s.

The country is currently in the process of another metamorphosis. For the most part the struggle is still seen in much the same terms, that is, a struggle between a colonial and settler regime, and a relatively united black opposition. These characterizations do accurately reflect some of the main trends of southern African history. However, they have missed, or at least partially obscured, two important features in southern African history which have helped to shape the country and which continue to play a role in contemporary politics and culture, both within South Africa itself and within the field of its relations with the rest of the world. These features take the form of tensions between poles or oppositions of the whole southern African polity. The first of these tensions is that between the creole European-derived populations on the one hand, and on the other the representatives of British imperial power. The second tension, closely related to the first, is between southern Africa as a unified political arena with a common historical pattern and set of problems, and the 'outside', represented most strongly by Great Britain and 'Europe'.[2] This second tension amounts to a form of occidentalism since it reified Europe and exploited this image of the European within the southern African political area.

The more obvious tension between black and white adds a third dimension to this set of political polarities. While this last polarity has attracted by far the most attention, a closer look at southern African society shows that it does not replace the others or overwhelm them. The historian W. M. Macmillan (1963) represented this complexity in terms of a triangulation between three terms, 'Bantu', 'Boer', and 'Briton', but this image emphasized their categorical differences, as if these social categories were fixed and obvious. The nature of and frequent ambiguity between boundaries of the social 'inside' and the 'outside' were analytically ignored primarily because they appeared to be obvious to a colonial historian early in the twentieth century. By dissecting the body of history as if it were composed of these three cultural polarities—that is, that between indigenous Europeans and imperial agents, that between South Africa as single political arena and the 'outside' represented by a reified Europe, and that between black and white—we can achieve an alternative view that exposes new historical trends which are still relevant to our understanding of contemporary South Africa.

I will examine the emergence and significance of the first two of these social-cultural tensions in the nineteenth century, especially that between the inside and the outside, in the context of south-eastern South Africa, in the imbricated regions of Natal and KwaZulu.[3] This is most relevant to the nature of occidentalism in the region, but is also of broader importance for understanding the emergence of the political culture of modern South Africa. Equally, however, this discussion reveals the complexities that can exist within an abstract notion like occidentalism as a 'conception of the West'. In partial contrast to the 'reaction to conquest' model (e.g. Hunter 1936) or 'resistance' model (e.g. Comaroff 1985; Comaroff and Comaroff 1992), I argue that the occidentalisms that appeared in southern Africa during the nineteenth century did not emerge in the neatly dichotomized field of intruding colonial power and indigenous residents. This is especially true in the Natal and KwaZulu region, but it is also true of the western Cape region. It is clearly less true of the Transvaal and the eastern Cape region, where white Boer voortrekkers ('pioneers') met black Africans directly in bloody conflict over distinct mutual borders or came into bipolar conflict over resources such as cattle or water.

In Natal–KwaZulu especially, indigenous people did not fix their gaze on a uniform body of intruders and, by a complex cultural process, highlight and essentialize its distinguishing features. Accounts of European survivors of shipwrecks from 1552 show clearly that the region was already complex, and had been absorbing people of European, Indian, Khoikhoi, and San origin from at least that time onwards (Morris 1992; Wilson and Thompson 1971: 78–86). Equally, Westerners in southern Africa did not see themselves as a homogeneous group uniformly representative of self-evident European power and culture. The field was not so neatly structured and the ways that cultural understandings emerged were not so orderly. The reality of southern African history and the identities and attributes of the contending parties were much too messy to sustain any neat tale of White vs. Black, Intruder vs. Indigene, the West vs. Africa. In one of the most insightful discussions of the regions yet written, based on field research in 1936–8 in the central regions of the old Zulu Kingdom, Max Gluckman wrote in his 'Analysis of a Social Situation in Modern Zululand' that the Zulu and the European

form together a community with specific modes of behaviour to one another. Only by insisting on this point can one begin to understand the behaviour of the people [during the opening ceremony of a new bridge in the Nongoma District near Ceza] as I have described it. . . . [H]ere I note only that the existence of single Black–White community in Zululand must be the starting point of my analysis. (Gluckman 1940: 10–11)

It is clear that a cultural and social dichotomy of white and black, European and African/Zulu did emerge and became essentialized, most especially during the period of 'colour-bar' segregation during the period of the Union government, and most cruelly exacerbated during the period of Apartheid legislation from 1948 until the beginning of the 1990s. But, to argue that this happened as a consequence of a 'reaction to conquest', or that it represented a direct form of resistance on the part of the Zulu, would be unjustified simplification, since it did not come about through any clear and original confidence in the superiority of the 'Europeans' in their contest with the Zulu. There were military successes, defeats, and stand-offs on all sides; culturally, each community was internally divided in many ways. These essentialisms took time to develop: they have a history. Moreover, the Zulu essentialization of the European—their indigenous occidentalism—took two quite divergent forms: that of rapacious white racism on the one hand, and on the other that of the ultimate source of justice and power. White essentialization of the Zulu was similarly divided between the view that considered them to be a warlike and aggressive nation, and one that cast the Zulu as the best, most docile kitchen boys and most reliable boss-boys of black labour in the mines.

In my description of some of the history that shaped the emergence of these essentialisms, and particularly Zulu occidentalism, three issues concern me especially. One is the development of southern Africa as a distinct political entity rather than just a dependency of Great Britain. With this development there emerged two distinct, and even opposed, sorts of white power in the area, one local and the other imperial. The second issue is Zulu and European conceptions of legitimate power. These conceptions differed greatly, which affected more than the ways that Zulus and whites understood and acted toward each other. Each sought to accommodate to and incorporate the powers of the other, but because of their different conceptions of power they sought to do so in different ways. The third issue, one I have mentioned already, runs through the two I have described. It is the complexity and contingency of the historical field at the time these essentialisms were emerging, which made it difficult for whites and Zulus to develop simple essential renderings of each other.

Emerging South Africa

Some of this ambiguity is apparent in political developments in the middle of the nineteenth century that coalesced to make southern Africa a common political arena, and therefore a unified object of social action and historical interest that was distinct from European identity. For example, the foundation of the Boer republics in 1852 and 1854 consolidated a distinct self-conception for their inhabitants, as creolized Dutch-speaking Europeans in Africa increasingly came to be called 'Afrikaners' (that is 'Africans' in their own language) or Boers ('farmers', and thus indigenous relative to the traders, miners, and colonial officials). Likewise, when the Cape Legislative Assembly was created in 1858 by Sir George Grey, the British Pro-consul and High Commissioner of the Cape and Natal colonies, and granted local autonomy in 1872 as the responsible government, it was under the leadership of farmers, hunters, traders, and light manufacturers who mostly were English speakers but who also were born in Africa. Theophilus Shepstone was one such person, the locally born son of a rural Wesleyan missionary who was a native speaker of Zulu (Colenso n.d.: 13). He was first appointed Diplomatic Agent to the Native Tribes (that is, the Zulu) in 1845, and was Secretary of Native Affairs for Natal from 1853 to 1875. A local public press had begun to produce literary magazines (such as *Cape Monthly Magazine*), church gazettes, almanacs, business guides, and newspapers, and these began to create and to express a local culture that gradually diverged from the (cultural-geographic) European, even though most English-speakers continued to think of themselves as 'European' (Thornton 1983*a*, 1983*b*).

The creation of southern Africa as a distinct entity, and hence as a basis for a distinct self-conception, was facilitated during the 1850s when, with very few exceptions, South Africa assumed the geographical form that it has today.[4] By the end of the following decade virtually all of the borders of the regions of contemporary South Africa had been either formally negotiated or practically acknowledged, or were defined by natural features such as rivers and mountains. Within this arena a distinctive politics and culture emerged, and the region largely ceased to be a European outpost in terms of its practical identity. Instead, it acquired a local identity, even though this was not always explicit or part of the awareness of the time. Thus, long before an Afrikaans-dominated government removed South Africa from the Commonwealth, it differed significantly from the other states that originated as British colonies. For example, the complex and formal patchwork of borders, languages, and identities among various version of 'the local' that characterized South Africa did not emerge in New Zealand because of the relatively small size of the islands and homogeneity of the indigenous population, as it did not emerge in Australia because of the political simplicity and demographic sparsity of its population. Southern Africa was perhaps most like Canada, where traders and some officials spoke Native American languages and where regions of relative autonomy emerged (Quebec, Northwest Territories). However, in terms of the sheer diversity contained in a single polity, South Africa is probably unique among the Commonwealth nations.

Internal sources of white power

The development of a southern Africa with its own political organizations and productive activities and with its own distinct, indigenous colonial or creole identity raised important issues then and now. By the last quarter of the nineteenth century, southern Africa ceased to be merely a bit of England (or even Europe) transplanted far to the south, wholly dependent on and reflecting British power. Instead, it became possible, even necessary, to distinguish between internal and external sources and uses of power. Like the American colonies, a distinctly colonial identity and culture emerged, with its own forms of political power and its own grounds for establishing the legitimacy of its exercise.

The external source of power, the intruding West of standard South African history, was imperial Britain. However, distinct from it were internal sources of white political power. Among the Boers in the Cape Colony, these included the institution of the commando, originally a self-defence levy led by a *veldkornete* or 'field lieutenant', and the local 'magistrate' or *drosdty*. Missionaries and wealthy tradesmen and farmer-landowners also constituted relatively independent centres of local power. In particular, the efficient and mobile military organization of the Boer commandos, especially when coupled with the judicial and administrative institution of the local magistrates, constituted effective organizations for territorial expansion. The commandos were loosely organized fighting

GRAMMAR SCHOOL (AMBIGUOUS LOSS)

María José Giménez

speaking of darkness
in this tongue I'll never own

I was staring at the ocean, feet pressed on white
sand, when your birthmark surfaced on my thigh

original scar, sorrow incarnate, elided in winter
visible only when twilight lingers late and summer

singes a jagged edge, a lake of light pierced by a shy moon
as if skin remembered where it came from in the sun

eyes hazed by smoke, hair glistening indian
and black blood, fingernails scratching labels

off bottles, sipping afternoons into oblivion, picking scabs
off stubborn wounds to forget how stories burst open

every dawn (dawn / sunrise / early morning
words that never quite add up to madrugada)

how many new phonemes would a tongue
need to explain ambiguous loss, to sing

las caras lindas de mi gente negra
what are the words for forgiveness

forces composed of free Boer farmers, transhumant pastoralists, and hunters. They provided their own mounts and arms and were available either to defend their own land or to fight on behalf of others, including black African kings and chiefs. In fact, as I describe later, it was such a commando group that played a significant role in Zulu politics when it came to the aid of Mpande, the Zulu King, in his successful consolidation of power. More formally, the Cape Parliament that was organized during the 1850s and the missionary organizations also constituted relatively independent groups of political actors, and hence internal sources of power during this period.

Through the 1850s the British Pro-consul, Sir George Grey, was unambiguous about his support for 'home rule' in the Cape, an important step for articulating local, as distinct from imperial, interests. His radically left-liberal position and his earlier experience in Ireland, where he favoured both home rule and the British Empire, led him to value moves that would reinforce the colonial element both as a balance to the imperial and as a reserve on which imperial interests might draw. This had been his previous strategy as a successful governor of South Australia and New Zealand, and he applied it zealously in the Cape Colony and Natal. In fact, he applied it too zealously, for when the Liberal government of Gladstone was replaced in 1858 by the Conservative government of Palmerston, Grey was immediately recalled on the grounds of fostering colonial interests that threatened the imperial interests that he was charged to guarantee. The division of interests, however, was by then well established, and Grey's recall had little effect in southern Africa.

The institutions of local government, whether of the independent Boer states or the Cape Parliament, had ideologies of power that were distinctly different from those of the missionaries, who were autonomous in practice and frequently acted on behalf of African interests and against both imperial agents and colonialists. One observer, Wilhelm Bleek, who was travelling in the Mahlabatini district in the heart of the Zulu Kingdom in 1856, noted that 'the Zulu believe that the Bafundisi ["missionaries", literally "teachers"] are a species of their own' (Bleek 1965: 68). The legitimacy of power for the governing institutions was based on the local settler 'democracy' of the Cape Legislative Assembly or of the Boer *volksraad* ('people's council'), while the legitimacy of the missionaries was based on the concept of a universal Christianity. Both were powerfully underwritten by the authority of texts and, especially with respect to claims to land, by the authority of maps, deeds of registration, and an emergent bureaucracy established to guarantee precisely these claims.

Internal and external politics

Under Grey, however, the polarity between Empire and colony became one that other indigenous peoples could exploit to good advantage. Those who were best able to exploit it were those who, like the Zulu, possessed relatively developed and centralized political organizations. The kings Dingane, Mpande, and Cetshwayo, even in the process of losing their autonomy, could claim to be like the British in their possession of royalty. Others, including the Griqua, the Nama, the Fingo, and the Gcaleka, although much more loosely organized, also attempted to exploit this polarity. Some, like the Nama and Fingo, were relatively successful in that they received guarantees from the imperial centre in the form of Crown Lands that were formally and legally beyond reach of the colonialists. However, others, such as the Xhosa tribes after the Great Cattle Killing, were not able to exploit this polarity. Differing success in identifying with the British Crown in opposition to the white colonialists and their allies, moreover, drove wedges between these peoples that remain today: Xhosa oppose Zulu, Fingo oppose Xhosa and Gcaleka, and the Nama—today fully assimilated to a coloured identity and Afrikaans-speaking—stand opposed to the blacks and the 'Africans'.

Thus, the emergence of these distinct internal sources of power is crucial to the understanding of the formation of a distinctly South African (and Zulu) occidentalism that continues to be relevant. This is because the interests and activities of the indigenized European peoples of southern Africa were distinct from the interests and activities of the imperial British. 'Europeans', 'whites' (*Blankes*), 'Westerners' were not unitary and homogeneous entities. This became clear-cut and obvious, even though it has not attracted commensurate attention from historians. Moreover, the meaning of these terms shifted subtly from one context to the other. Sometimes opposed—as for instance non–Afrikaans-speaking 'foreigners' from Europe, or *uitlanders*, were opposed to Afrikaners in the Transvaal Republic before and until well after the Anglo-Boer War of 1899–1902— and sometimes united in opposition to black Africans, the various terms for the European-derived population in southern Africa always referred to ambiguous and overlapping categories.

All, however, began to recognize the difference between the powers and potentials that existed within the arena of southern Africa and those that existed outside of it. This was the pre-condition for the development of two southern African politics: the politics of the inside and the politics of the outside. South Africa is unusual in the world today in the extent to which its politics has become transnational. While there are many examples that could be cited, the Commonwealth Mission to South Africa of 1986 provides a good illustration. As the Secretary-General of the Commonwealth, Shridath Ramphal, wrote in his foreword to the report of the seven 'Eminent Persons':

Over the last six months a remarkable thing happened in one of the saddest corners of our small world. A group of seven people from five continents, black and white and brown, gave everything they had to—holding back a darkening storm. For a brief moment—South Africans of all races glimpsed a path of negotiation to a more worthy future. (Commonwealth Secretariat 1986: 13)

South Africa's many and contradictory political goals and its methods for achieving them—recently especially Apartheid, but before that the international furore over the British attack on the Boer republics, the South Africa 'Native Question', the Zulu War, David Livingstone's castigation of the Boers, the outlawing of slavery, and the subsequent Great Trek in 1838—have all been part of the politics of other nations and of internationalism *per se* to a much greater degree than is the case for any other African country. In comparison with the atrocities in the twentieth-century European wars of nationalism (called 'World Wars'), or of such wars elsewhere in Africa, in South America, and in South Asia, it is not at all obvious that South Africa's policies and political actions have, in themselves, been more brutal or more outrageous than many others. South Africa has nevertheless taken on the role of a sort of generic political passion play that could be equally useful to capitalists or communists, socialists or democrats. South Africa's politics have been part of debate far beyond the borders of South Africa itself, and for far longer than any particular event would seem to warrant. Political actors within South Africa have long been aware of this. There has developed a strong dichotomy between the politics of 'home' and the politics of external representation which have involved the rest of the world. Moreover, these divergent politics—one internal, one external—have been used by all sides in the political struggles that have characterized southern African society for the last 150 years.

One corollary of this polarity has been the construction of 'the West' as a unique source of power and as a coherent political entity to which appeals could be addressed and which could be imagined as a single moral actor. This construction has been crucial to the development of a politics *of* southern Africa and a politics *for* southern Africa. The European and the African were constructed as separate and opposed categories, not only in Europe, but in Africa, and a politics *within* South Africa became separated from a politics *on behalf of* South Africa. The emergence of these categories of Europe and Africa, and of and for South Africa, shaped and was shaped by concepts of the sources of power, legitimate or otherwise.

Concepts of power and southern African essentialisms

It was not just divergent sources of power that shaped the history of southern Africa. Also important were divergent concepts of power and how it was distributed. In particular, people in southern Africa did not, as Westerners commonly did, limit 'power' to mere administrative power or the ability to effect real changes in some thing or person. Instead, often they had a more diffuse understanding of power as a fundamental quality of life or status. In southern Africa this was expressed in notions of witchcraft, the errant sexuality of witches and their familiars, powers to make or withhold rain, and differing concepts of the relative status and powers of different genders. Such powers were combined in complex ways with political powers of Zulu (and other African) chiefs. While a chief's or king's administrative powers were essential to the maintenance of the polity, they were not essential to his moral status as a chief. In was otherwise for the Europeans, however, since moral and administrative powers were closely linked in their own political cultures. While the organization of the Boer commandos and the British settlers was significantly different, they depended on commonly held notions of legitimacy, legality, and community. Consequently, the relationship between and among leaders and their subjects had different cultural bases for the Zulus and the Europeans.

Certainly the economic interests of the imperial government, the colonists, and the Africans were involved in shaping the emergence of the specific and perhaps unique politics of southern Africa. However, interests that are in every way similar to those that existed in South Africa have existed elsewhere without creating a politics that was driven as much by the moral and political interests of the world community as by its own internal dynamics. The peculiarity of southern Africa springs in part from the developing occidentalist construction of the West, a development in which conceptions of power played an important part. The complex and diffuse understanding of the nature of power that I have mentioned, an understanding that fuses spiritual and other forms of non-material power with the Western understandings of instrumental and administrative power, made it possible to create 'the West' not merely as an ethnic, national, or geographical category, but as a source of a special sort of power.

Under both British and Zulu customary legal norms, the powers of royalty stand outside and above the powers of ordinary government. In both cases, individuals are subjects of the monarch, but equally are members of the political community. That is, they are citizens of legally constituted territories or polities ruled by governments. But while British and Zulu norms were similar in terms of their form, they differed in terms of their content.

In the case of the Zulu Kingdom, African individuals were subject to the king, who formally controlled aspects of their person, while each was also a member of a smaller polity. The types of power that were available to the leader of these smaller polities—the headman (*induna*) or regiment leader—were restricted to control over individuals' labour, their access to land and pasturage, and to other economic resources such as trade goods and, later, education. The king, in theory and at least since the time of Shaka and until the conquest of the Zulu state in 1879, controlled life, death, and the expression of sexuality—especially the right to marry. In the case of the British, royalty commanded political allegiance but did not claim to control the person. In general, the Church did that through its control of the rituals of life's passings and its strictures on expression of sexuality, its regulation of gender roles, marriage, rules of descent, and inheritance. Local leaders of various kinds could control labour, but individuals' sexuality was controlled only by their immediate senior kin (that is, parents) and by those individuals themselves in terms of their relation with God as mediated by the Church. This British concept of sexual regulation characterized all of the European-derived populations in southern Africa, and contrasted sharply with the African concepts and divisions of these rights and powers over the person. In other words, Zulus and Europeans saw the rights to exercise control over person, life and death, property, and sexuality as being quite differently distributed.

This cultural difference was to prove critical, since the Zulu kings' claims to control the sexuality of their subjects were flatly contradicted by the European views. During Mpande's reign, this led many Zulu men to leave the regiments and wander south into the regions of the Natal Colony, where the monarch and government did not claim rights to control when and whom they could marry. In order to marry in Zulu terms, however, men had to exchange cattle for wives according to the practice of *lobola*. But under European concepts of the differences between power over property and power over persons, *lobola* implied that women were being sold in marriage, a form of transaction specifically forbidden by English morality and by British law, and was specifically disallowed.

The result of this mismatch of categories of person and property and of concepts of power was the creation of an enduring mystery, as well as significant demographic shifts and new negotiated loyalties. Indeed, to this day these differing concepts of person, power, and sexuality bedevil understanding and politics in the Natal and KwaZulu region, but in the middle of the nineteenth century they were entirely implicit in the form of practical accommodations and understandings. Like other cultural accommodations, this one was resolved through the reification of powers and categories. For the Zulu, this meant the reification of 'the West' and the emergence of the category of whites, conceptions that function quite differently in South African politics from other, similar constructions that emerged at roughly the same time, such as Indians or coloured. For European settlers and imperial agents, this meant the reification of the Zulu. Because Westerners saw the Zulus as having a state-like polity with a recognizable centre, they could reify and essentialize the Zulu in ways that were impossible for most other African societies they encountered (Martin 1984). The result was that 'Zulu' became the name for a special kind of Africanness, a primordial and powerful autochthony and strength, that did not attach to similar categories, such as 'Sotho' or 'Tswana', 'Hottentot' or 'Kaffir'.

While Westerners tended to see the Zulu as a unitary entity, the situation for the Zulus was different. They confronted missionaries, teachers, traders, and agents of institutional 'powers' (in the European sense), each of whom represented, deliberately and explicitly, some different form of essentialized spiritual, gendered or sexual, material, and organizational powers. The culture of the Zulu, like the culture of southern African societies more generally, already possessed concepts and terms for many types and sources of power. White power quickly became another of these, and 'white' became a name for particular kinds of power that required particular kinds of access. Consequently, it was possible for the Zulu to essentialize the West as wholly powerful, as a source of complex powers that, in Zulu terms, were capable of being manipulated and hence were available to be appropriated. During the middle of the nineteenth century the Zulus refined their conception of this welter of powers into a polarity between the white power of the 'outside', generalized as a form of occidentalism, and the white power of inside, generalized as a form of racism.

These two forms of a single reification of the European—on the one hand as a generalized source of goods and moral authority, and on the other as a form of virulent otherness and violent exclusiveness—continue to shape the political culture of southern Africa. I have already noted that it is customary to speak of southern African history in terms of a more or less 'black and white' struggle, with the phrase echoing a moral dichotomy of good and evil as well as a perceptual dichotomy between people who are relatively dark-skinned and relatively light-skinned. However, it is perhaps more accurate to speak of these dichotomies in ways that allow us to conceive more readily the cultural and historical complexity that they gloss.

The categories of white and black in southern Africa are not simple structural oppositions except in so far as they serve to structure complex semantic fields, any more than they are merely labels for perceptual colours of skin, hair, and eyes. These terms have functioned in the twentieth century to name a particular form of cultural and economic struggle between groups and political communities whose social constitutions have changed over historical time. Most importantly, because the colour terms imply a simple oppositional politics, they have obscured the ethnographic detail of real social relations in actual contexts of daily life. These are important in themselves, but they are also important for understanding the complexities and contingencies of the historical development of social arrangements and accommodations by different sets of people within the region, arrangements that have been shaped by the emergence of cultural concepts and categories that are held in common, or shared as opposed terms in polarities that are constructed out of a common historical experience.

Historical contingency and southern African essentialisms

I said that the story of Natal and the early colonial encounter is perhaps unique, and certainly unusual, in comparison with other histories of colonial encounters. Partly this is because the colonization of Natal was quite late in historical terms. It began only in the third decade of the nineteenth century. Only some fifty years later it ended, in the sense that the main features of social and cultural reference and the main features of political structure came to exist more or less as they continued to exist until April 1994. With experience of the Americas, Asia, Australia, New

Zealand, West Africa, the Cape Colony, and India already behind them (Laband 1992: 7; Thornton 1983*a*), the British traders and tradesmen, missionaries, soldiers, and governors knew what they were doing, so to speak. They were implementing a script for domination that had played well to countless audiences around the world, audiences who—often in spite of themselves—accepted the broad principles of a colonial social order that was imposed sometimes by force of persuasion and sometimes by force of arms, but usually by a sophisticated combination of both that was made possible by clocks, maps, and books, and occasionally enforced by the less certain technology of firearms.

In the region of Natal or KwaZulu, the force of arms was not decisive until the defeat of the Zulu Kingdom at the hands of the British army around 1880. This defeat brought an end to Zulu independence and established the broad principles of territorial and political order that continue to exist today. Before that, while there were many local engagements, there was no general, regional warfare or concerted military engagement. Some of these local engagements were extremely bloody, such as the Zulu King Dingane's attack on the Boers that killed some 200 families in 1838, and the subsequent battle at Blood River that caused the death of 2,000 Zulu soldiers. These, however, remained 'events' in a larger process, both in the eyes of participants and in the eyes of subsequent historians.[5] It was not until the Anglo–Zulu War of 1879 that large-scale military involvement occurred. By then, all of the fundamental structures of domination and accommodation were already in place. The war was almost completely unnecessary. It simply confirmed, with the loss of many lives, an arrangement that already existed.

The history of Africa is frequently told in terms of broad sweeps of peoples and tribes and armies across large, seemingly empty territories. However, the history of the foundation of Zululand and the Colony of Natal cannot be easily or accurately told without constant reference to one or another of a handful of individuals whose personal actions and decisions directly shaped the subsequent history of this part of Africa. One of the reasons they could do so was that both the colonial and the imperial presence was so complex and uncertain that no renderings of the West or the whites seemed predetermined or self-evident. Equally, though I devote less attention to it in this chapter, the diversity within what came to be known as the Zulu Kingdom has been radically underestimated or misconceived. This is partly because the rapid conquests of the Zulu state presented to the first European observers what seemed to be a unified front, behind which real social, cultural, and linguistic diversity was simply suppressed by the violence and wartime exigencies of the period. Also this is partly because historians have, until recently, failed to inquire into the nature of this diversity (Cobbing 1988; Hamilton 1992; Wright 1989).

The diversity the Zulus confronted is illustrated, first of all, by the fact that there were three distinct European-derived communities in the area. These communities had distinct histories and confronted the Zulu in different ways. They were the Portuguese of Delagoa Bay to the north-east, the English traders and frontiersmen of Port Natal (later D'Urban, or Durban) on the coast to the south-east, and the Boers on the western and south-western flank of the Zulu Kingdom. Second, there was already considerable diversity within these communities and a surprising degree of flexibility and mobility among them: English, black and white Americans (Bleek 1965: 70), Dutch and Central European Jews, and other Europeans, 'Hottentots', Indians, and Malays (Bleek 1965: 68), and other Africans. Itinerant tradesmen, cattle herders, hunters, freebooters, transport riders, and scouts added to the more stable groups of farmers, missionaries, imperial agents, a few professionals such as doctors and surveyors (the latter especially important for appropriating land and legitimizing land claims), and the officers of a local colonial government still in its infancy. In the Port Natal settlement from the 1830s were people from most of northern Europe, the British Isles, and America, as well as some Indians and Malays. In the Portuguese settlements were tradesmen, artisans, slaves, hunters, adventurers from Portugal, India, and the Indonesian archipelago, as well as agents of the Portuguese Crown. Circulating among these were escaped and freed slaves, refugees from conflicts that continued to be fierce and destructive long after Shaka's death, as well as escaped prisoners, both white and black. There were, finally, African work-seekers, traders, farmers, herdsmen, and labourers from the interior and from along the coasts to the north and south.

Under these complex and even confused conditions, it was by no means a foregone conclusion that there should emerge any particular reification of Western identity. There was then, as there is today, no obvious single polarity of power, colour, nationality, or regional identity. Moreover, the incorporation of European frontiersmen as chiefs among the Zulu, such as John Dunn and Theophilus Shepstone, as well as the early use of Zulu-speaking catechists and teachers by missionaries, further blunted many polarities that might seem obvious today. As one might expect in such a variegated setting, from the early 1830s to the 1850s racial and ethnic categories in Natal had not yet formed conclusively, and the differences in powers between persons, it appears, always seemed larger than the differences in powers between groups and settlements.

This ambiguity is apparent in assessments of the military power of the many forms of organizations that existed at the time, such as the Boer commando, the Zulu regiments (*impi*s), British garrisons, chiefly retinues, and private means of defence. The relative strength of commandos and small British garrisons had been tested, but without conclusive results.[6] Military power became, of course, increasingly significant as it became increasingly unbalanced, but the outcome of battles was by no means certain as late as the last quarter of the century. The annihilation of the British regiment at Isandlwana in 1879 by the Zulu regiments (Laband 1992: 3, 98), like the convincing defeat of the British column that had been sent to enforce the annexation of the South African Republic (the Transvaal) at Laing's Nek and Majuba Hill in 1880, made it apparent that the balance of military power between the British imperial forces and the forces of the Zulus and the Boer republics was still very much an open question.

This military uncertainty had important consequences for the Zulus. They were not roundly defeated and forced to capitulate. Instead, they managed to 'surrender' to the British with a degree of honour (Laband 1992: 247–52). This made it possible for them to continue a strategy aimed at incorporating some aspects of British powers even while they themselves were being incorporated into the British administrative structures of Empire. Similar, but in a kind of inversion of the Zulu accommodation with the British, was the alliance between the Boer commandos of the voortrekkers' short-lived Republic of Natal, and Mpande, Dingane's brother and claimant to the Zulu paramountcy.

In 1837, the voortrekker column under the leadership of Piet Retief had reached the western marches of Zulu land and attempted to settle there. Dingane evidently agreed to a treaty—or so Retief believed—that ceded land to the Boers. Dingane, however, repented of this action before Retief reached his wagons, and Retief was killed in an act that is memorialized as a special moment of treachery in the formation of Afrikaner identity. The Boers rallied after this event and under a new leader, Andries Pretorius (after whom the capital of contemporary South Africa is named), defended themselves against the Zulu armies that had been sent to annihilate them. Against apparently insuperable odds, the Boer defences held at the Ncome River, with a tremendous cost to the Zulu attackers. Again, these events at what came to be known as Blood River ('Ncome' was the previous Zulu name) were incorporated as formative

in a tongue that twists nada es gratis into nothing is free
a land where freedom oozes tar and bile from black bodies

how to speak of unspeakable sorrow, a life alive but gone
what sound do roots make as they grow inside an empty ribcage

all I've learned from all these suns here is how
to stuff my pockets with words and black stones

when anyone asks where I'm from, I pull them out
and show them your obsidian absence in my hand

elements of Afrikaner foundation myths and helped to solidify an Afrikaner identity and self-confidence. Ironically, this confidence made them available as military allies of Mpande, who used the alliance to overthrow Dingane.

The relative balance of military forces meant that outcomes were always uncertain, and this provided the motive for attempts to form alliances with Boer forces rather than merely to resist them or to accept subjugation to them. In 1828, Shaka, the founder of the Zulu Kingdom, was killed by his half-brothers Dingane and Mhlangana. After he secured his position, Dingane began to relax the strict military discipline of the *amabutho*, the age-grades on which the military regiments were based. Unlike Shaka, however, he permitted two of his brothers to survive his own consolidation of power. One, Mpande, seemed too ineffectual to present a serious threat, but it was he who eventually overthrew his elder brother Dingane. While his motives were complex, his means were simple. In 1839 Mpande fled to escape the dangers of living within striking distance of his brother the King. Subsequently he allied with the Boer commandos on the borders of the Zulu realm, and with their assistance mounted a force that defeated his brother. Mpande was recognized as king by the Boers, and later 'crowned' by the British Native Affairs Agent Theophilus Shepstone.

The events of the thirty years from the 1830s to the 1860s illustrate the fragmented nature of the emerging political arena and reveal a strategy of attempts at mutual incorporation as often as they do attempts at outright domination. The Boers believed that they had ample reason to seek to punish the Zulu. The fact that they did so in alliance with another Zulu chief demonstrates the strategies of mutual incorporation that all sides attempted.

However, it was not only the whites who presented a complex and ambiguous appearance. The same was true of the Zulus. From the 1830s, British settlers had established a trading settlement at Port Natal on the coast. Zulu people, or those people who had recently been incorporated into a kingdom that had come to be known as Zulu only a few years earlier, were already seeking to escape Dingane's demands for labour and for warriors. Sometimes whole regiments, sometimes smaller groups or individuals, fled to the south to seek more peaceful lands, trade goods, and protection along the margins of European and Boer settlements. Eventually, Theophilus Shepstone was established as paramount chief of the 'Exiled Zulus' and prepared to lead them south into the Colony of Natal. By 1848, Shepstone, as one of several Zulu-speaking white people who were fully integrated into the Zulu political structure, was recognized by the colonial government as chief of those Zulu who lived outside the 'kingdom' under Mpande.

Thus, by the beginning of the 1850s the region was divided into a southern tract and a northern Zulu Kingdom. The former was annexed by the British imperial government acting from Cape Town, and the Zulu living in it were placed under the chiefship of a white Zulu-speaker. Although formally designated a Native Agent, Shepstone understood his role in African terms, and was accepted by many Zulu as a chief in the indigenous idiom. In fact, each had captured aspects of the powers of the other's polity. This capture involved consolidation and some redefinition of categories and roles such as 'chief', 'king', 'native agent', and so on. But the choices open to the actors in this context were limited. Unable to establish unambiguous domination in any sphere, it was necessary to reify peoples and to pursue strategies of alliance and accommodation with them and with the powers that they were taken to possess.

Occidentalizing England and the West

Such a reification is the concept that I will call the 'Imperium', a construction of the West, and more particularly England, that allowed the Zulus symbolic access to Western powers in their struggles with encroaching Westerners. Reflecting both the contingent nature of the way occidentalisms emerge and the importance of individuals in southern Africa, this concept of an authoritative, external Western power did not spring from the Zulu themselves. Instead, it was provided largely by the British missionary John William Colenso. Colenso represented himself as coming to the Zulu directly from the Queen herself, not from the Cape or Natal Colony. He spelled this out explicitly in letters written back to English congregations:

[The Zulu] welcomed [me] in the most friendly manner as one sent by the Queen of England 'who loved her black people as well as her white', to see their condition, and devise plans for their improvement. . . . The kafir names . . . given to their Bishop . . . *Sobantu*, 'Father of the People', names which are entirely of their own invention [are] constructed out of the notion which they have formed of the Bishop's duties from what they have been told about them. A powerful chief, Langalibalele, in reply to my question, 'Would he like his children to be taught?', replied 'We are the children; we wish to be taught. We came here to save our lives from our enemy [Mpande], and now we wish to know what our protectors know.' (Colenso n.d.: 8)

Colenso had been a biblical scholar, a mathematician, and a Christian-Socialist follower of the teaching of Frederick Dennison Maurice. He arrived in Natal as bishop of the Anglican Church in 1854 together with his wife, other British missionaries and assistants, and a young Prussian student of African languages, Wilhelm Bleek. Bleek was the son of a prominent German biblical scholar, one of those whom Matthew Arnold later called the 'Higher Critics', and intended to serve as the Bishop's linguist. In the next two decades, Bleek did indeed define the grammars of several South African languages, including the Bantu languages (Bleek chose the name of this family, which included Zulu), and the Khoi (Hottentot) and San (Bushman) languages. But his role in Colenso's party was to act as what we would today recognize as an anthropological linguist. He proceeded immediately to live with Mpande in his own home *umuzi*, or kraal, to learn Zulu and construct its grammar. Bleek's success in this endeavour, and Colenso's success in learning Zulu, permitted early and direct communication between Colenso and the Zulu. It also contributed to the reification of the Zulu as a single linguistic unit. In the preface to the second edition to Colenso's *Zulu Grammar*, published in 1872 and based on Bleek's early linguistic work, Colenso acknowledged that the 'dialect' that was represented by the dictionary was only that of a

small tribe, the amaZulu, who under their famous chief *uTshaka* (Chaka) [Shaka], and his brothers and successors *uDingane* (Dingane) and *umPande* (Panda), have acquired and maintained . . . the supremacy over the natives along the S.E. coast of Africa, excepting, of course, those who have been living under British protection since Natal came under our government . . . On this account it has a right to be considered the standard dialect of this part of Africa. (Colenso 1872: 2)

Colenso was the most important catalyst in the formation of the occidentalism of the Zulu, which is precisely what he set out to do: create an image of 'the West' as an abstract power of justice and light. Indeed, Colenso believed that the missionaries were 'bound to teach' the Zulu all of the benefits of European science, law, and industry, and not just those of religion.

We are bound to teach him, as God shall give us opportunity for so doing, what we [that is, Englishmen] ourselves have learned, not only what we have been enabled to acquire by our own exertions and industry, but what we have *inherited*, and received through the hands of others, from the Father of all, the Father of lights, the 'giver of every good and perfect gift.' Most of all are we bound to impart that highest knowledge . . . of God himself. (Colenso 1864: 16) earlier European teachers invented classicized Greece and Rome. In other words, the teaching practices of the missionaries led to the creation of a particular format of Western Civilization and its codification in a form in which it could be taught. (It is still taught thus today.) Colenso's occidentalism was the result of a specific knowledge practice.

> I had brought to me, for instance, a number of native boys who were given up by their fathers after considerable hesitation for five years education. At the end of that time I was obliged to allow them to return to their homes, according to our agreement. . . . [But], like many a working man in England, [these boys] would desire that their own children should receive a better education than themselves. (Colenso 1864: 18)

The Zulu, perceiving these knowledge practices as powerful, accepted them as access to power. As Colenso reported it, one chief, Nongoza, who brought his children to be educated by Colenso at Ekukanyeni, 'the place of light', declared, 'I should like to be the last fool of my race!' (Colenso 1864: 18).

Teaching not only served to communicate knowledge, but became in itself an emblem of being 'European', hence the occidentalism of the Zulu. But since the knowledge that was communicated, together with the means of its communication, was from outside, from beyond, from the other (as the Zulus saw it), this occidentalism represented an external recourse to power that could be used in the real struggle that existed between the Zulus and the colonialists, the 'creolized' settlers who were in direct competition with them. The occidentalism represented by religion, by the Queen (especially Queen Victoria) and the British royal family, and by the 'outside' as an abstract and moral source of power thus became consolidated as a cultural reality. The nature of this early occidentalism explains in part why South African internal politics has so often sought a resort to forms of moral coercion from the outside, when a delicate balance of violent coercion and its limited potentials for real change restricted recourse to attempts at military domination.

This occidentalism has played an important role in the international condemnation of South African racism. This is because, in its stress on an idealized justice residing in external moral authority, it enabled a politics of an appeal to moral justice that is clearly seen in Colenso's own direct appeals to the Queen or, later, in the Anglican Zulu lawyer Pixley Seme's addresses to the newly organized African National Congress (Rive and Couzens 1991), as well as in Gandhi's formulations of 'protest politics', and up to the present, in the world spread of the Anti-apartheid movement. It has had a vast impact far beyond Zululand.

Naming his bishop's manse 'the place of light', he bypassed the colonial structures, which he feared would interfere with his efforts to communicate the gospel as directly as possible to the Zulu. This aim was shaped by his Broad Church Protestantism and was made possible by the rapid progress that he and Bleek made with the Zulu language. This occidentalism, this reification of the West, was deliberately planned and set into action as an educational strategy by a man of pedagogical training. During a recruitment drive in England in 1857, Colenso argued that the Zulu actually had a 'claim' on England that required their education since they had already been 'heavily taxed' and governed without their consent, received 'as subjects', and given a partial taste of religion. 'Happily,' he claimed to those prospective missionaries who listened to him,

[t]he present moment is full of encouragement. The light is beginning to break at length out of the thick clouds. . . . [The] appointment of his Excellency Sir George Grey . . . [as] our new Governor in Africa . . . [will] aid the efforts of Christian teachers, while publishing the Name of God and the wonders of His Love among them, and to direct the energies of this spirited and intelligent people [that is, the Zulu] into the channels of peaceful industry! . . . [T]he Church of England has the work now in her own hands. (Colenso n.d.: 19–20)

Colenso had been a master of a house at Harrow School under the headmastership of Thomas Arnold, a man who had once remarked that the Empire was won on the playing fields of Eton and Harrow. But the content of the Zulu occidentalism was specifically religious and owes its form to the institutions of the Anglican Church and the Society for the Propagation of Christian Knowledge.

Thus, this occidentalism was not an all-encompassing construction of the West formed in opposition to a unified Zulu identity. It was not the consequence of a conflict between a black and a white ('creole') African identity, or the reflex of resistance to domination, or the reification of the 'oppressor' by the 'weak'. It was not, in other words, generated in the process of a struggle between the Zulus and the forces of imperialism, the British Crown and its pursuit of Empire. Instead, it was specifically designed for the purpose of teaching, rather like the reifications of Ancient Greece and Rome that emerged first during the later Middle Ages, when the methods adopted for teaching Greek and Latin as keys to knowledge led inevitably to the reification of the classic civilizations associated with them.

To pursue his plan to teach the Zulu the knowledge of the West, Colenso self-consciously invented an occidentalized West, just as the

Naming his bishop's manse 'the place of light', he bypassed the colonial structures, which he feared would interfere with his efforts to communicate the gospel as directly as possible to the Zulu. This aim was shaped by his Broad Church Protestantism and was made possible by the rapid progress that he and Bleek made with the Zulu language. This occidentalism, this reification of the West, was deliberately planned and set into action as an educational strategy by a man of pedagogical training. During a recruitment drive in England in 1857, Colenso argued that the Zulu actually had a 'claim' on England that required their education since they had already been 'heavily taxed' and governed without their consent, received 'as subjects', and given a partial taste of religion. 'Happily,' he claimed to those prospective missionaries who listened to him,

[t]he present moment is full of encouragement. The light is beginning to break at length out of the thick clouds. . . . [The] appointment of his Excellency Sir George Grey . . . [as] our new Governor in Africa . . . [will] aid the efforts of Christian teachers, while publishing the Name of God and the wonders of His Love among them, and to direct the energies of this spirited and intelligent people [that is, the Zulu] into the channels of peaceful industry! . . . [T]he Church of England has the work now in her own hands. (Colenso n.d.: 19–20)

Colenso had been a master of a house at Harrow School under the headmastership of Thomas Arnold, a man who had once remarked that the Empire was won on the playing fields of Eton and Harrow. But the content of the Zulu occidentalism was specifically religious and owes its form to the institutions of the Anglican Church and the Society for the Propagation of Christian Knowledge.

Thus, this occidentalism was not an all–encompassing construction of the West formed in opposition to a unified Zulu identity. It was not the consequence of a conflict between a black and a white ('creole') African identity, or the reflex of resistance to domination, or the reification of the 'oppressor' by the 'weak'. It was not, in other words, generated in the process of a struggle between the Zulus and the forces of imperialism, the British Crown and its pursuit of Empire. Instead, it was specifically designed for the purpose of teaching, rather like the reifications of Ancient Greece and Rome that emerged first during the later Middle Ages, when the methods adopted for teaching Greek and Latin as keys to knowledge led inevitably to the reification of the classic civilizations associated with them.

To pursue his plan to teach the Zulu the knowledge of the West, Colenso self-consciously invented an occidentalized West, just as the earlier European teachers invented classicized Greece and Rome. In other words, the teaching practices of the missionaries led to the creation of a particular format of Western Civilization and its codification in a form in which it could be taught. (It is still taught thus today.) Colenso's occidentalism was the result of a specific knowledge practice.

I had brought to me, for instance, a number of native boys who were given up by their fathers after considerable hesitation for five years education. At the end of that time I was obliged to allow them to return to their homes, according to our agreement. . . . [But], like many a working man in England, [these boys] would desire that their own children should receive a better education than themselves. (Colenso 1864: 18)

The Zulu, perceiving these knowledge practices as powerful, accepted them as access to power. As Colenso reported it, one chief, Nongoza, who brought his children to be educated by Colenso at Ekukanyeni, 'the place of light', declared, 'I should like to be the last fool of my race!' (Colenso 1864: 18).

Teaching not only served to communicate knowledge, but became in itself an emblem of being 'European', hence the occidentalism of the Zulu. But since the knowledge that was communicated, together with the means of its communication, was from outside, from beyond, from the other (as the Zulus saw it), this occidentalism represented an external recourse to power that could be used in the real struggle that existed between the Zulus and the colonialists, the 'creolized' settlers who were in direct competition with them. The occidentalism represented by religion, by the Queen (especially Queen Victoria) and the British royal family, and by the 'outside' as an abstract and moral source of power thus became consolidated as a cultural reality. The nature of this early occidentalism explains in part why South African internal politics has so often sought a resort to forms of moral coercion from the outside, when a delicate balance of violent coercion and its limited potentials for real change restricted recourse to attempts at military domination.

This occidentalism has played an important role in the international condemnation of South African racism. This is because, in its stress on an idealized justice residing in external moral authority, it enabled a politics of an appeal to moral justice that is clearly seen in Colenso's own direct appeals to the Queen or, later, in the Anglican Zulu lawyer Pixley Seme's addresses to the newly organized African National Congress (Rive and Couzens 1991), as well as in Gandhi's formulations of 'protest politics', and up to the present, in the world spread of the Anti–apartheid movement. It has had a vast impact far beyond Zululand.

Conclusions

The occidentalism of Natal and KwaZulu thus took a number of forms, and was founded in the complexity of a few decades of intense but confusing conflict among a variegated collection of groups and individuals of diverse cultural backgrounds in a broad but relatively sparsely populated landscape. Military force and violence, while more or less continually present, were almost always inconclusive. Out of this emerged a dual occidentalism that served to order a cultural landscape within a confused political and social reality.

The essential European of the occident could stand for the virulent racism of colonial farmers who found themselves in intense conflict with black Africans, or of the British regiments that punished Zululand severely in the aftermath of the Zulu War of 1878–9 by burning many of the homesteads and grain-stores of central Zululand. Since the outcomes of these violent struggles were usually ambiguous, leaving a complexly interwoven landscape of Zulus and whites, the emergence of absolute categorical racism that fully excluded the participation of each in the other's polities never emerged. As Gluckman commented in 1940:

The schism between the two colour groups is itself the pattern of their main integration into one community. They do not separate into groups of equal status: the Europeans are dominant. . . . The two groups are distinguished in their inter-relationships in the social structure of the South African community of which Zulu land is a part, and in this inter-relationship one can trace separation and conflict, and co-operation, in socially defined modes of behaviour. (Gluckman 1940: 14)

In the middle of this century, and in the middle of the last century, Europeans and Zulus knew something about the codes and expectation of each other's cultures, and used what they knew—or thought they knew—to attempt a cultural accommodation that maintained the cultural distinction, but permitted practical interaction within the local arena.

On the other hand, in the international arena in which southern African politics have long played a role, the essential European was represented by the missionaries as a source of external justice and of power that could be appropriated and used in the local arena. Today, this occidentalism of external recourse may be represented—somewhat ironically, since they are neither white nor European by now—by the Group of Eminent Persons of the Commonwealth that toured South Africa in 1986. They represented the power of the outside in South African politics, a source of external justice and a locus of ultimate appeal, much as appeals to Queen Victoria were made by chiefs and bishops in the nineteenth century, and much as Colenso insisted that he was sent by the Queen herself, not by the colonial government or even by Whitehall. 'I thank God,' he wrote in 1864, 'that I *am* commissioned by the Queen of England, in the name of our national Church, to be a "preacher and a teacher"' (Colenso 1864: 16). What he preached, of course, was a form of occidentalism. The reification of the West as both villain and saviour was perhaps already present in the combination of lust for wealth and land among one segment of the European population, and the equally forceful lust for salvation and light that drove the missionaries, who, Bleek said, the Zulu believed were 'another species'. As Bishop Colenso stated in 1864, Europeans had a 'duty' to 'strive to impart the blessings as they assuredly will impart the evils of civilization' (Colenso 1864: 16).

In the light of the real uncertainty of violence as the instrument of domination in Natal and KwaZulu, it would seem too simple to account for the construction of the occidental out of a process of resistance or reaction. Similarly, the notion that the reification of either the Zulu or the European was both thematically unified and unproblematic deserves at least to be seriously questioned. This chapter has not exhausted the full impact of the polarities and complexities that I have sketched, but it does show that the indigenous occidentalism of this part of South Africa was a complex historical product, with ample cultural life yet to drive a new politics in a new South Africa after Apartheid.

Notes

1 I use the term 'creole' here in a very broad sense to describe a community of complex and mixed European, African, and East Indian origins that became indigenized in Africa. This is not part of the usual vocabulary of South African history, and I use it to highlight, by the implicit comparison with other creole peoples, an aspect of southern African history that has been difficult to address for many reasons.

2 'Europe' and 'the European' are terms that carry special meanings in southern Africa. They are easily misread by people who are actually recently arrived from Europe and by Europeans and North Americans today. In South Africa from perhaps the last quarter of the 19th cent. through the first three-quarters of the 20th, 'European' was used somewhat ambiguously to distinguish European-derived indigenous populations from black African populations, as well as to refer to recent immigrants. Context usually made the different usages clear. Hendrik Verwoerd, a psychologist and one of the principle architects of Apartheid, however, confused these usages, perhaps deliberately, but certainly to his political advantage. Since he was in fact born and partly raised in Europe (not South Africa), it was necessary for him to fuse these separate connotations

in order to acquire the political power he sought. By adapting the European linguistic and cultural nationalism of his day to the African context, he was able to unify an Afrikaans—that is, 'African'—political party of African-born whites who spoke the indigenous dialect of Dutch, by appealing to their common 'European heritage' and supposed common interest. It obscured an important difference in local usage, however, and thus has muddled scholarship to this day.

3 Natal is the name given to this coast by the Portuguese explorer Vasco Da Gama around Christmas in 1488. The first European trading settlement on the coast was called Port Natal in 1824, and the Boers named their settlement in the region the Republic of Natal in 1838. This was annexed by the British in 1843 as the Natal Colony. KwaZulu or Zululand, more or less equivalent terms, refers to lands inhabited by the Zulu, a congeries of peoples unified under Shaka, a war-leader from the small 'Zulu' clan, who became king and gave this name to the areas of his conquest by the beginning of the 1820s. The history of settlement, conflict, and administrative laws created a region in which the border of these two political entities became jigsaw-puzzle–like.

4 While the main outlines of the Cape, Natal, the Free State, Transvaal, and Transkei were all defined by the end of the 1850s, the exceptions included Basutoland (later Lesotho), declared a protectorate in 1868; Bechuanaland (Botswana), annexed as a protectorate in 1885 (Rotberg 1988: 172–9); and Swaziland, whose borders had been defined in 1874 by the Transvaal government and ratified by conventions in 1884 (Laband 1992: 6; Wilson and Thompson 1971: 275–8).

5 Indeed, Zulu and Natal history does seem to have a special kind of 'event-ness' rather than structure, trends, or even a *longue durée*. Shula Marks comments, for instance, that, in contrast to a 'tendency . . . in some social history to discount "events", the essays [in her *Ambiguities of Dependence*] unashamedly centre around events'. Citing Max Gluckman's (1940) 'Analysis of a Social Situation in Modern Zululand', she notes that her history focuses on 'the kind of "specific, bounded happening" usually associated with anthropology' (Marks 1986: 9).

6 Compare the similar case, discussed by Bronwen Douglas, of the uncertainty of French military dominance in their Pacific colony of New Caledonia (Douglas 1992).

References

BLEEK, WILHELM H. (1965). *The Natal Diaries of W. H. I. Bleek*, ed. O. Spohr. Cape Town: Balkema.

COBBING, JULIAN (1988). 'The Mfecane as Alibi: Thoughts on Dithakong and Mbolompo', *Journal of African History*, 29: 487–519.

COLENSO, JOHN W. (n.d. [*c*.1854]). 'Church Mission among the Heathen in the Diocese of Natal, the Earnest Appeal of the Bishop of Natal on behalf of the Heathen Tribes within and on the Borders of the Diocese'. Publication in the